From Jailer to Entrepreneur

Paul Ward

Prologue

My name is Paul Ward and I was born on the 4th July 1957 in Seacroft, Leeds to a police officer father and a mother who was a buyer for Elida Gibbs.

I am the youngest of three boys, having two brothers who are twins and are two years and three months older than me.

I have been married to my beautiful and very understanding wife, Jenny, since 1978 and we are as much in love today as the day we married.

I am at the time of writing this a father of two grown up children, Alastair and Katy, and a beautiful granddaughter, Ava Rose.

I had a normal upbringing in a normal family surrounding of the time. Neither of my parents were very gushing when it came to emotion but we had good discipline, enough freedom and a secure environment to grow up in. We did not have a lot of money, but the world was a slightly different place in the '50s and '60s and our financial needs were not as demanding as they are today. As long as I could get out on my pushbike, play football and generally be outside I was more than happy. My school years were not particularly memorable as I was not the brightest student in the world and had my cheeky side or, some would say today, rebellious side. Therefore, how I ended up working in the Prison Service I am a bit unsure really.

I left school at 16 years of age in 1973 and did as all my peers did and started an apprenticeship, in my case in mechanical engineering at Kirkstall Forge Engineering, Leeds. The rest of my conventional working life was spent working in the Prison Service for 33 years, until I saw the light and retired early to become an entrepreneur property investor and developer.

The purpose of this book is to let people know what actually happens in our prisons without the political slant, as it is factual as far as I witnessed it. I would also like to get the message across to people who are stuck in a job they hate, working for a boss they would rather not be around and moaning every day about their life, that there is a way out of that world.

The only person you should be blaming for your life is you, as you have control over what you do with it. I want to tell you how I completely changed my mindset from a negative civil service one to a very positive business one, and how that has given me a much better outlook on life.

I hope you enjoy my journey and if some of it changes your attitude from the traditional school, exams, job, retire, to one of freedom and a more positive way of thinking, that would make me feel great.

Enjoy.

Chapter 1

1973 – 83

I left Cross Green Comprehensive School in July 1973 with a few CSEs to my credit and low self-esteem of my academic abilities, but proud of my sporting prowess.

I feel I let myself down academically but most definitely, the education system let me down badly. This I put down to the loony left that was a product of the liberal '60s and this notion of politics of envy for the elite, so they thought it would be a great idea to bring everybody down instead of giving people like me something to aspire to. These progressives brought in comprehensives and were determined to rid the country of grammar schools, as they were seen as elitist. I was never destined for a grammar school, but I maintain we need to nurture our brightest people in the formal educational sense and people like me would have benefitted more from a less formal education but one aimed at life skills, financial skills, more work- or self-employed-based skills instead of being cooped up in a classroom where all I wanted to do was dream and get on the football field or sports field. At the age of 13, I represented Yorkshire at gymnastics but this was seen as just a hobby by the establishment rather than a potential career and something I was particularly good at. How times have changed; now sport is a massive cash cow and the best sports people are hero-worshipped. Sport and particularly team sport can give young people invaluable skills for the working world, not to mention the financial benefits and job creation it provides. First political lesson over.

I would just like to point out I now have an honours degree thanks to my own determination and the Open University, however the Prison Service just ignored this fact, putting no emphasis on this as an achievement or how it would improve me as a person or help the Service to grow into a better place.

My father was born and brought up on a farm in Shropshire, then joined the Army at a very early age and went on to be a police officer for 34 years. He was a very influential person in my life and as much as I loved him he was of the old school in relation to 'go to school, get a job for life, retire, just accept that as your lot, and know your place in life'. Although I fell in to this life (I had no other idea how to get out of it), I would never accept my place in life and was a little bit rebellious through my young life.

An apprenticeship it was. I started my working life in a big dirty factory that manufactured heavy-duty axles for lorries, buses etc. I slogged away in this filthy factory for four years as an apprentice, going to day/evening classes at Kitson College of Technology until I passed out of my apprenticeship. I stayed for another year, but I could see the writing on the wall with the unions bullying people into strike action and Japan, Germany etc. starting to modernise and overtake Britain as the workshops of the world. I will try not to do too much politics but anybody who wants strong powerful unions again, be careful what you wish for. I appreciate not everybody will agree with this, but in my opinion Margaret Thatcher was the best thing to happen to this country at that time. I for one will not be voting for Jeremy Corbyn so he and his '70s cronies can take us back to these days of strikes, three day weeks, lights going out, rubbish piling up in the street. All you young people out there who have a romantic notion about equality, read the political and industrial history of these times and believe me, you will not want this again.

I actively started looking for a different career. My first dalliance with being an entrepreneur was when I was 19 years of age and I tried to buy a newsagents' and had visions of being a millionaire by the time I was 30 years of age with a string of newsagents. When I went to the bank manager he just laughed at me, which did nothing for my confidence and self-esteem and to my shame I gave that idea up; instead of saying, "Right, you arrogant bastard, I will show you," I went back to 'knowing my place'. It makes my blood boil just writing this.

I got married on the 29th July 1978 at 21 years of age and we bought a house in Yeadon to the west of Leeds for £10,500; oh, how times have changed. After numerous times on strike from the factory I thought I couldn't see any future in this and now we had a mortgage, it was even more important to take some positive action about our future.

The Prison Service

With my father being a police officer I thought that seemed a pretty cool job driving around in fast cars chasing villains (as a mad James Bond fan, MI5 was beyond me!). I applied for the police, knowing I may have a problem being five foot seven-and-a-half inches tall and the minimum height for getting in the police at that time was five foot eight inches. As expected, I was rejected for half an inch (I bet there are a few dirty minds putting another connotation on that?). Another disappointment, another day, so move on.

My father asked me if I would consider the Prison Service. At first, I said not a chance I was going to work among all those two-headed monsters that prisons are full of. After a little time I thought again about this idea and came round to the idea I could teach engineering to the two-headed monsters. My father knew the Chief Officer (I will explain later the hierarchy structure of the Prison Service) at a prison near Leeds and said he would arrange for me to speak to him. When I met the Chief Officer he was a huge bald-headed man who looked more like what I imaged a prisoner to look like, however he was very helpful and gave a very good picture of the Prison Service as a great career.

After this chat I went away to give it some thought. After a couple of weeks I thought, why not, what is there to lose apart from my good looks? I made enquiries about joining with an intention to teach engineering. In mid-1979 I filled out the application form to become a prison officer. In these days you had to join as a prison officer first and then apply to become an instructor in the workshops when you had done your 12 months' probation as an officer.

I put my application in and eventually got an invite to attend Wakefield Prison to take a knowledge test to see if I was bright enough to go further in the process. I turned up at Wakefield Prison at 9am sharp around September 1979. Wakefield was a Category A prison full of the worst kind of criminal, from murderers to rapists, very old and quite daunting to a 22-year-old.

We walked through the grounds of the four-storey prison, the wings made up of dark brick with bars on small windows, and prisoners shouting obscenities at us. I really did wonder at this stage, "What the hell am I doing?" Stiff British upper lip Wardy, I said to myself, you can do this. We entered the administration building and went into a classroom with about 30 other people. I looked around and felt very young compared to the others. The average age of people joining the Prison Service in 1979 was 28 with 75% coming from the Services, particularly the Army.

The tests were on English, Maths and Reasoning, and lasted for about 90 minutes. We sat in this room for another 30 minutes while the papers were being marked. A rather stern looking man walked in to the room with a sheet of paper and explained what was going to happen. He said he would call out names and they were to leave the room. At least three quarters of the people in the room had left when the man finished calling out names. I thought they must be the ones who had passed, as I felt the test was not that hard and my immediate thoughts were once again how thick I was. To my surprise and relief we were the ones who had passed. For once in my life at this time I felt proud of an academic achievement, even if only a small one.

We then went for some lunch and were told we would be having a medical in the afternoon before being interviewed as the final part of the process. The one thing in life I had no doubt on was passing the medical as I was very fit and healthy, and so it proved. As there is a W at the beginning of my surname I was always last, and I finally went to be interviewed at 8.30pm. I walked into this large office that reminded me of a headmaster's study in a private school, where two men were sat behind a big desk. I was told to sit in the single chair about four feet from the desk. I was grilled for 30 minutes about my life, my thoughts on what I would do in certain situations and other random things. I genuinely had no idea how I had done but after some deliberation between the two of them they offered me a place as a trainee prison officer. I thanked them and got up to leave when one of them said, "Goodness knows what they will think when you turn up at Leeds Prison." I took that to mean my small stature and very young fresh-faced looks. After over 12 hours since I walked in to Wakefield Prison, I walked out of the big imposing gate and punched the air as if I had scored the winning goal in the cup final for Leeds United.

After about a month I received a letter telling me I was to start at Armley Prison, Leeds on the 21st December 1979 at 8am. It was a fantastic feeling telling my present employer I was leaving, but also a nervous feeling. About two weeks later I was told I was not to start until 21st January 1980. My pay was to be a basic weekly wage of £63.63 with an index-linked Principal Civil Service Pension. On top of this there was as much overtime as you wanted. I was earning about £40 a week in engineering with very little overtime and no pension.

My appointment letter.

HOME OFFICE
Portland House
Stag Place
LONDON
SW1E 5BX

Our reference:
Your reference:

Telephone 01-828 9848 ext *190*

692/w/79

Paul Michael Ward

2.1.80

Dear *Mr Ward*

I am writing to offer you formally an appointment as an unestablished prison officer.
You are therefore requested to report on *21.1.80* to the Governor of
HM Prison *LEEDS* , who will send you further instructions. The enclosed
'M' form should be completed and handed in on the above date, when it will also be
necessary for you to produce your birth certificate. Your appointment will be on
a conditional basis, pending receipt of satisfactory replies to references and other
enquiries as may be made, and the completion of the Civil Service Department's usual
enquiries into age, health and other matters. If the outcome of the Department's
enquiries is unsatisfactory, your appointment will normally be terminated, unless
the Civil Service Department are able to recommend the continuation of your employment
on different conditions of service from those outlined in this letter. In such a
case a new offer of appointment will be made to you. If the outcome is satisfactory,
you will be notified accordingly and your appointment will be continued on an
established basis. You will be on probation for a period of 12 months and confirmation
of your appointment is dependent upon the satisfactory completion of this probationary
period (which may under certain circumstances be extended). If your work and/or
attendance during the probationary period is not satisfactory, your appointment will
be terminated. Your appointment may be terminated at any time during the probationary
period in case of misconduct or if your service is unsatisfactory and it is clear
that you will not be able to reach the required standard before the end of the
probationary period. Normally for the first 12 weeks you will be under training,
the first 4 weeks at the above named establishment, and the following 8 weeks at
Leyhill/~~Wakefield~~ Officers' Training School. At the end of the training period you
will be posted to one of the Prison Service establishments in England and Wales, and
you will have a continuing liability to be transferred to any other such establishment.
You will not be permitted to receive any gratuity or perquisite whatever, or
without special permission, take any other occupation or employment, or hold public
office.

The following paragraphs and the schedule attached to this letter summarise your
main conditions of service as they apply at present. Any significant changes will
be notified by means of Notices to Staff. Details of conditions of service
applicable to Civil Servants are to be found in the Staff Rules Handbook, a copy
of which will be handed to you at the training school.

PAY

You will be paid weekly in arrears. Your basic starting pay will be £63.63 a week,
plus rent allowance. Full details of prison officer rates of pay are provided on the
attached statement. You will receive extra payment for all hours worked on a
Saturday or a Sunday, within the normal 40 hour week. Your pay may be subject to a
reduction if you are in receipt of a Civil Service pension.

At establishments where bachelor accommodation is available a single officer will normally be expected to occupy it: if it is not available he will receive an allowance of £5.40 a week. (A Supplementary allowance of up to £1.48 for inner London and £1.00 in outer London may also be payable.) If a married officer needs to occupy bachelor accommodation because he does not live within reasonable daily travelling distance he will be charged £5.03, including VAT a week: he will, however, receive a rent allowance of an amount not exceeding £10.80 a week in respect of his own home. (A Supplementary allowance of £2.95 for inner London and £2.01 for outer London.)

If it is at all practicable, a married officer is advised to live at home and travel daily to his first place of appointment since this arrangement will have a bearing on the extent of his entitlement to removal and other related allowances if subsequently he is transferred on permanent appointment. On permanent appointment you may be entitled to removal and certain other related allowances. The circumstances in which such payments may be made are described in paragraph 13 of the accompanying notes. An officer under training is advised not to move his home in advance of permanent appointment.

Officers do not wear uniforms whilst under training, but are paid a cash allowance instead.

HOURS

You will normally work a 5 day week of 40 hours (net) excluding meal breaks, usually with opportunities for overtime as soon as training is completed.

LEAVE

In addition to public holidays and privilege holidays which total 10 days and are detailed in the Staff Rules Handbook, your annual leave allowance will be 4 weeks with pay, rising to 4 weeks 2 days with pay after 7 years total service, to 5 weeks with pay after 17 years total service, and to 6 weeks with pay after 27 years total service.

PENSION SCHEMES

Establishment appointees (including conditional appointees) are covered from the outset by the Principal Civil Service Pension Scheme, details of which are included in the schedule to this letter.

If you are willing to accept employment on the basis of the terms contained in this letter and the attached schedule, you will be required to sign a copy of this appointment letter when reporting for Prison Officer training.

2

1980

Monday 21st January 1980 finally came and I woke up after a very nervous night with little sleep in plenty of time for my journey to Leeds Prison. I lived near Leeds/Bradford Airport, which is the highest airport in England and very prone to snow in winter. I opened the curtains to find a heavy fall of snow. I was so nervous about starting that I never really gave the snow a thought.

After attempting to eat some breakfast I said goodbye to Jenny and jumped in to the car. I lived on a bit of a hill which took some getting out of due to the snow and this should have set alarm bells ringing for the general road conditions, but my only thought was on the day ahead. As soon as I got to the main road to take me in to the centre of Leeds the traffic was in absolute chaos. Panic set in but thought I would be OK as I had left myself plenty of time (or so I thought!). No mobile phones in those days.

I was supposed to be at the prison for 9am and turned up at 9.30am, but I thought nothing of it as they would understand with the weather being as it was. I knocked on the big prison gate in my best suit and tie looking like a little lost schoolboy and said to the imposing figure who opened the gate, "My name is Paul Ward and I have come to start as a prison officer." He looked me up and down then said, "You need to go over there," pointing to an administration building. I said thank you and went on my way.

I tried to open the door but found everything locked. First lesson, you stupid boy, it was a prison after all. I rang the bell and a nice young woman let me in after I explained who I was and why I was here. She took me through to a room where three other people were sat at desks and a uniformed man was standing in front of them. I walked in and said, "Hello, I am Paul Ward, sorry for being late but the snow was terrible." He took one look at me and said, "Very good of you to turn up halfway through the day, and if you should survive the day, let alone the next few weeks, make sure this is the last time you are late." Welcome to the Prison Service. Mr Dunnett was his name and at that point in my prison career he was the scariest person I had ever met.

I sat down and was introduced to the three other recruits, who were all as nervous-looking as me. We spent the morning being told what we could expect from the next four weeks. At this time, you spent four weeks in civilian clothing at Leeds Prison learning the basics, being introduced to prison life, visiting other types of prisons and preparing for eight weeks at a training school at a place called Leyhill. This was next to Leyhill open prison in Gloucestershire.

Before going in to the prison we had to sign the Official Secrets Act:

Official Secrets Acts

Declaration To be signed by members of Government Departments on appointment and, where desirable, by non-civil servants on first being given access to Government information.

My attention has been drawn to the provisions of the Official Secrets Acts set out on the back of this document and I am fully aware of the serious consequences which may follow any breach of those provisions.

I understand that the sections of the Official Secrets Acts set out on the back of this document cover material published in a speech, lecture, or radio or television broadcast, or in the Press or in book form. I am aware that I should not divulge any information gained by me as a result of my appointment to any unauthorised person, either orally or in writing, without the previous official sanction in writing of the Department appointing me, to which written application should be made and two copies of the proposed publication to be forwarded. I understand also that I am liable to be prosecuted if I publish without official sanction any information I may acquire in the course of my tenure of an official appointment (unless it has already officially been made public) or retain without official sanction any sketch, plan, model, article, note or official documents which are no longer needed for my official duties, and that these provisions apply not only during the period of my appointment but also after my appointment has ceased. I also understand that I must surrender any documents, etc., referred to in section 2 (1) of the Act if I am transferred from one post to another, save such as have been issued to me for my personal retention.

Signed   P. M. Ward

Surname *(Block letters)*   WARD

Forename(s)   PAUL MICHAEL

Date   21 - 1 - 80

E 74 (5-74-0)

Extracts from the Official Secrets Acts, 1911 and 1920

Section 2 of the Official Secrets Act, 1911, as amended by the Official Secrets Act, 1920, provides as follows:—

"2 (1) If any person having in his possession or control any secret official code word, or pass word, or any sketch, plan, model, article, note, document, or information which relates to or is used in a prohibited place or anything in such a place, or which has been made or obtained in contravention of this Act, or which has been entrusted in confidence to him by any person holding office under Her Majesty, or which he has obtained or to which he has had access owing to his position as a person who holds or has held office under Her Majesty, or as a person who holds or has held a contract made on behalf of Her Majesty, or as a person who is or has been employed under a person who holds or has held such an office or contract,—

(a) communicates the code word, pass word, sketch, plan, model, article, note, document, or information to any person, other than a person to whom he is authorised to communicate it, or a person to whom it is in the interests of the State his duty to communicate it, or,

(aa) uses the information in his possession for the benefit of any foreign power or in any other manner prejudicial to the safety or interests of the State:

(b) retains the sketch, plan, model, article, note, or document in his possession or control when he has no right to retain it or when it is contrary to his duty to retain it or fails to comply with all directions issued by lawful authority with regard to the return or disposal thereof; or

(c) fails to take reasonable care of, or so conducts himself as to endanger the safety of the sketch, plan, model, article, note, document, secret official code or pass word or information:

that person shall be guilty of a misdemeanour.

(1A) If a person having in his possession or control any sketch, plan, model, article, note, document, or information which relates to munitions of war, communicates it directly or indirectly to any foreign power, or in any other manner prejudicial to the safety or interests of the State, that person shall be guilty of a misdemeanour.

(2) If any person receives any secret official code word, or pass word, or sketch, plan, model, article, note, document, or information, knowing, or having reasonable ground to believe, at the time when he receives it, that the code word, pass word, sketch, plan, model, article, note, document or information is communicated to him in contravention of this Act, he shall be guilty of a misdemeanour, unless he proves that the communication to him of the code word, pass word, sketch, plan, model, article, note, document, or information was contrary to his desire."

Section 1 (2) of the Official Secrets Act, 1920, provides as follows:—

" (2) If any person—

(a) retains for any purpose prejudicial to the safety or interests of the State any official document, whether or not completed or issued for use, when he has no right to retain it, or when it is contrary to his duty to retain it, or fails to comply with any directions issued by any Government Department or any person authorised by such department with regard to the return or disposal thereof: or

(b) allows any other person to have possession of any official document issued for his use alone, or communicate any secret official code word or pass word so issued, or, without lawful authority or excuse, has in his possession any official document or secret official code word or pass word issued for the use of some person other than himself, or, on obtaining possession of any official document by finding or otherwise, neglects or fails to restore it to the person or authority by whom or for whose use it was issued, or to a police constable: or

(c) without lawful authority or excuse, manufactures or sells, or has in his possession for sale any such die, seal or stamp as aforesaid

he shall be guilty of a misdemeanour."

(2523) 3 604896/834286 1/74 300m NCS 821

We had some lunch, then we were to be taken inside the prison. We entered through the wicker gate, which is a small door within the big gates, and the sense of anticipation was strange. We were then let through another set of gates and in front of us was a huge building in rather a depressing dark brick with a big clock in the middle. Leeds is an old Victorian prison that houses prisoners awaiting trial and some newly convicted. There was a distinctive sound of keys rattling which were attached to the officers by long chains, which were fastened to a large belt around the waist. We went through about four locked metal gates and wooden doors before entering a corridor with offices either side. There were names and titles on the closed doors, including The Governor.

We went up some steps and through another set of metal gates and wooden doors into the centre of the prison. The noise and the smell were the first things that hit you. The smell was of body odour and food (not food Gordon Ramsay would be proud of) and the noise was lots of people talking, officers shouting orders, and it reminded me of a human warren. There were four long buildings in front of us called wings which were on four storeys and each one held around 250 prisoners, although they were originally made to hold 100 prisoners each. There was wire across the second floor that I found out was to stop people hurting themselves if they jumped from the fourth floor or were thrown over. OK. let's move on. As the four of us walked in in our shiny new suits, looking as green as grass, you could feel hundreds of eyes on us as everybody knew what we were.

This was one of the toughest months of my life with sessions in the gym every day, often joining in with the prisoners, getting the odd word in our ear at best or a sly punch at worst and I felt sure the instructor purposely turned a blind eye to this, possibly to toughen us up. Constantly writing loads of notes and taking in so much information.

When I joined the Prison Service the rank system was as follows:
Officer
Senior Officer
Principal Officer
Chief Officer II
Chief Officer I
Assistant Governor
Deputy Governor
Governor

So you can see the career structure was pretty good and gave you something to aim for.

At the end of the four weeks at Leeds we had to meet the Chief Officer in his office. He was a huge man sat behind a huge desk and the top Chief position was one to behold and aspire to. We did not sit but stood in a line in front of his desk. I stood there with my arms folded, which seemed to upset him as he told me to unfold them and show some respect otherwise he would wrap them round my neck and tie a knot in them. They did not stay folded for long. I soon began to realise discipline was a big part of this service, and whether one saw this as bullying or discipline you had two choices: live with it or go now. I chose to live with it as I began to see something positive happening in my life.

The four weeks passed quickly and I had learned so much in this short space of time. We were measured for our uniform and sent for a few days off to prepare for eight weeks away from home at Leyhill Training School.

I said goodbye to Jenny on a cold February day to travel the long distance to Leyhill. I felt really strange and sad leaving Jenny on her own knowing I was going to be away for some time, but it had to be done and I was excited as well as a bit nervous. After about a four hour drive we arrived at Leyhill. It was a fabulous country house in its own grounds with the open prison at the side of it and I was completely in awe of these surroundings.

Entering the building, it was as impressive on the inside as it was on the outside with a fabulous wooden staircase, glass chandeliers and other things you would find in a stately home. For a lad from a rough estate in Leeds this was like another world. We were allocated our rooms, and mine I shared with three other blokes from different parts of the country. It overlooked the beautiful gardens and further on the Gloucestershire countryside. We were shown round the building and grounds then had an evening meal before going to bed in anticipation of the eight weeks ahead.

The following day we then had to go to the parade ground to learn how to march, which was very comical as many recruits had service experience and this came as second nature to them, mixed with people like me who had never done this before. People were going in different directions at different paces. Keystone Cops sprang to mind and I was just glad it was not being filmed. As amused as we were, the tough and aggressive instructor was far from amused, which actually made it even more amusing.

The eight weeks was full on, learning the academic side of laws, regulation, policy etc. mixed with the physical side of keeping fit, doing work in the dojo, putting on handcuffs, how to use a two-way radio and many other aspects of becoming a prison officer. In between this was the odd evening getting a bit too drunk and regretting it the following day, but it was all making me a stronger person both physically and mentally. These eight weeks also taught me about teamwork and looking out for each other.

At the four-week period we were given the weekend off to travel home, but before this we were given our letters with the prison we were posted to. This was the bit most people dreaded as we had no idea where we would be going. Most who were single were given London prisons regardless of where they came from. I opened mine and it said HMP Manchester, commonly known as Strangeways. To be honest I was quite excited but was unsure how Jenny would take this.

When I got home the first thing was give Jenny a big hug as I had missed her so much and second told her where we were going. Jenny being Jenny took this in her stride and accepted this was my career and it had to be done. She has never really been career conscious so seemed to be OK at leaving her job with the Yorkshire Water Authority. I went back after the weekend to complete my eight weeks' training to prepare me for the big bad world of a real prison. On the final passing out the Chief Officer in charge of the Training School gave a rousing speech, but the thing I remember most was at the very end when he said, "Prisoners: they will lie to you, cheat you, hate you, threaten you, may even assault you but the main thing is don't let the bastards get you down." I don't think he would get a job in the Prison Service I left 33 years later, but never a truer few words were said to me in all those 33 years, as what he said was exactly how it was. The only thing he missed off was some of these sentiments could also relate to some people working in the service, especially lying and cheating.

I made my way home after this eight weeks a much more confident person ready to take the world on, or at least a few of Britain's finest characters. I had a few days off before I had to prepare for travelling to Manchester to find my digs and start my career for real. You are on a 12-month probationary period, and during this time you can be told to leave if you do not come up to standard or do not pass your probation at the end of 12 months without any recourse.

Manchester Prison:

On Monday 21st April 1980 I set off early from my home in Leeds to travel across the Pennines to the dark side (Lancashire). I can remember this day as if it was yesterday as it was a day that changed both mine and my wife's lives.

I came off junction 19 of the M62 and joined the long straight road in to the centre of Manchester. You can see the big tower from the prison for miles and then the imposing huge building comes into frame, then the nerves really started to rumble. I parked my car and walked up the side of the grim prison wall to the huge main gate. I knocked on the gate with the massive doorknocker, an officer opened it, and with some authority said, "Yes, can I help you?" I explained who I was and he pointed me to the training department further up the wall. So 50 metres further on I knocked on the training room door and a small man wearing a Principal Officer's uniform said, "Hello, can I help you?" in a very friendly way. This took me aback a bit as most people of any rank I had first met in a prison usually had an air of superiority and fairly gruff manner. This man, whose name to my shame I cannot remember, was really nice and treated me as a person rather than a subordinate, which made me feel quite relaxed.

There was about 12 other people starting as a prison officer with me which again made me feel a bit more relaxed. At this time Manchester Prison had taken the management of courts over from a prison called Risley, therefore a lot of new officers were required to service them.

Today the court cells and transport of prisoners is managed by private companies but in 1980, prison officers did this role. I will cover this later.

We spent the morning in the training room having lots of information put in to our brains and being provided with our uniforms. We were given five blue shirts with razor sharp collars, four clip-on ties, so prisoners did not strangle you, three pairs of trousers, two pairs of shoes, two prison jackets with HMP insignia, five pairs of socks, an overcoat and two hats, two belts, a chain for your keys and a baton, or truncheon as the police call them. This went into a long pocket on the right side of your trousers. We put our uniforms on and I felt taller than my five foot seven-and-a-half inches and strangely quite proud.

In the afternoon we were split into two groups and taken for a tour of the prison. Manchester Prison was very similar in age to Leeds and just as dominating and gruesome but was much bigger as it had five wings in the main prison and another four in what was called the Borstal Allocation Centre (BAC), making at this time around 1600 prisoners – two or three to a cell designed for one. For those of you who are not old enough to remember the borstals, these were establishments where young people went who were given a sentence of borstal by the courts. Borstal was a sentence of six months to two years depending on the individual's behaviour. If they behaved they could do six months, if they were a bit naughty they could end up doing two years. This was a very effective way of managing a prisoner, but as with everything that works, the establishment some years later abolished it for something that didn't work.

The BAC at Manchester was one of two in the country where offenders given borstal by the courts were initially taken to be allocated to borstals around the country. I will explain how this works later.

I was very impressed by the cleanliness of the prison and what appeared to be order but there was still that smell of body odour and nice food that you eventually get used to. Just like Leeds there were orders being shouted and general noise of over a thousand people living in one space. Manchester is designed on a rotunda style with a large centre with five wings off the centre. The BAC is a copy of this on a smaller scale as a separate but attached building. At meal times a Principal Officer stands in the centre like a conductor of an orchestra instructing officers to send prisoners for their meals in rotation. Watching this for the first time was quite something. Prisoners would come down under instruction a landing at a time down one staircase to the ground floor under the centre, where there were serving areas for food set out in a circle. Prisoners did not even stop as food was literally slapped on a metal tray by an army of other prisoners who worked in the kitchen, then up another staircase back to their cell to eat their meal. Sixteen hundred prisoners were served their meal in about 25 minutes. Seeing was believing.

The kitchen was a hub of activity with loads of worker prisoners in white overalls seemingly knowing exactly what they were doing, and it all came together like clockwork. I think at that time the kitchen manager had about 25p per prisoner per day to provide three meals a day. Although prisoners complained about the food it was better than a lot of hospitals and most prisoners probably never ate as well outside. More about food throughout the book.

The workshops were again very busy places full of prisoners beavering away, albeit at pretty mundane work including the archetypal stitching of Royal Mail bags.

We finished our tour and those of us who were going to find our digs were allowed to go early. I was staying in a B&B just up the road so I made my way there. It was not the most salubrious of places but it was clean; however, the rooms were not much bigger than the cells I had seen in Strangeways. I had to find a pay phone to call Jenny, no mobiles in these days, to tell her about my day and let her know everything was OK and ask how she was doing, as this was the second time we had been apart since being married ("Aah," I hear you saying). I spent the evening watching TV with a load of brickies and other builders talking football and other blokey stuff. Well, they were talking about Man Utd and I was talking about football, Leeds Utd of course.

I must say I did not sleep too much that night and went down for my breakfast in civilian clothing, as I was not too sure the other guests would appreciate what I did. Maybe that was unfair, but I did not want to take a chance.

I put my uniform on and took the short drive to the prison. We all met in the training room again as we were having a week's induction before being thrown in to the deep end. All officers at this time were allocated to a sub division and there were 10 sub divisions with 20 officers in each sub division. I was allocated to sub division 5 and given my shift pattern that I would follow for the immediate future.

My week's induction was over and I was given the weekend off to go home. I took great pleasure in driving east on the M62, soon seeing the white rose of Yorkshire and the smell of fresh air. We had a great weekend and I was on a bit of a high discussing my week and the future of looking for a home in Manchester. We agreed to put our house on the market. We bought our house in 1978 for £10,500, this was April 1980, and we put it on the market for £18,000 and eventually got £17,500, not a bad profit in two years; about 75%. Maybe this is where I got my love of property from for my future years that come much later in this book.

I returned to my digs on Sunday evening for an early start on Monday morning. In these days we used to start at 7am to unlock prisoners for them to get their breakfast and lock them up again so we could go and get our breakfast, before unlocking the prisoners at 9am for work etc. I never really got my head around the fact we started work at 7am, unlocked prisoners to 'slop out', locked them back in their cell and then we went for a breakfast for three quarters of an hour. The breakfast most officers had was a full fry up with all the trimmings for next to nothing cost-wise. On top of the big drink culture, long hours of overtime and a stressful job, there is no wonder not many prison officers made it to retirement or only had a couple of years before leaving this world. That is good for the Government, as they do not have to pay much in pensions.

I was allocated to a wing, D Wing, which was a convicted wing made up of a mixture of prisoners serving different sentences from a few days for non-payment of fines to a life sentence. Although this was my allocated wing, it was hit or miss if I worked here. As a new officer I was sent up to the fourth landing. There was a hierarchy within the officers depending on years in the job, so I had to get to know my place and make my way to the '4s' as the fourth landing was known. When we unlocked the prisoners at 7am, they had three quarters of an hour to 'slop out' and get their meal and be locked up again while we went for our breakfast. My role was to stand next to the sluice where prisoners threw the contents of their night's ablutions away and used the toilet. The reason for an officer standing here was that it was one of the areas where prisoners tended to sort out their little squabbles. It was not the best place to be if you had been out the night before, as you don't need me to tell you the smell that was generated.

Slopping out was a term used when prisoners emptied a bowl of urine and sometimes other bodily functions into a sluice, of which there are two on each side of a landing. As well as a sluice, there is a urinal and a toilet with a half door so you can see the person in there. So overall, there were two toilets, two urinals for around 100 prisoners. A civilised prison system for a 20th century rich country? I will leave you to make your own mind up on that one.

After some time living at the B&B I was getting a bit fed up with this way of living. I happened to be talking about it once to a colleague, Malcolm, and he offered to put me up in his house as he said he had a spare room. I thought I would give this a go. He lived in a very nice area of Manchester, Didsbury, in a nice house. He had two daughters, one of which still lived at home, and his wife. Malcolm explained to me that he was out quite a bit but just to make myself at home. His wife was a lovely woman who insisted I came to sit in the living room with her rather than in my bedroom. I did spend many evenings looking for a house for Jenny and myself, so did not impose much on them.

I realised after a while the relationship between Malcolm and his wife was a strange one. I had an inkling from work that Malcolm was a bit of a lad with the ladies and a few officers made some suggestions I should be careful as Malcolm's wife was not getting 'looked after'. It did not take me long to get used to the humour within prisons at that time. It is a mix of black humour, mixed with a macho, sexist and often crude humour. A lot of this was a coping mechanism mixed with the drink culture. By the time I left the service it was a complete different culture going full circle and very politically correct (PC). In 1980 I had never heard the term PC, in fact I don't think it had been invented yet.

I was taken aback one evening when Malcolm's wife started to open up to me about her marriage, saying she and Malcolm had a very open relationship which basically meant he went off sleeping with other women and she for some strange reason put up with it. I do not think she was interested in other relationships but seemed happy to do her own thing.

After months of looking for a house in various parts of Manchester, we eventually bought one in Timperley, which was South Manchester near Altrincham. We moved in November of 1980, which was a real relief for both Jenny and me. We were now part of the Cheshire set, all frills and no nickers. The only drawback to living here was I had to pass Old Trafford every time I went to work which was a horrible experience. I have to admit to a very childish act one day on my way to work. I had stopped at the traffic lights right next to Old Trafford. A big flash car came up at the side of me and I realised the occupant was Ron Atkinson, the then manager of Man Utd. He looked over at me just as the lights were turning green so I pulled my tongue out and pulled a funny face at him. He just laughed and I felt absolutely stupid, but did smile to myself, just glad he did not know me.

I could not believe what the Prison Service paid for over and above my salary. I was getting a nightly subsistence allowance for the time I was living on my own, travelling expenses back home on my days off to the extent I was hardly touching my wage. When we moved house the Service paid for everything. All removal expenses, solicitors. When we moved in they paid what was called a carpet and curtains allowance. This covered everything from new curtains, carpets, plumbing white goods in, TV aerial, and many more. On the day we moved I even got a travel allowance for the dog. What do you think the taxpayer of today would say to that? At least a lot of this stopped well before the MPs were found out about their expenses years later. While I am talking about money, another way of adding a few pounds to our wages was subsistence for going to court with prisoners. As I explained earlier Prison Staff used to manage the Crown Courts: transporting prisoners to court, managing the cells and providing security in the dock with them. We also took them to the Magistrates Court. We used to get subsistence of over five hours, over 10 and over 12. This encouraged prison staff to hang around at court as long as possible to ensure they got the highest subsistence plus overtime. I have on a number of occasions driven round and round Manchester town centre in a big 56-seater coach with up to 12 prisoners on board to ensure we got at least the over 10 hours subsistence. I am convinced the management of the service knew this happened, but the Prison Officers Association (POA) was very powerful in those days and it was easier to let this happen than deal with it.

The year was rolling by and I spent most of the time listening, learning, and getting used to the culture, humour and the different styles of prison officer. At this time as I explained before about 75% of prison officers had come from the services, so many of them were older than me and more worldly wise. There were a lot of tough guys who were not particularly good at listening to prisoners, as in their mind prisoners were there to do as they were told and shut up. The one thing I did find was no matter how much they may take the mickey out of you as the new boy, they would always be there if I got into difficulty with a prisoner(s). The camaraderie was very strong.

After about two months I was called to the number one Chief's office. I was really worried as this generally only happened when you had done something wrong, so I was racking my brain to think what this could be. I knocked on the Chief's door and there was a light system, like traffic lights on the wall. The green light went on and I walked in the office. The Chief was called Williamson but to me it was Sir or Chief. As I walked in the Chief was sat behind his desk. He stood up, shook my hand, and told me to sit down. He was a big bald headed man with a strong Yorkshire accent. I was completely confused and had no idea what was coming. He asked me if my father was called Bob Ward, Inspector Bob Ward from Leeds City Police. I said yes, he is. At this he relaxed in his chair and said my father was a friend of his whom he got to know when he was working at a prison near Wetherby, where my father spent time as an inspector. He then went on to say, "If any of these Lancastrian bastards have a go at you for being a Yorkshireman you come and see me." I said, "Thank you, I will," even though I had no intention at all of doing this. I left the office with a big grin on my face and a bigger sense of relief.

It was great to get moved in to our house before Christmas and this brought up the end of a very interesting and eventful year that was quite stressful in many ways both from a personal and working point of view.

1981

I did not particularly have a big celebration drink-wise on New Year's Eve as I was working on New Year's Day from 7.45am to about 9.00pm. This was something we had to get used to for the foreseeable future. Can you imagine the miners' union putting up with these hours on a national holiday?

I passed my probationary period on the 21st January 1981 so became an established prison officer, and at that time I could not imagine doing anything else for the rest of my working life as the career prospects seemed quite good so I resolved to climb that ladder as best I could. This, I guess, was the brainwashing the likes of me had from parents, teachers, the establishment etc. To be fair at the time this was far better than working in some smelly, hot factory where the prospects for bettering yourself were very limited.

I noticed a yellow Triumph Spitfire with a soft top in a car showroom just up the road from the prison. I think with Jenny's blessing I bought this fun car and as uncomfortable as it was it was initially a lot of fun to drive, particularly with the roof down. I say initially because with the notorious Manchester weather (lots of rain), I found the roof leaked and no matter what I did I ended up with a wet lap, so often getting out of the car looking like I had wet myself. We used to drive along with bits of tissue, rags and anything else stuck in the spaces where water came in. I felt like a millionaire even though I was very far from it, but it is good to dream sometimes and it made me feel good at the time. I was only 23 years old after all. We lasted about 12 months with this car and decided our youth phase was over as far as cars were concerned.

At the beginning of the year there was a bit of a buzz around the prison as a notorious London gangster was coming to the prison for what was termed a 'lay down'. This was a month away from a long-term prison to give them a rest from him. He arrived and was placed in a single cell on A Wing; it was unheard of that someone had a single cell, but if he was with another prisoner there would be a good chance he would kill him.

This prisoner had been in prison for many years and was still potentially very violent and had a history of assaulting prison staff, other prisoners and basically anybody who upset him. I cannot name this person but he was one of the Kray twins' gang with a reputation for being extremely violent on their behalf.

When I first came across him I was really surprised as he was about five foot three inches tall, not particularly well built and well into his 50s, and was very polite. He stayed for a month causing no problem at all, was generally very respectful and when he left he shook hands with a few prison staff and off he went. I read up on this guy after this and his record in and out of prison was terrifying, which completely had me baffled as to the man I had dealt with over this month. If you saw this guy in the street you would not look twice at him as he was very insignificant, but in the London professional criminal world he was to be feared and someone you would not want to get on the wrong side of. So much for the romantic notion that London gangsters of this era were nice people.

As an officer just out of his probation I then had to earn my spurs doing what they called 'general duties'. This was where you did all the work around the prison such as bath house duties, workshops, supervising exercise, Crown and Magistrate duties, hospital watches, supervising visits and many more which I will explain later. As you progressed, you could apply for a 'fixed post' which was areas like reception and again I worked in many of these areas, so I will explain later.

I will explain the general duties I did throughout 1981–83. The bathhouse was where the prisoners were allowed a shower and a change of clothing. Due to the number of prisoners and lack of facilities, prisoners were allowed a shower once a week, except for certain prisoners who worked in areas like the kitchen. As an officer you sat outside the shower area at a desk booking prisoners in and ensuring clothing exchange was done fairly. You had to have eyes in the back of your head as this was a classic area for prisoners to resolve disputes and for payback time, so the prisoners who 'slipped' in the shower and came out with a black eye were quite numerous. A number of officers would turn a blind eye to this as they found it quite amusing. Duty of care was not particularly high on the agenda at Strangeways for officers or managers.

One of the most boring jobs I found was sitting in a workshop. The officer sat on a raised platform so he could see everything that was going on and at his side was an alarm bell. This alarm bell was to summon other officers if an incident occurred. There were usually two officers in a workshop with up to 60 prisoners. I once witnessed an alarm bell situation in a workshop where a mass of officers ran to the workshop, and they were quite a distance from the main prison, so when most of them got there they were out of breath and unhappy at having their tea break upset; they were ready for a fight (yes, I am talking about the officers). They could not decide who was the cause of the disturbance so the senior officer in charge said, "Take him out, as he is the biggest and ugliest." This prisoner protested his innocence and resisted so was surrounded by a large number of officers and physically removed, being manhandled all the way to the segregation unit (I will explain what this is later). The senior officer was really chuffed, saying, "That will make them think in future." What he meant was that was a lesson to anybody thinking it funny to press an alarm bell for fun. One of the workshops at this time was the archetypal sewing of Post Office sacks. I thought this was just on films but here was I sat watching 40–50 prisoners sewing mailbags. All I could think about was the old gangster movies. Many of the workshops were nicknamed 'noddy shops' as they were such tediously boring work for prisoners.

Another general duty was supervising exercise. Prisoners were allowed an hour exercise a day. This was on a yard that had five circles where prisoners walked round and round. Each alternate circle the prisoners had to walk in the opposite direction. Why this should be I never did know, as it was just one of those things that happened and nobody questioned. As the new officer I had to stand outside the toilets. My main role was to ensure prisoners did not congregate in here, so I was forever having to go in to a smelly area to remonstrate with prisoners who were hanging around smoking or talking, and they often felt brave in there as the officer was quite isolated and as the young newbie some of them tried it on with you. This was actually good for confidence as I put on an air of authority and used my training to project my voice and show a level of assertiveness. All five foot seven-and-a-half inches of me with my uniform and big cap trying to look the part (I often smiled to myself about the act I put on). Once prisoners realised they could not intimidate you they soon gave up and did as they were told, not necessarily because of me but the consequences of not doing as they were told was not worth the hassle. This was not such a good job in the middle of winter as you were stood in one place for an hour and by the end of the hour you were nithered. For you Southerners, that means it was bloody cold.

Supervising visits was OK, at least it was warm. Convicted prisoners were allowed a visit with their family and friends once a month, technically for one hour. The visits hall for the convicted prisoners was set up with individual tables and prisoners could have a maximum of three visitors. There was a small canteen run by the Women's Royal Volunteer Force (WRVS) where prison visitors could purchase tea, coffee and snacks.

Visits were the times when prisoners tried to get illegal goods into prison, usually drugs of some nature. Even though visitors are searched, quite often some of the female visitors would hide items in their underwear or even inside their vagina. They would then pass the item(s) when they kissed at the end of the visit and the prisoner would swallow it or conceal it in their mouth. If they swallowed it, it would come out when they went to the toilet and retrieved it. Desperate and sad people, but I suppose being locked up often three to a cell for long periods of time, it was a relief from reality. In my early days in the service there were relatively few drugs in prison compared to many years later, and today there are more drugs in prison than in the NHS.

Supervising visits was generally a pleasant task as the prisoners were usually in a good mood and by and large the visitors were OK, particularly convicted visits. Prisoners on remand or trial were allowed visits on a daily basis for 15 minutes and as they were technically innocent at this stage, both prisoners and visitors had a different attitude towards prison staff. They were allowed to wear their own clothing, which made supervision harder, and they were allowed to bring in more goods. They were also allowed to bring in food, which was a nightmare as this was such an easy place to hide contraband. Remand and trial visits were much less pleasant a feel, as there were a lot more of them and they were in two long lines separated by a long table and a barrier from touching. Officers sat on high chairs at the end of the row. I was once sat on one of these chairs when a small boy of about five years of age came up to me and said, "Fuck off screw." I looked at his father who had a stupid grin on his face as he had obviously sent him up to do this. I actually felt sorry for this young boy as he was only doing what his father said, and my thoughts were, in another ten years this boy would be in the same place as his father. After the visit I had a little chat with his father who thought this was hilarious. It was pointless trying to reason with him, so I just said I would have the last laugh, and he was kept locked up for the next 48 hours as he was on my landing and I forgot to unlock him for his meals or exercise. He did apologise after this. As I have children who were once that age, I contemplated how different a life they had. This brings up the debate, nature or nurture. I know which argument I side with: definitely nurture.

One of the worst jobs on these visits was taking the food that prisoners were allowed to have from their visitors. We worked from a little cupboard with a shutter on each side, one for visitors and one for prisoners. The food was brought in in all kinds of containers, usually Tupperware, and we had to search the food with a fork, which usually annoyed the visitor and caused many arguments. This room absolutely stank of different foods and I usually did not eat until the following day. I love a good curry, but this was enough to put you off forever. Prison staff argued for years to stop this practice due to the ease with which contraband could be smuggled in to prison, but the people who managed the service took no notice of this until many years later when ministers had to put a stop to it. Weak, pathetic managers who only cared about their own careers and not rock the boat.

Hospital watch, or as it was more commonly known, bed watch, was when a prisoner had to go to an outside hospital due to the nature of their illness. This involved two prison officers sitting at the bedside of the prisoner 24 hours a day, so six officers doing 8-hour shifts.

The prisoner would at this time be cuffed to the bed and when he went to the toilet or had a bath he would be put on a closeting chain, which was a long chain with cuffs on each end. The prisoner would be cuffed to one end and the officer to the other, which then gave the prisoner some privacy when using these facilities.

Quite often, the nurses would feel sorry for the prisoner being cuffed to the bed with two hairy arsed prison officers sat with him for all to see what he was. On a number of occasions, the nurses would be quite hostile to prison staff as the bad guys who were treating this 'patient' like an animal. I found this attitude quite strange as this person could easily have burgled their house or stolen their car. We used to have a bit of fun with nurses who took this attitude by telling them the prisoner raped a nurse. This usually worked in changing their sympathies. Not very professional I know, but some of the nurses deserved no less. I know you will be thinking: well, what about the prisoner who is totally oblivious of this? At this time not many prison staff would care about him. Cuffing prisoners to the bed ceased to be allowed so had to be cuffed to an officer at all times.

One of the most comical bed watches I ever did was with a prisoner who had fallen from a roof while running away from the police. He said the police pushed him off, as he would. This roof was three storeys up so the prisoner broke nearly every bone in his body. He was in plaster from head to foot and could not move anything other than fingers and toes, and we spent months round the clock sitting at his bedside. What an absolute waste of taxpayers' money, but we were more than happy because it was mostly overtime for us and what an easy way to earn it. On some occasions, we agreed that one of us would turn up about two hours late and the other would go two hours early. Management checks were rare if non-existent. Happy days! Although I knew this was wrong, it was custom and practice in these days and everybody turned a blind eye. By the way, to make this particular bed watch even better, the prisoner was very compliant and actually quite good humoured under the circumstances.

Another role we did was to service the Crown Courts. We used to do two weeks at a time on this duty. The courts that Strangeways managed were Manchester Crown Court (MCC), Crown Court Manchester (CCM), Knutsford CC, Oldham CC and Bolton CC. We also escorted prisoners to Magistrates Courts around the area, which I will mention later.

The big Crown Courts were basically mini prisons in that they had cells, visits areas, a reception area to process prisoners, kitchen and exercise area. During the day up to 200 prisoners would leave the prison to go to court of some type, be discharged from prison and on some days be transferred to other prisons.

The cost of escorting and running the courts by qualified prison officers was pretty high. The number of officers who attended just one big Crown Court was high. Many jobs were pretty mundane and should not, in my opinion, be done by qualified prison officers whose training was to work with prisoners in a prison environment. We used to have two officers assigned to cooking for the staff and prisoners. This was a popular job as it had a number of perks. And to think the taxpayer was paying for this.

We left the prison for the Manchester courts around 8.30am so we could get the prisoners settled in, given a cup of tea and given the opportunity to speak to their legal team before courts starting at 10.30am, or whenever the judge decided. As a new officer I had to sit in the dock with the prisoner, with another officer who would be in charge of the dock. This in effect was still part of a prison. At first I found this part of my work really interesting, but after about a year of sitting through mostly mundane cases, it became very hard to keep awake. On one occasion I was sat in the court with a mundane burglary case that went on and on with the barristers doing what they always do and talking and talking round the houses using language that nobody could understand, in particular the poor scrote in the dock whom this whole charade was about, when the other officer in the dock fell asleep on his chair and leaned back, suddenly disappearing down the steps to the cells with an almighty crash as he rolled down about 20 steps. The whole court stopped in disbelieving silence as the officer staggered back up to the dock where he bowed to the judge and with a bright red face, hair all over the place and torn uniform apologised to him. The judge looked over the top of his glasses and said, "Thank you officer, I think we were all falling asleep, so now we are all awake can we carry on please." And that was the end of it. Even judges have a sense of humour and show a human side. You can imagine I did not keep this to myself and we had a good laugh about it later. There is always a good cartoonist in every prison and this was too good to miss for the resident artist at Strangeways.

One of the most interesting but saddest cases I sat through was a young man who was burgling a house at night and someone called the police. The police arrived and he appeared to panic, and stabbed a young police officer with the screwdriver he had tried to force the window with. Although the offender admitted manslaughter of the policeman he pleaded not guilty to murder, as he said he did not intend to kill him, so a full trial had to take place. With this every detail is gone through with pictures that are not pleasant to see. I do not often feel sorry for criminals but I had some sympathy for this guy as he was a two-bit burglar who genuinely seemed to panic and from what I listened to, he certainly did not go out with the intention of killing anybody, let alone a police officer. He was found not guilty of murder but guilty of manslaughter, which I think was the correct decision. He was, however, given a 15-year sentence because it was a police officer in the execution of his duty. I am a bit unsure we should treat one life taken different to another, but that is how the law worked in those days, and possibly still does.

Another interesting and quite comical day I had was at Knutsford CC. In the dock was another little scrote burglar. As this was a very small crown court, only one dock, we escorted this prisoner in a taxi. On the way he was telling us he had done a number of burglaries in the Knutsford area. Knutsford is a very affluent area to the south of Manchester. He said he was going to plead not guilty as he felt like playing with the court. As it turned out this was not the brightest thing to do as the evidence was very conclusive and he was found guilty within an hour. The judge gave him three years' imprisonment which was just, in my opinion, but very severe compared to other comparative crimes. The judge then went on to say during his sentencing, "We do not want the likes of you coming here and burgling our houses, you should stay in the city and burgle in your own area." As someone from a council estate I found this statement an absolute disgrace and it said a lot about how the privileged people of our society really feel about the rest of us. The arrogance was disgraceful. As we went down to the cells, the prisoner turned to me and said, "I wouldn't mind, none of the houses had anything worth taking." That tickled my sense of humour.

Oldham CC was an eye opener. It was not a very big Crown Court but a busy one. For those of you who do not know Oldham, it is not a very affluent part of Greater Manchester and crime is a way of life for many. In saying that, like everywhere there are good people who may not be financially well off but it does not make them bad people. I would say about 70% of trials in Oldham ended in an acquittal and I put this down to the difficulty in finding a jury that was sympathetic to the judicial system. This is of course my opinion, but it is based on sitting through many trials of people I knew to be guilty because they told me and the evidence against them was generally overwhelming and they were still found not guilty. The good old British judicial system with its trust in the jury system.

I mentioned earlier about the payment system for being out of the prison. We used to get additional payment for being out of the prison on escort duty and different rates of payment for over five hours, over 10 hours and over 12 hours. This was measured from when you left the prison to when you booked back in. This meant not only did you earn extra money for being out for longer, you also earned some overtime.

When we went to the bigger Crown Courts it was easy to ensure you stayed out for the 12 hours as you had to wait for the next day's court lists from the court staff, and also we processed prisoners who had been convicted and a game of cards was a must, so it was easy to justify the time. At the bigger courts you had a Principal Officer in charge who was more than happy to ensure he got his extra payment. I have even driven round Manchester City Centre a few times in a 56-seater bus full of prisoners to ensure we did not get back to the prison too early. Who said you cannot get money for nothing? On top of this you nearly always incurred at least two to three hours' overtime. This lasted for two weeks so you can imagine these duties were very popular. Oh, happy days for weak management who buried their heads in the sand to the abuse of the public purse that was taking place under their noses.

The Magistrates were not quite as lucrative but you could still get your day out of the prison and collect your subs. The Magistrates were very boring as at this time the police ran them so we were basically just left sitting around for hours on end. It always took two prison officers for this task and on occasions when there was a particularly nasty character we had three. Basically our role was to deliver the prisoner to the court around 9am. We went this early so they had access to their legal person. You had no idea what time they would appear in court, as the courts were as organised as a group of six-year-olds. You could be sat around all day and the prisoner would appear in court at say 2.30pm for about ten minutes so he could stand there and say, "Not guilty," then be remanded in custody. We then sat around for another hour or more for a remand warrant from the court offices and then took our time to call a taxi to take us back to the prison. Often this duty was performed on your rest day so it was all overtime, and on top of that you got your subsistence for being out of the prison. I used to think of my former colleagues at times like this, who worked in a smelly dirty factory on an eight hour shift with one hour for lunch with the rest of the day hard at it at a machine. As you can imagine I had no regrets making my decision to join the money machine called the Prison Service.

On a different note one of the most comical times I had in a Magistrates Court was when we escorted a rather notorious Liverpool gangster to Manchester Magistrates. He was generally OK with us unless he felt he had not been treated properly, and then became rather a difficult person to deal with. He was a very tough person who was not really affected by being physically dealt with as that is all he had known most of his life. When we took him to the court he was OK on the journey, however when he was due to go in to the dock we went to the cell and he was stood there as naked as the day he was born. We told him to put his clothes on as he was going in front of the Magistrate. He was not particularly respectful in his opinion of the Magistrate or the court system but was still relatively calm. We tried to talk some sense in to him but he politely declined our advice and said he would only go in to the dock with no clothes on, as the police had stitched him up and taken his liberty when he was innocent so he said they could have his clothes as well, as they had taken everything else.

Discussions took place with the Magistrates to see if there was another way to deal with this but they were adamant he had to appear in court in person. We explained that to him and he said, "Fine, but you will have to take me up as I am." So this is exactly what happened. He stood in the dock with his tackle waving around for all to see. I am sure the Magistrate had a twinkle in her eye as it was probably some time since she had seen such a specimen. As soon as the Magistrate began to speak the prisoner turned his back to show her where she could park her bike, but the main reason for this was wanting to demonstrate his lack of faith in the judicial system. It was very hard to keep a straight face but we all remained very professional and he was remanded in custody, taken down to the cells where he put on his clothes and politely said, "Boss, can we go back to the prison now?" Prisoners used to call officers 'Boss'. I have no idea whether he was guilty or not but the courts found him guilty and he became quite a notorious prisoner for his rejection of the rules, and caused a lot of problems throughout his fairly long sentence.

I hated going to Salford Magistrates as the court was in a very rough part of Salford and surrounded by a warren of terrace houses. The taxi had to park just outside the court and we had to walk along the street for a short while handcuffed to the prisoner. On many occasions we would be surrounded by local thugs who tried to intimidate and generally made us feel uncomfortable. This was mostly intimidation and was to them a bit of fun. Thankfully nothing serious happened for me, but an officer escorting a prisoner to the court in late 1981 was badly assaulted and the prisoner they were escorting escaped. It took this to finally get the court to upgrade security and we were allowed to offload our prisoner in a secure courtyard.

1982

I had to work on Christmas Day at the end of 1981 which was a bit of a culture shock for me being the first time, but one good thing was that there was no traffic on the road. As compensation I had New Year's Day off so we could celebrate the New Year in our new home in Timperley as Mancunians (Yorkshire ones, of course).

As a keen young officer I took the opportunity to apply for a 'fixed post' in the New Year. A fixed post is where you do a specific role for a period of time as opposed to general duties as explained previously. I applied for reception and was accepted. The first 12 months was learning the role and filling in when permanent reception officers were not available, then 12 months as a full time reception officer.

Reception was where prisoners were processed when they came from the courts and transferred in from other prisons. Prisoners also were processed through reception when leaving to go to court, being transferred to other prisons and being released from custody after serving their sentence or released on bail.

The process was making sure a prisoner had a committal warrant, either a convicted one or remand. This is from the court, signed by the court clerk and is the legal authority to hold a person in custody. Once this was checked and we ensured we had the correct person in front of us they were strip searched, their property and clothing logged and given prison clothing. None of this was done with much privacy or dignity, but nobody seemed to complain too much. The prisoner took a quick shower and came out with their ill-fitting clothing of blue denims, blue & white striped shirt and denim jacket. They were then taken up to the main body of the prison where they were allocated a cell and locked up for the evening. At this time there was very little information for prisoners, and for those new to prison this must have been quite a stressful and frightening time. No wonder quite a number of prisoners harmed themselves in these first hours, but there was little sympathy from rough, tough prison officers who felt their role was merely to lock people up who deserved it.

So 1982 was spent doing periods in reception learning this role and doing general duties within the prison.

Jenny fell pregnant and was expecting our first child in April of this year. On the 12th April at 3.25am our son, Alastair, eventually arrived after Jenny was in labour for an eternity. She was completely washed out after this, but Alastair had all the right tackle and another part of our life was just beginning. I felt so proud to be a father but my admiration goes out to Jenny and all the mothers out there after what they go through on our behalf. Men think they are tough but after what I witnessed we are nowhere near as tough as women. Hats off to you, and particularly my lovely wife.

I don't think anybody is ever really fully ready for parenthood and we were certainly not ready for this little bundle of joy depriving us of so much sleep over the next 18 months to two years. I often had to start my shift in reception at 6.30am and sometimes worked until after ten in the evening. This was on top of having my sleep broken at least four or five times every night; I was constantly tired but happy as well. I am glad I was in my early 20s to be fit and able to cope with this. A lot of officers used to work for weeks without a day off but I never worked my weekend off as this was precious family time to me, and I earned enough money with the overtime I did. I could see how many of the officers were divorced or going through marital issues as they were never at home and those that had children must never have seen them awake.

We used to do nights about once every ten weeks. I did not particularly like nights as they upset my digestive system but they were good for time off. The night shift was a 12-hour shift. There was one officer for each wing. You started your shift by checking that every prisoner was in their cell and alive. During the night at set periods you had to pass a pegging point where you recorded the time you passed it to prove you were patrolling. This was recorded in the Chief Officer's office. To get round having to stay awake all evening we used to split the night between all of us so one officer used to do an hour walking round the whole prison doing the pegging on every wing while the rest did what they wanted. Some officers took the opportunity to sleep, some just read or basically did what they wanted. The two managers on nights knew this was going on and turned a blind eye to it as long as the pegs were recorded.

There was one Principal Officer who used to do other Principal Officers' nights and ensure certain officers did the same so they could have a poker school. I am aware of some officers losing some serious money at these poker nights and getting into real difficulties. In fact, I was told one officer lost his car one night. I am not sure if this was true but I would not put it past some of the officers of this era.

On my first set of nights in 1982 I had my first suicide. It was a young man who had only been in prison for a few days and it was his first sentence. For one so young and inexperienced, he was very calculated in the way he took his life. He lay in bed with the bed sheets up to his neck, and then cut his wrists lengthways cutting the artery and then hanging his arms over the side of the bed with two containers catching the blood so he would not be detected. He was very much beyond help when we found him in the morning and this was the first of many prisoners who took their lives over the next 33 years. As much as it was very sad to see a human being take his life, the sad reality of prison life is you become a bit immune to the emotion and just act in a professional manner. Or, shall I say, I and many others did but there were those who just did not care.

The year passed very quickly with a lot happening in my life with learning a new role in reception, working long hours and having a new member of the family. It was a mixed year as the joy of having our first child was fantastic but my beloved Leeds United were relegated to what was then Division 2. After being brought up with the Don Revie team this was almost unbelievable and to add insult to injury I was living in the heartland of Manchester United supporters. To say I got some stick was an understatement. It was at this point I nearly got my friendly Chief Officer to sort them out, but toughed it out and let the petty little glory hunters have their day.

1983

1983 was not my best, because after being ill for nearly two years riddled with cancer, my mother died at the age of 52. My mother was a smoker for much of her life and I don't know if this caused the cancer but it certainly would not have helped. Watching my mother deteriorate to a virtual skeleton when she died certainly convinced me never to smoke, even though I wouldn't anyway because they are the most disgusting things and thankfully I couldn't stand the things. Even if I wanted to smoke I just couldn't as they made me puke. It was a great decision when they banned smoking in public places, as I could actually go to a pub or restaurant without coming out smelling like a tramp and my eyes watering and stinging. So I said goodbye to my mother at such an early age it does bring life in to perspective. My father had been very much a family man and this really affected him even though he tried to hide it. My father dealt with this in his own way and as ever he came through the grief to start a new life for himself. He did something I never thought he would and had a couple of holidays on his own, then joined a singles club for older people. This is where he met Margaret, whom he later married and had a great life with until his death in 2012, and Margaret has been like a mother to me and still is to this day. She made my father's life a good one and devoted many years to his welfare after he had his stroke and was incapable of doing anything for himself. A wonderful woman.

Back to the prison and one of the roles I did not particularly like was doing the exercise in the Segregation Unit. The Segregation Unit (seg unit, as it was called) was a small unit on the bottom of D Wing. It was a small unit separated off where prisoners were located when they were too dangerous or unruly to be with the main population or prisoners who had been placed on report and given Cellular Confinement (CC). A prisoner was placed on report for breaking prison rules and went in front of the Governor, who adjudicated on him by asking if he was guilty or not. If he pleaded not guilty, the Governor would listen to the evidence of the officer placing him on report and any defence the prisoner had. In these days the prisoner was very rarely found not guilty and really it was just a 'kangaroo court'.

Back to the exercise before I explain more about the seg unit itself. The exercise yard was a small dingy cage where prisoners would walk round in silence. Some prisoners were so dangerous they had to be exercised on their own and often they spent the whole exercise trying to wind you up or just being a pain. On one occasion a particularly obnoxious prisoner refused to come off the yard, which was a rather stupid decision as the seg unit staff were generally handpicked for being rather large, very tough and not averse to a bit of violence. This prisoner lasted about ten minutes of refusal and a bit of gentle persuasion by the officers until their patience ran out and he was physically removed from the yard. All I can say about these times is prisons like Strangeways were not pleasant places. Many prisoners somehow generally accepted being treated like animals, or they felt they had no choice as trying to fight the 'system' was futile. In saying that, some prisoners behaved like animals and had no regard for anybody, including themselves.

The seg unit itself was a grim place that thankfully I never worked in at Strangeways. Many of the officers working here at this time were just legal thugs in my opinion, and again so-called managers just turned a blind eye or actually condoned the way prisoners were treated. You may ask why people like me did not say anything about this. As much as I would like to have made my feelings known I had to protect myself, my job and my livelihood. This may appear to be a bit of cowardice, but I felt at the time it was futile and I would certainly not have been able to continue working in the service being an outcast.

I spent a good part of this year working in reception which I found really interesting work, dealing with lots of different situations and learning some legal issues around holding people sent to us from the courts. I also learned a lot of organisational skills as the movement of prisoners through a big local prison reception needed to be done with good systems in place as it was not a good thing to discharge the wrong prisoner, particularly if you were releasing him to the street. Thankfully I never did this and it was not something that happened very often but some prisoners would try anything. I was working in reception once when a prisoner was brought down from the wing to be discharged. You have his record in front of you and ask certain questions like date of birth, prison number, and address on coming in to prison, etc. and also there was a picture of the prisoner. This particular prisoner was being discharged by a colleague and answering all the relevant questions and not too far from being released when a prison orderly (a prisoner trusted to work in reception) said to me, "Boss, that is not Joe Bloggs." I said, "What do you mean it is not Joe Bloggs?" He said he knew the prisoner who should be released and that was not him. Alarms bells rang and we eventually looked further in to this and found the person who should be in front of us was still in his cell and the prisoner in front of us was his cellmate.

What had happened is the prisoner who was to be released had a similar look to the other prisoner in the cell, and when the officer went to the cell he asked for the prisoner being released by name. At this point, unbeknown to the officer the other prisoner said that was him. The officer asked him for his prison number which he gave as the other man's in the cell. To be fair to the officer at this stage, he may not have known the correct prisoner so accepted this was the correct person and took him to reception. The two of them had worked out a plan where the wrong prisoner would pretend to be the real one who was to be released by learning all the details about his cell mate, and they realised they had a look of each other so he could use his identity. Once he was released and gone the real prisoner to be released would then call the officer and say he should have been released from his sentence but the officer took the wrong one. As we would then be unable to legally hold someone who had served their sentence we would have had to release him as well. I am not sure why the reception orderly did what he did, but we were very thankful to him, and in the same vein you had to give the two prisoners hatching the plan some credit for their audacity which nearly worked.

Both prisoners were placed on report, one for attempted escape while the other was charged with assisting an escape. As these were serious charges which carried a prison sentence, they were referred to the police and charged with a criminal offence. This way the one who should have been released was taken to police custody, then returned later after being remanded in custody by the Magistrates Court. A valuable lesson for us, and procedures were changed after this.

As my time in reception was coming to an end halfway through the year, another opportunity came up to work in the Observation Classification and Allocation Unit (OCA) on a fixed post basis. This time for two years as a reserve and two years in post. I applied for this post and was successful. This was a real prestigious role within a local prison so I was really chuffed, and put a few more experienced officers' noses out of joint as they wanted it. I will explain what this role is later.

So when my time came to an end in reception I carried on doing general duties until joining the OCA. One experience I need to share with you is quite a comical one, but did not seem like it at the time. I was given the task of escorting a prisoner to visit his partner who was serving a sentence in a women's prison to the south of Manchester called Styal. At first I thought this would be interesting and was looking forward to the experience. We arrived at the prison and had to initially go through reception. It seemed quite strange to see women in uniform and women prisoners. At this time it was all male staff in male prisons and female in female prisons (this changed around 1987). We had to walk through the grounds of the prison handcuffed to the prisoner to the visits room. As Styal was a less secure prison than Strangeways, prisoners were wandering around the grounds going to different parts and the looks we got made us feel like we were in a goldfish bowl. As we passed one of the wings there was a group of women prisoners at the windows shouting and whistling at us as we passed. The sexual innuendo that came from these women was something I had never experienced from a woman in the past, and some of the suggested sexual positions we were propositioned with I did not think were physically possible. Even the prisoner we were escorting was beginning to feel uncomfortable and said, "Come on Boss, can we walk a bit faster?" I think the female officers escorting us were having a bit of a chuckle at our expense and once we got in the taxi to go back to Strangeways we all burst out laughing, and looking back, a good day was had by all and it gave me yet another life experience.

I had joined the Manchester Prison Golf Society in this year. Every few months we would arrange a society day out to a nice golf club where we started with a fat boy's breakfast, nine holes in the morning, a light lunch, and 18 holes in the afternoon and then showered and changed for an evening meal. I did feel a bit guilty on these days as I worked a lot of hours and Jenny was at home with Alastair but it was a release for me and I think Jenny recognised this and was very understanding and unselfish, as she has been throughout our marriage (and still is). These days out were really enjoyable and I even got reasonable at golf.

There were around 30 of us on these days and I used to hate it when I was one of the first ones to tee off, as everybody stood round watching, so you can imagine the pressure of getting the first shot off the tee as the laughter was deafening if you scuffed it. In saying this there were some very good golfers and when you played with them they were very patient with you, offering help and advice on the way round.

I remember one day we had arranged a day at The Mere Golf and Country Club near Knutsford. This was a very posh club. We had a good day's golf and after showering and changing into our suits we went for the evening meal. We shared the restaurant with a group of solicitors who were obviously on a similar day out. As the evening went on and the drink was flowing this group of solicitors started getting louder and louder, swearing and being objectionable to the young female waitresses. Some of my colleagues were getting a bit fed up of their behaviour and it came to a head when one of the solicitors put his hand on the backside of a young waitress. She was very uncomfortable with this and unsure how to deal with it. A couple of our group stood up and asked them politely to stop their rowdy and unacceptable behaviour but their arrogance was such that they carried on. As I explained earlier I worked with some pretty tough, uncompromising people, and a few of these stood up and politely explained who they were and if they did not act in a respectful manner to us and the golf club staff they would have no choice than to remove them physically. A bit of a standoff took place for a short period, then I think the solicitors took a look at the rest of us and decided discretion was a good option. I think that was one of the best decisions they had taken in a while and probably since. They left soon after with their tails between their legs and we were given a few bottles of wine on the house by a very grateful manager. Some prison officers might be rough tough people, but obviously knew how to behave in the right circumstances. Maybe some solicitors spend so much time with criminals that they become like them, or it is just pure arrogance. I guess, as with everything in life, it is a small minority that give the majority of decent people a bad name.

I had Christmas Day off, which was nice, and was on night duty over the New Year period. This was a strange experience as at midnight all the prisoners bang on the cell door with plastic cups. This is like being in a riot with the noise and shouting and puts the hairs up on the back of your neck. It lasted about 30 seconds then stopped and peace and quiet took over again. Strangeways is more or less in the centre of Manchester and you can look out of the windows to see everyone enjoying the night, with fireworks going off and people going about their celebrations. What a place to spend New Year, was my thought. Yet another life experience.

So another year comes to an end.

Chapter 2

1984 – 87

So I started 1984 looking forward to working in the OCA. This, as I said, was one of the best roles in the prison and generally one for more experienced officers than me. It was where prisoners were interviewed the day after they came to prison after being sentenced or convicted. They had an induction interview to assess them for work, category of prisoner they were and ascertain any issues they had, or not as the case may be. The main type of issue was generally family related. One guy once told me he had been arrested and committed to prison and his dog was left in the house. He said the dog had been there about three days on its own, so we asked the police if they would help in this matter. The police officer I spoke to was not too sympathetic, as the prisoner was not too popular with the police, but I finally reasoned with him that it was not the dog's fault he was owned by such an irresponsible person.

For those who qualified as requiring a parole dossier due to the length of their sentence, one was opened at this point. Each officer working in the OCA was allocated certain prisoners who became our responsibility to do parole reports for throughout the time they were at Manchester, and to instruct other people to do likewise such as probation staff, medical etc. In effect we managed that prisoner's sentence while he was in Manchester, from behaviour reports to allocating them work and eventually moving them to a training prison where they could continue their progress to eventual release.

The ones I enjoyed the most were life sentence prisoners, as you had to go in to some depth of their offending and past life. Reading the notes of the case was interesting and at times quite distressing. Sometimes you could not equate what you had just read to the same person who was sat in front of you, as often you would be interviewing someone serving life and they would be polite, co-operative and not in the least what you would expect from someone who had taken another person's life, often in very violent circumstances. All in all the OCA was a very responsible role as we had a lot of power over a prisoner's life while they were in the prison.

As I was a reserve at this time in the OCA, I did other general duties. One of these was working in the hospital ward. As a basic officer you were classed as a Discipline Officer and some officers chose to become specialists. One of these was what we called a Hospital Officer. In effect they were nurses, but the training they got was nothing as comprehensive as a nurse in the NHS and nothing like as compassionate. A lot took this as a way to earn a bit extra and get out of working in the main prison and all its issues. In saying that, I did not envy them their role as there were some real fruit bats in the prison hospital who were very unpredictable and often very violent. A quick jab with some jungle juice usually calmed them down. As Discipline Officers we helped in the hospital by collecting patients for the surgeries and patrolling the Ward as additional security. This was a proper funny farm with seriously mentally damaged people. I have always maintained throughout all the time I spent in the Prison Service there have been many people who should not be there due to their mental state, as prison staff were not qualified to deal with this kind of illness and in my opinion many of these people were made worse in prison due to the fact they were not understood by the average prison officer, so were treated like any other prisoner who became unruly or violent. That usually meant isolating them in the seg unit and when they were not in the seg unit they would be locked up for long periods, by and large without work or any other kind of stimulation. To add to this they were often treated even worse by other prisoners which often went unnoticed by prison staff. I will no doubt touch on this subject later as for whatever reason the number of prisoners suffering mental illness got larger and larger throughout the years. In my layman's opinion this had a lot to do with drug use. Some politicians want to legalise them? I guess this is a never-ending debate which I will leave you to decide which opinion you have.

On one occasion I had to escort a prisoner who was appealing his conviction and sentence. We had to take the prisoner to HMP Brixton to be held overnight before going to the Court of Appeal at the Old Bailey. Going to Brixton itself was very interesting, as it was and probably still is one of the most famous prisons of this country. You will read later how I ended up working there for three years. Brixton was a very old Victorian prison that made you feel you were going back in time. We dropped the prisoner in reception in the afternoon and all seemed pretty orderly, even though the reception area was a warren of small corridors and cells with little room to work effectively or give prisoners any privacy.

We had booked some digs somewhere in Streatham. In these days we were given a set overnight allowance so we usually booked the cheapest digs we could so we had more money for ourselves left over. We even shared a room to make a bit more. Tight Northerners, I can hear you Southerners saying. I cannot argue with you as we are a bit tight with money and I think Yorkshire people more than Lancastrians.

We got up bright and early to make our way to Brixton and pick our prisoner up to take to the Old Bailey. As we entered the reception area at Brixton it was absolute pandemonium with prison staff and prisoners everywhere. The number of discharges to various courts was mindboggling and how each prisoner got to where they were going was a massive credit to the staff at Brixton.

We arrived at the Old Bailey, passing the front of this impressive and famous building only to drive in at the side of the building and in to what can only be described as dungeons. Romance over. The court cells were nearly as chaotic as Brixton reception with prison staff, prisoners and barristers all over the place. It was fascinating just to sit and watch what was going on. Once again, amid the chaos, everything seemed to slip into place and court proceedings got under way. We took our prisoner up the stairs from the cells into the dock and we entered this magnificent courtroom with all its pomp, and sat down to wait for the judges. As this was an appeal court, there were three judges. What a cost this all must be. I know we would all want the protection of the law if we were ever wrongly accused of a crime but there must be a cheaper, more efficient way of doing things. Getting any kind of change within the law courts is virtually impossible as judges in this country are all powerful and very few politicians will take them on; also, a large number of MPs were and possibly still are from a legal background so they are going to look after each others' interest, not to say back pockets.

Our prisoner had his appeal dismissed so we took him back down to the cells. The Principal Officer in charge of the cells asked us what we wanted to do, did we want to get off or leave it a bit to get more subs? We decided to take the opportunity to look around the building so we went upstairs and had a good look round this beautiful building before making our way back up to Manchester. All in all I would not like to think how much these two days cost. The taxi fare, two officers on overtime and subsistence, three high court judges, two barristers, court staff and more just for one person who was allowed to play the system by making a spurious appeal. I do appreciate there has to be an appeal process, but when you know most of the urchins who appeal are doing it because they can, and it is a bit of a day out for them at no cost to them, it does make you a little bitter and twisted.

1984 brought another wonderful addition to our family. My wife gave birth to a beautiful daughter, Katy, on the 12th September, which meant we had the perfect family with a son and a daughter. I truly felt on cloud nine at this point in time. I even forgot how poor my football team were, I was so happy. Thankfully Katy slept at night but due to the fact Alastair was such a poor sleeper we thought there was something wrong with her so we still got up to see that she was OK. She is in her thirties now and can still sleep for England.

1985

Most of 1985 was spent working in the OCA where I continued to do some really quality work with prisoners in relation to their rehabilitation and progress towards eventual release, or towards moving to a less secure environment where there was more opportunity to do better quality work. It was quality work for the time, but compared to the service today it was pretty basic I guess. I really enjoyed the work with the lifers helping them to progress and eventually move on to a long term prison, where the facilities were much better for someone serving a long sentence.

By this time I was starting to think more about my career from a point of view of promotion. The first process was to take a Senior Officers exam. You had to have four full years' service in the January of the year the exam was sat to take the exam and because I joined in January 1980, I had to wait an additional year. So the exam date was set for the 3rd April 1985 and I applied to take this. Working in the OCA was a great place for me to be as there were interview booths where we interviewed prisoners, and it was also good for getting some peace and quiet to revise. I have never been a lover of exams but this meant a lot to me so I put in an awful lot of effort and time.

By the time the exam date came round I don't think I have ever been as ready as I was for this. I went in to the exam with a high degree of confidence. I turned the paper over and for three hours gave it all I had. Because of the work I had done and the fact I actually enjoyed learning about my job I came out of the exam room as confident as I went in. Sometime later we received the results and I had passed with some room to spare. I was so chuffed with myself and this meant so much to me and what I could achieve for myself and my growing family.

In these days we used to have a national promotion board for all promotions. Having passed my exam I was entitled to apply for a promotion when the boards were announced. A promotion board was announced not long after I got my exam results so I applied for the chance to be interviewed. I got a letter in November 1985 telling me I would not be called for interview. I appealed this decision but was equally unsuccessful. I later found out that almost nobody with less than ten years' service was given the opportunity of an interview. What an anachronistic system where promotion was based on years of service rather than ability. This was a large promotion board and unbeknown to me there would not be another one for a number of years. I just had to accept this and get on with my job and accept that time was on my side.

As this year was generally fairly uneventful in terms of things happening in the prison, I will relate about the shocking attitude of some sections of the prison officers at Strangeways at that time. It was mostly the older end of the officers, but there was a large minority of officers wearing National Front badges under their ties or jacket lapels. Some of these were managers and one was a Chief Officer. I personally found this hard to accept and tried to distance myself from the people I knew were openly racist, as this was not acceptable to me and totally unprofessional. Once again I am sure senior managers in the service knew this was going on and turned a blind eye to ensure they did not get on the wrong side of the POA. Thankfully most, if not all, of the younger newer officers did not come in to the service with these Neanderthal thoughts, so I could see some hope for the future.

So 1985 came to a close with a bit of a bang, literally, as I used a motorcycle to get to work leaving Jenny with the car to help her get around with the children. On Saturday 30th November I was riding home from work. My route to the south of Manchester took me through the centre of the city and the main shopping street of Deansgate. As I set off from some lights at the end of Deansgate a taxi decided suddenly to brake for no apparent reason and in my haste to avoid him, the bike skidded on the wet surface and the bike, with me on it, landed in a heap on the road. I stood up and tried to lift my bike up and found my right arm was dangling down by my side with me unable to move it. I realised I had dislocated my shoulder. At this point there was no pain and I just sat on the side of the road with people fussing around me trying to help as best as they could.

The ambulance arrived and the ambulance man assessed me then he put an oxygen mask on me for the pain, even though at this stage I was not in pain. I was put in the ambulance and taken to hospital. I was put on a trolley in a waiting booth and I asked the hospital staff to phone my wife to let her know where I was. By the time Jenny arrived I was starting to feel some pain. Jenny had to get our two children ready just around their tea time, get them in the car and try to find the hospital. I had no idea where the hospital was but Jenny said it was in a really rough area. The hospital was called Ancoats.

I had an all-in-one bike suit on which the nurses struggled to get off me without inflicting high levels of pain. I had my uniform on under the suit and with it being winter I had a jumper on. I told the nurses to cut the jumper off as I would get another one, but for some reason they seemed to want to inflict more pain on me and boy, was it painful. After about four hours I was in absolute agony and was told they could not do anything until I had had an X-ray – but because it was a Saturday there was no radiologist on duty, so they had to call one from home. I told Jenny to take the children home as I was going to be in overnight and the children were getting fed up. By the time I had my X-ray I was in excruciating pain. The X-ray showed a bad dislocation and they said I may need a pin in my shoulder, so they put me to sleep to see if they could put it back without this.

I woke up the following morning with my shoulder back in the position it should be and the pain had gone. The doctor told me they did not have to put a pin in my shoulder but it was a pretty bad dislocation and I should not be surprised if I would suffer arthritis in later life. What a jolly person he was!

Jenny and the children came back in the morning to pick me up and take me home. I was more than happy to leave this hospital, as I felt my treatment the previous evening was pretty poor and did nothing to endear me to our precious NHS. The only positive thing that came out of this was the fact I was off for the whole of the Christmas and New Year holiday and in fact I did not return to work until 19th Feb 1986.

1986

Throughout 1986 there was talk about new working practices being discussed. Finally it looked like the management of the service were looking to bring the Prison Service into the modern era and professionalise it. I must admit I thought the Prison Officers' Association (POA) would put up a lot of opposition to change as they were one of the last bastions of the archaic unions (or associations) of the 1970s. No doubt Mrs Thatcher had something to do with this as she was working her way through the groups who were keeping Britain from becoming a modern workforce. As you can probably tell, I was and am a fan of Margaret Thatcher and the strength she showed in changing this country from a strike-infested, union-dominated socialist state that was going bankrupt, to a private enterprise, aspirational and meritocratic society that allowed skilled and entrepreneurial people to thrive and make this country a place to be proud of, and encouraged hard work instead of the demoralising welfare culture engendered by the socialists. Look what happened to the Eastern Bloc countries; after years of depressing socialism they have seen the light and see capitalism as the way forward for the majority of hard working people. I am not saying capitalism is perfect and I do not like greed, but you have to give people some aspiration in life. Unfortunately wherever you have human beings some will always want to take advantage for their own greed. Capitalism has its minority of greedy business owners and socialism has its union bosses looking after their own type of greed.

The rest of 1986 passed with little incident as I continued my work in the OCA. Later in the year there was a notice came out for officers to apply to work in a new prison being built in Yorkshire called Full Sutton. Full Sutton was located about 12 miles east of the beautiful city of York and was due to be completed by October 1987. I asked Jenny if she would like to return to our native Yorkshire and she did not hesitate in saying yes. Full Sutton was to be a Dispersal Prison, which is a long term prison holding the worst offenders in the country. I saw this as another step in my career development. I applied for Full Sutton and received my acceptance letter on the 15th December 1986. This was really exciting news and was to be another chapter in both my career and family life.

HM Prison Service All correspondence should be
Headquarters   addressed to:
Cleland House   The Governor
Page Street   HM Prison
London SW1P 4LN   FULL SUTTON
Telephone 01-211 3000 Moor Lane
Direct line 01-211   Full Sutton Village
                   Near Stamford Bridge
                   Humberside YO4 1HS

Home Office
HM PRISON SERVICE   50
                              100 plse.

Officer P.M. Ward
HMP Manchester

Your reference

Our reference   BS/RMH

Date   25.2.87

Dear Mr Ward.

I thank you for your recent letter requesting permission to live out
of quarters on your posting to Full Sutton.

I have no objection in principle to your occupying your own property.

Obviously when you are in a position to do so you will tell me where you
intend to live. I shall then need, as outlined in Manual 1, Section 1 -
Quarters, to be satisfied that you will be able to attend punctually
for duty from that address and that satisfactory arrangements can be made
for you to attend for duty in the event of an emergency or a requirement
to attend for unscheduled duty.

Though there is no requirement for you to install a telephone, I must
advise you that if you do so I shall require that the number is
available to me for the purpose of contacting you in an emergency or for
unscheduled duty, unless, of course, you can offer some other means by
which you can readily be contacted.

I look forward to welcoming you at Full Sutton in due course.

Yours sincerely

B V SMITH
Governor designate

My transfer letter to Full Sutton

1987

So 1987 started with the Ward family looking forward to returning to their beloved Yorkshire. I was not sure when this would happen but realised it would be later in the year as Full Sutton was not due for completion until sometime around late summer. I continued to work in the OCA but was taken out around March due to my impending transfer at some point in the year, so I was put on general duties as a bit of a dogsbody.

I mentioned previously how the management of the service were looking to modernise and professionalise the service. This was not before time in my opinion, as an incident happened that had no place in a modern Prison Service. I was patrolling the landings on B Wing when I came across an incident where two prisoners had barricaded themselves in their cell due to a perceived injustice they felt had occurred against them. In a modern civilised service a level of dialogue would take place to end this situation with the minimum force and minimum potential injury to staff or prisoners. This was not the Strangeways way, however. A little bit of dialogue took place until the manager in charge said, "That's enough pussyfooting around, get them out." The Deputy Governor was stood on the centre viewing what was happening when the Chief Officer turned to him and said, "I don't think you want to witness this anymore, Sir." The Deputy Governor agreed with this and returned to his office like a good boy.

This incident was on the fourth floor of the wing so the prisoners had to be taken to D1, which was the seg unit located on D Wing, quite a distance from the cell location. The rest of the prison was locked up while the heavy mob were mobilised to remove these two. I will explain what Control & Restraint (C&R) is later in this book as at this time it did not exist, but I will just say there was no skill involved in removing the two unreasonable prisoners. These prisoners had offered no violence at this stage, as they were requesting to see the Governor over their grievance. After a short period the door was removed (cell doors have hinges that can be removed so the door opens outward) and the officers piled in to remove the barrier and get to the prisoners. At this stage the prisoners attempted to resist the officers but were overpowered and what happened next was not something I would like to see happen by a professional body again, but it made some of those American police look like children playing games. I am not professing to be an angel, but I would class myself as a professional person doing my job to the best of my ability within the rule of law. Neither am I saying anybody here committed a criminal offence, but I would say some were being a bit unprofessional.

We put our house on the market for £39,500 which was an increase of around £18,000 from when we bought it in 1980. You can see why I eventually got in to property later in life. I still have the receipts for the solicitor and removal company; the solicitor was £460 for sale and purchase, removal was £372. How times change. We were not too long in getting a buyer but because I did not have a transfer date we tried to drag it out a bit. We eventually had to sell before I got my transfer to Full Sutton, so Jenny and the children had to go on their own for about five weeks before I could join them, so it was back in to digs for me.

We bought a brand new house about two miles from the centre of York. This was a lovely big four-bedroom detached house which we paid £54,500. This was about 12 miles from Full Sutton. Once again I received all expenses for this move from solicitor's fees to carpet and curtains. Thank you, your majesty.

I was put to work in the prison hospital for my last few months. I hated this as all I did was run around picking prisoners up for appointments, sitting with them while they waited and taking them back. When not doing this I assisted the hospital staff with in-patients, where many of these were mentally ill and very difficult people who were unpredictable and I had no qualifications or training to deal with this type of prisoner. Boy, was I glad when October came and I was transferred to Full Sutton to get away from the fruitcakes (and that was just the staff).

While all this was going on the changes to the way we managed prisons was being introduced. This was called 'Fresh Start' and completely changed the way the service was managed. Fresh Start changed the grading system by removing the Chief Officer grade leaving three uniformed grades, Officer, Senior Officer and Principal Officer, and created five non-uniform managerial grades. At the beginning of Fresh Start all these grades were given a number, from I to VIII. Throughout the years the names of these have changed and been fiddled around with, but the basic model of three uniformed and five non-uniformed management grades has remained since this time to when I left the service. Overnight Chief Officers lost a lot of their status and had to spend a bit of money on cheap suits and learn how to manage strategically rather than bully. One of the main changes that sold the deal to the POA membership, apart from the bribery of £200 as one-off payment, was the removal of overtime and more or less doubling the basic salary. This meant staff could take a two week holiday without losing a lot of money in overtime and being paid a poor basic salary. At first, uniformed grades could contract in to do nine additional hours a week which reduced over five years to a basic 39 hour week.

Another major change was the introduction of mixed staff in prisons, so men could work in women's prisons and vice versa. A lot of the Neanderthals were truly shocked at this and were adamant it would lead to all sorts of problems and a softening of prisons with discipline going out of the window. What it did do in my opinion is make male prisons much less testosterone filled, which initially reduced violence and probably did soften prisons, but they needed softening, or shall I say less confrontational. The strange part of this was the average prisoner's attitude was one where they showed more respect to women officers than many of their male colleagues. On many occasions I heard big roughy toughy prisoners apologising to female officers for swearing. By the time I left the service it would seem strange not having mixed gender staff. It just shows you how change eventually becomes the norm until the next change. Life and business are about mindset, something of which I will discuss more later, but thank goodness the higher management were finally having the courage to change the mindset within the service to a more positive one.

Manchester was one of the first four prisons to adopt Fresh Start in July 1987. As the week started on a Sunday in the Prison Service, Fresh Start came in on Sunday 4th July, my birthday. It was very strange as on the Saturday there were loads of staff around with officers taking the chance to work overtime on their rest day; the following day the staff compliment was much less. This was a strange experience for staff and prisoners. As I was working in the hospital I was kind of out of the main part of the prison and a bit sheltered from the problems this initially caused. As with any change, and this was a big one, there are always going to be teething problems.

Jenny and the children moved to our new house in York in September so I had to move in to digs until the beginning of October, when I was given my date to move to Full Sutton. So after nearly eight years we moved back to our beloved Yorkshire and the beautiful city of York. A lot of houses around us were still being built so we were living on a building site for some time. We experienced our first ever burglary within weeks of moving here. The patio doors that had been fitted by the builders were an absolute disgrace in that you could virtually lift them off their rails once you broke the lock, and that is how they got in. Ironically one of the empty houses had the patio door forced a couple of days before, which we presumed was the same people doing a practice. Welcome back to Yorkshire.

I started my first day at Full Sutton in early October. The prison had no prisoners in it at this time, which was a bit weird. There were a number of us starting at the same time, so we were given a tour of the prison. There were four wings, each wing holding around 108 prisoners. This was going to be a different experience for me as in long term prisons prisoners did not share cells, unlike in Strangeways where they could be three to a cell. Each wing was very poorly designed as they were on a square, on two floors with three landings, or spurs as these were called, with 18 cells on each spur. The fourth spur was for administration on the top floor and the dining room on the ground floor. Each spur was like a hotel corridor, and separate from each other so you could not see what was happening on another spur or between each floor. The stairways were very dangerous as they were also blind spots, so initial thoughts were quite worrying considering the type of prisoners that would be held on these wings.

There was a very big workshop and education area with very well stocked workshops, which were set up to be more vocational than the noddy workshops I experienced at Strangeways. There was a huge sports field which would be used by prisoners to play football, rugby, run etc. This was big enough for a small plane or helicopter to land so there was wire across to prevent this. There was a hospital which was to NHS standard, with rooms for all different medical disciplines and a smallish ward for in-patients. Within the grounds there was a prison within a prison. This was called a Special Secure Unit (SSU) which had a maximum capacity of ten cells. This was all electronic. The doors to get in, the cell doors and internal doors were all operated from a small control room within the unit that was state-of-the-art technology for this time with buttons and cameras everywhere. It had its own visits room, gym, exercise yard etc. I will say more about this when I get to the part when I worked here.

As this was a new prison we immediately operated under the new system of Fresh Start. I was assigned to the group that operated reception, the canteen, library, labour liaison (where work was allocated to prisoners), and one other which I cannot remember. Due to my previous experience I was allocated to reception but as the prison was empty we did quite a bit of training and spent a lot of time putting furniture into offices, cells etc.

At the end of October we took our first prisoners. Most of the officers who were allocated to reception were very experienced and the majority had previously worked in local prisons, many of them Northern people who took the opportunity to move out of London. So most of us working here had a local prison attitude, which was one where prisoners do as they are told without question. This led to a bit of a clash when we started receiving prisoners as most came from other long term prisons throughout the country, therefore the prisoners had a long term attitude, which was one where things were much more relaxed and they were used to speaking to staff in a different way and were entitled to a lot more property.

During the first few weeks where we took in about 50 prisoners, there were a number of nose to nose confrontations but we were determined to start off being in charge and set the culture that was to be Full Sutton. Some of the prisoners coming from prisons such as Long Lartin had boxes and boxes of property, which was ridiculous, and much of it was taken off them and stored, which caused many a confrontation. This again was a bit of a culture shock for many of the officers, including me, as local prisons were very strict with the amount of property a prisoner could have (virtually nothing).

One thing that was new to many of us was the fact this was the first time we had experienced working with female officers. To be fair to the majority of male officers, the small number of female officers that were at Full Sutton at this time were accepted and as I described earlier, in my opinion female officers added some real positives to the male environment; in particular they made the culture less aggressive and female officers were more capable of defusing aggressive situations with reasoning and talking, where many times when you get two males together they do not want to be seen to back down and feel they need to prove their 'manhood', whatever that is in the Neanderthal world.

The year ended with D Wing about three quarters full with staff and prisoners preening for position and trying to get a culture in place that was unique to Full Sutton. This is not easy when you have a large number of uniformed staff and managers coming from prisons all over the country used to working in different ways in different types of prisons. This is where strong leadership is required.

The first Governor was a man called Barry Smith who was a very experienced man with a career in the armed services before the Prison Service. He was OK, but I got the impression he had no intention of staying too long and this turned out to be true. I think Mr Smith was only at Full Sutton less than a year when John Staples arrived. Mr Staples was a very bright man and a gentleman. I believe he had an academic background and was certainly not from the old school of armed forces-type discipline.

Chapter 3

1988 – 1990

1988

The first three to four months of 1988 was a very busy period in reception with weekly influxes of prisoners. There is no love lost between prisons, and this meant many of the other local and long term prisons took the chance to get rid of all their rubbish and difficult prisoners, which meant more confrontation and quite a difficult time for all of us. Professionalism at its finest. I cannot complain as we have all done it at times, as you get so fed up of certain prisoners it does everybody some good to have a change. What comes around goes around.

It took a bit of time to realise what you were dealing with until the prison started to get more and more prisoners in. At Strangeways a lot of the prisoners were low key burglars, car thieves etc. mixed with a number of more serious prisoners who just melted into the large number of prisoners without being noticed too much. In a long term prison all the prisoners are pretty serious offenders and in some cases very serious and infamous, and are given more freedom within the prison so it makes you a bit more aware of the potential of these people.

Being a high security prison and having an SSU, Full Sutton held the highest security of prisoner. There are three types of Category A prisoner. Normal Category A, these prisoners had to have a book with their picture in and this was like a diary kept wherever they went. These prisoners were allowed to go to work etc. with the rest of the prisoners. Then there was a high risk Category A. These prisoners had to be escorted by an officer when they left the wing to go to work/education. They also had their own visits area where visitors had to be vetted by the prison and police. Finally there was exceptional high risk Category A prisoners who were kept in the SSU. All these prisoners, when being moved outside of the prison, were escorted in a specially equipped van and depending on the type of prisoner or specific intelligence at times had an armed police escort.

Halfway through the year I was told I was being moved to the canteen from reception. The canteen within a prison is not what the general public know as a canteen. It is basically a shop where prisoners purchase items with their wages. In a prison like Strangeways the prisoners could only buy basics like tobacco, sweets, biscuits, toiletries etc. In a long term prison prisoners at this time were allowed to cook their own food on the wing, so working in a canteen in a high security prison was more like working in a real shop. The general public would not believe the time and money spent in this area. Each week after taking orders from all the prisoners we had to spend nearly a full day taking the prison van in to York to shop at supermarkets, and other specialist shops to get the items prisoners ordered. Some items, like fresh vegetables and eggs, were delivered from local suppliers. I used to enjoy canteen shopping day as it was a day out of the prison; sometimes I would go and have a cuppa at home or we even called at a local pub for our lunch. I always did want to run my own newsagent since being a young man so this job suited me doing orders, stocktaking and all the things that go with running a shop. The entrepreneur coming out of me. The bit I did not like too much was when prisoners came to get their orders as invariably they would be unhappy with something, which meant confrontation. I remember one day when a prisoner who called himself Charlie Bronson after the famous actor came to the canteen. Charlie was a very dangerous prisoner who started serving a short sentence but ended up extending this considerably due to his violence and hostage taking. Charlie once came to the counter and started making a nuisance of himself over an order. Eventually it became a bit heated and he started throwing things around, shouting and making general threats. Charlie is not a particularly tall man but is a very keen body builder and very unpredictable. Eventually after the alarm bell was pressed and a body of officers came, he calmed down and was escorted back to his wing. Contrary to what the popular press would have you believe, Charlie was not too brave when confronted by a number of prison officers willing to take him on. As far as I am aware, Charlie is still in prison and will probably be in for the rest of his life.

In June of this year I did a fire officers' course. I am not really too sure why I did this as I have never had any interest in being a firefighter, but it was four days out of the prison at the West Yorkshire Fire Service training centre in Wakefied. It turned out to be a great experience and I thoroughly enjoyed it, but still had no desire to be a firefighter. The training was very physical and at times quite scary. We had a morning in the smoke room where you donned all the breathing equipment and went into a smoke filled area which was small rooms and corridors where you could not stand up. Once the thick black smoke filled the area it went pitch black, and getting used to breathing through the mask was pretty scary and you lose all sense of where you are. I was glad to get to the end of the four days and it left me with nothing but respect for the real firefighters who do a difficult, physical and dangerous job on our behalf.

My first duty of nights at Full Sutton was on the gate. This is the front entrance to the prison. With this being a modern high tech prison the gate lodge was full of buttons, cameras etc. and once the overrides were put on from the control room nobody could enter the gate lodge without me letting them in. You had to start by checking that all the keys were in place, and then you had to write up the following day's diary with the names of staff that had to be booked in, then it was basically up to you what you did. So close the blinds, make up a comfy area and have a nice sleep until early the following morning when the night manager came to open the prison up ready for the early staff on duty, such as the kitchen staff. Then you had a week off after the seven nights. I didn't particularly enjoy nights as it used to upset my whole digestive system and sleeping pattern, plus the fact they were pretty boring, but the week off was really good, especially if you added some holiday time on the end. Happy days.

I decided to apply to the Open University to study for a degree. The Prison Service at this time paid for me to do this so it was a bit of a no brainer (no pun intended) to improve my chances for promotion or give me skills to do something else. I applied for this and was given funding, so started my first year taking a social studies course. I really enjoyed doing this. Most of it was done on your own at home but we did have an evening each week where we had a tutor to help us. I found this type of learning really good and for one of the first times in my life I actually enjoyed education. If I am honest I never really expected to complete the four years it would take me to do a degree, but in the end I did six years and took an Honours Degree. It was a really proud moment for me when I walked on the stage at the Harrogate Exhibition Centre with my cap and gown on and my family watching me receive my degree. So I can add BA (Hons) at the end of my name now. This achievement is even better in my eyes as I did this doing a full time job, and bringing up two young children. I must praise my wife, who never complained when I disappeared to the dining room every night to study and do my assignments. During the six years I did two summer schools at Norwich and Nottingham Universities. These were a great experience for me being in such wonderful places of learning, and I felt some slight anger with myself that I did not concentrate more during my school years and go to university from school. However I do now have a slightly different view on life as I think we should be encouraging more young people to be business people or entrepreneurs rather than go to school, university, get a job, retire, out to pasture. We need more free thinkers, risk takers and wealth builders, not just people who are conditioned to make wealth for a tiny majority. More of this later.

I always tried to get Christmas Day off, particularly since having children, and was happy to swap with officers who preferred New Year's Eve as I was not bothered about this. Getting drunk for the sake of it has no real appeal to me and it is just another date in the calendar. So I was off again for Christmas of 1988 with my lovely family.

1989

In February of this year I left my group to work on B Wing. As I said before, the wings were a terrible design in the fact the spurs were like hotel corridors, where you had no sight of other spurs or your fellow officers and they had no sight of you. After working at Strangeways, where they were modelled on the Victorian style of a rotunda where you could stand on the centre of the rotunda and view every wing and landing, I am not sure who had oversight of the design of Full Sutton from a prison point of view but they need shooting allowing such bad safety and security for staff and prisoners. It was patently obvious whoever it was had no idea about the way prisons are managed and what goes on inside them.

It took me some time to get my head around prisoners being in a cell of their own and the amount of possessions they were allowed, including budgies. It really did take some time to get used to opening the cell door just a slight way, just in case the budgie escaped. It also took some time to understand the type of people we were surrounded by, with around 25 lifers on B Wing at this time out of a population of 108; some of these were Category A prisoners and the rest were all serving long determinate sentences. There were some pretty nasty people housed in one little area. The idea of a long term prison is that the outer area is secure so they are given more freedom inside. This in most people's terms is called appeasement. I am all for treating prisoners with humanity in decent conditions, but some of the things prisoners were allowed went beyond that. It seemed a strange concept that the worst type of criminal is treated the best.

On the spur that I was allocated, you are given a certain number of prisoners who you do parole and lifer reports on, so you get to know these prisoners quite well. One of my prisoners was one of the Birmingham six. He was actually quite a nice person to talk to and it was very interesting talking to him about his arrest, trial and subsequent conviction. All the time I knew him he was constantly appealing against his conviction, and as we all know they were eventually released on appeal. I have no idea if they are guilty or not, but I have my own opinion which I will keep to myself. The one thing I will say: although he was angry at the system for locking him up for many years, he was nearly always OK with me and generally with prison staff. I would generally say this about many of the IRA prisoners I encountered. They saw themselves as prisoners of war and had nothing personal against us, as their argument was with the political system. In saying that, if the upper echelons of the organisation told them to kill a prison officer or start a riot, they would do it without thought of their personal hardship or consequences. I guess in a strange way you admired them for their beliefs, but you could not accept that they were prepared to kill innocent civilians for their cause.

Another thing that took me some time to get used to was prisoners cooking their own food in an evening. We actually gave them cooking utensils to do this, including knives to cut the food up. We let them have pots, pans, tins of food with sharp edges when opened, glass bottles and other things to do damage with. But to be fair, by and large the prisoners respected this privilege and there were few incidents as the more influential prisoners did not want to lose this privilege. Some of the smells were really nice, particularly the curries some of the Asian prisoners made. One Asian prisoner used to regularly put a bit of his curry on a plate for me. I should not have allowed this, as it could have had anything in it, but it was rather nice and I am still alive.

During the August of this year I attended my first Open University Summer Camp at Nottingham University. This was a new experience for me and I went with a little nervousness, thinking there would be all these clever people there who made me look a bit thick. This was not the case and I had a great week with really nice people and very helpful tutors, who taught me to think in a different way, i.e. ask questions, be intuitive and keep an open mind to other views. I wish my school days had been like this instead of the boring, "Do as you are told, don't try to think for yourself and learn by rote to pass an exam, not to teach you about life and preparing you for the real world." I learnt how to use a university library, how to write about different paradigms, how to put your view forward in a well thought out way and the art of debate. It really opened my eyes.

After three years of there being no promotion opportunities the service finally held national promotion boards for Senior Officer, which was the grade next up for me. I applied for this and was granted a board on the 15th March of this year. A promotion board at this time was made up of three people. It was usually two Governor grades and an HR person. They were held at what was Prison Service Headquarters at this time, Cleland House, Westminster, London.

So off I trotted to London looking like a tailor's dummy in my shiny new suit, shirt and tie. I had worked very hard learning about interview techniques and listening to people who had been through this process and the type of question I would be asked. I sat in the waiting room for my turn to be grilled, getting more and more nervous until I was summoned. I walked in to this big room where three people were sat behind a desk and a single chair in front facing them. I was invited to sit down, offered a glass of water and asked if I had had a decent journey down. This was supposed to put me at my ease. The last time I had done anything like this was in 1979, when I was interviewed for the job. The first question I was asked was, "What newspaper do you read?" My initial thought was, what the hell has this got to do with managing in the Prison Service? To this day I don't have the answer to that question. Anyway as I did not particularly read a newspaper I said *The Daily Telegraph*, as this was the paper my father read on a daily basis. The next question was, "Why do you read that newspaper?" I felt like saying, because it has the best sports page, but knew this was the wrong answer so I said: it is a quality paper that gives a balanced view of the world. How sickly was that answer. They just nodded and moved on. Most of the questions were around how I would deal with various situations, from disciplining officers to managing people. By the time I came out after about 40 minutes I felt like I had been put through a wringer.

They kept us waiting for ages for the outcome, as they cannot tell you if you have passed until the last person has been interviewed. A couple of months later I got my answer and I had passed, which was a great relief and sense of achievement. The next bit was that you were invited to apply for a posting. Although they could technically post you to any prison in the country, they did try to place you in one of your choice. It took them until January of 1991 to tell me I had been posted to Full Sutton. Don't you just love the bureaucrats in government agencies? Can you imagine these people running a business where you had to make a profit? The only good thing about this was they gave me a seniority date from 1989, which meant I could possibly go for the next promotion earlier.

So I continued being an officer for the rest of year and all of 1990 with the occasional acting up to Senior Officer. On the 10th December I was transferred to the SSU. As explained earlier, this is basically a prison within a prison. Due to the type of prisoner in there and the potential for being conditioned, corrupted etc. the maximum tour of duty was six months. As explained earlier, this was state-of-the-art for the time, with everything operated electronically and cameras everywhere. Basically the prisoners' living accommodation was one corridor with ten cells, a gym at the end, a games room, sitting room, kitchen, shower area and an enclosed exercise area led off from the corridor. When I started here there were eight prisoners who were classed as exceptional high risk category A. There were two Italian Mafia, three top IRA, one of the Brinks Mat robbers and two London gangsters. Although they did not always get on with each other there was a kind of mutual agreement to tolerate each other, and us.

As in the main prison, the prisoners in here could cook their own food. Because the senior management wanted to keep these people happy in such a confined space they were more or less allowed to spend whatever they wanted on food. One of the tasks for officers was to go to the external shops for the prisoners' order, as in the main canteen described earlier. I went in here a few weeks before Christmas and I could not believe what was purchased by the prisoners for their Christmas dinner. One of the Italians was reputed to be worth around £40m so money was no object. On Christmas Day the table was laid out with the biggest piece of salmon I had ever seen in my life, a huge turkey, every single trimming you could wish to see and the most expensive chocolates and Italian cakes. The only thing they were not allowed was alcohol. Who said crime doesn't pay? The good thing about all this was there was far too much for the prisoners to eat, so they invited the officers to share with them. If only the general public knew what was going on. These were the most dangerous prisoners in the system and they were treated like lords. Christmas over and in to a New Year.

1990

After about a month in the SSU I was starting to get a bit restless as the novelty had worn off and it was becoming very boring and claustrophobic for me. Basically your whole day was spent sitting in a corridor while the prisoners just went about their business. As they did not want for anything, they were more or less self-sufficient and all we were there for was security. The prisoners by and large were polite and often held us in conversation. One good thing about working here was we were allowed to read, so I took the opportunity to bring my Open University books in and read them. As I was reading a book one of the IRA prisoners looked at it and said he was doing the same units as me. We got into conversation about the work we were doing and he asked me how I was getting on. I explained I was doing OK but having to work and bring up a young family it was hard work. He had all the time in the world and offered to help me. I asked the Senior Officer's permission if I could sit with this prisoner to discuss our studies, which he allowed. After this I spent many an hour sat on his bed, going through the units and offering each other advice and help. So I guess not many people can say they were helped to pass their Open University year by a mass-murdering IRA Quarter Master. I must say I just scraped through and he passed with flying colours. I would love to name some of these people but I think the thought police would come knocking on my door. I did not last my six months as I found it so boring it was driving me crazy, so I asked if I could come out early. I had to find my own replacement and as this was seen as a cushy job there was no shortage of takers.

The service moved away from what we called in the early days Minimum Use of Force Tactical Intervention (MUFTI) to Control & Restraint (C&R). Both of these were to be used on violent or refractory prisoners or riot situations when all other forms of persuasion had been exhausted. MUFTI was basically 'hit them with a big stick' and C&R was a bit more sophisticated, where the prisoner was put under restraint in a manner that was painful but generally no real harm was done to the prisoner or staff. In March of this year I did four full days of C&R training. This involved learning various hold techniques to restrain a prisoner, working in a three man team to remove a prisoner from a cell or room and generally to do this type of work in a more professional way. Later in my career I did the more advanced stuff dealing with major riot situations where you work in teams and units. All C&R is carried out in protective clothing, shields and helmets. Although this week was quite demanding, and sometimes painful, it was really enjoyable. I have used these skills on many occasions and later in my career managed situations. Once you are trained in the larger type training for riots etc. you are liable to be called under something called Tornado, which is the mobilisation of C&R teams from around the country in the event of major disturbances. I attended a number of these but the worst and scariest for me was at Everthorpe prison in East Yorkshire. The noise and confusion of a major riot situation is not something you want to experience very often. Many of you will remember the Strangeways riots, which I did not attend, but from people I have spoken to this has to go down as one of the most frightening for prison staff as well as many prisoners. We need to understand that most prisoners just want to get on with their sentence and get out and want no part in this kind of activity. It is much more frightening for the ordinary prisoner to be in a situation where the psychopaths have taken over the asylum.

When I came out of the SSU I spent most of the rest of the year acting up to Senior Officer on a role called movements. This was where we managed the movement of prisoners to work, education etc. We were also alarm bell response, so if an officer or other member of staff was in trouble, or prisoners were fighting, they rang an alarm bell which showed in the control room and they sent officers to the scene via a message on personal radios. The rest of the year was not overly exciting, apart from a trip I did to Broadmoor Special Hospital.

Some prisoners are diagnosed as mentally ill with treatable illnesses, so are allocated a place in a special hospital, or as many know them, mental institutions. The crazy part of this system is if a prisoner is mentally ill with an untreatable illness they remain in prison with medically untrained staff, and in my experience the ones with an untreatable mental illness have been the worst, most violent type. I guess it does make some sense as they are hospitals so if you cannot be treated then there is no point in going to a hospital. There should, however, in my opinion be separate places for the untreatable mentally ill prisoner where specially trained staff can manage them. In October of this year I escorted a prisoner who had been deemed mentally ill to Broadmoor. Broadmoor is a long way from Full Sutton so we spent a long time in a van with this man. As it turned out he never said a word to us all the way down. We arrived at Broadmoor, which looked more like a prison than a hospital, and entered reception. It was very different to a prison inside as all the staff had white coats on and spoke to the prisoner like a patient rather than a criminal. We took him in to a ward where 'patients' were wandering about freely, some I must say like zombies, who I was informed were drugged up to the eyeballs (legally). We were offered a cup of tea which was brought by a trusted patient. I found out this trusted patient had murdered and cut up into bits three members of his family. I must say I was glad to get out of here and have much respect for the people working in this environment.

This was the first Christmas Day I had worked in the 10 years I had worked in the Prison Service. I did a late shift which was starting at lunchtime and finishing at 8pm. At least I could see my children opening their presents, but it was strange to have to go to work on this day. All you people who feel sorry for prisoners should see what they had for Christmas dinner and tea. I can imagine many people in care homes etc. not eating half as well and they have not committed horrendous criminal offences. Of course you still get some prisoners complaining about the food.

Chapter 4

1991 to 1994

1991

14th January 1991 was the date I was finally officially promoted to Senior Officer, having waited over 12 months. I was messed around a bit for a few months doing work here there and everywhere until I was allocated permanently to D Wing.

D Wing was a wing full of what are known as 'main wing prisoners'. Basically this meant they were not under protection due to their offence, i.e. a sex offender, but your basic murderer, robber, and drug dealer etc., really nice people. My going to D Wing coincided with the prison slowly taking a turn for the worse. Some of the original staff and managers had used Full Sutton as a way to get to the North, or get a promotion then take the opportunity to move to other areas or get further promotions, leaving Full Sutton with a lot of very new officers, and for some reason some very poor senior managers who were incapable of managing difficult prisoners – so appeasement was the order of the day for them, leaving the uniformed staff to face the difficult situation that was growing worse each day. These types of prisoners are not stupid, and they sensed there was an opportunity to intimidate the inexperienced staff, and gradually found that the senior managers were equally open to being intimidated and backed off.

The type of prisoners on D Wing at this time ranged from London gangsters, IRA and major drug dealers to murderers and other serious criminals, so you can see if you give them an inch they will take advantage of this. One of the worst areas was the use of pay phones, which was a relatively new concept in prisons. They were only allowed to use them at certain times of the day and even though there was a booking system, there were not enough phones for the amount of time they had and as you can imagine the bullies and big boys had more than their fair share of time. This led to confrontation with wing staff and again the answer from the senior managers was to let them use the official prison phones, which went against all the rules as these did not have the ability to be recorded and you had to ask the prisoner to finish his call and put the phone down, where the pay phone had limiters on them, so once again this created confrontation.

As a junior manager on the wing, you were directly in line with the prisoner complaining and the officer looking to you to back them up against the prisoner. With the senior managers totally backing off, I was on a hiding to nothing. There were many areas of confrontation where prisoners tried to make no go areas so they could do their dealings and bullying. The TV rooms was one area of confrontation and intimidation, as officers had to go in to the room at lock up times to switch the TV off and tell them to leave. If there was a programme on they wanted to see, it was another chance to intimidate and push the boundaries. Another flashpoint area was the servery where meals were served. The food, in my opinion, was of a good quality and they had at least four choices, but obviously this was an easy place to create a situation for intimidation and potential violence. Some prisoners used to take any chance to complain about the food, and again, as much as wing staff would tell prisoners everything was OK so they should take their meal or leave it, this often ended up in a stand-off where a Governor grade would eventually come and invariably tell the officers to get more food or change the food. They rarely stood up to the prisoner(s). Morale began to get thinner and thinner.

This was a very testing time for me as a fairly new manager and a real baptism of fire. You got very little, if any, training on management skills, there was certainly no mentoring or support, just an attitude of get on with it, you have passed a promotion board, haven't you? Yes I did, but I lied about reading the *Telegraph*! Maybe that's where I was going wrong.

I did my first set of nights around March of this year as a senior officer. As a senior officer doing nights was pretty good as you based yourself in the centre office, which was away from the residential wings, and you had a Principal Officer in charge to make the decisions. My role was to visit each wing periodically to ensure the night staff were OK and doing what they should. I had to put a double lock on the outer wing doors at the beginning of the night and take them off before the day staff came on. This was for additional security. Thankfully we did not have too many issues during this week which helped me to ease my way in to the management of the prison at night, learning the dos and don'ts, rules and regulations.

I will tell a few stories of incidents throughout the next 18 months which may leave some of you wondering why we did this job. I can tell you I questioned it many times myself.

One major problem that emerged was the brewing of hooch. This is illegal alcohol that prisoners make from all sorts of things like bread, orange juice, fruit, sugar and many other items prisoners could easily get hold of. This is dangerous stuff for both the prisoners' health and prison discipline through drunkenness, which we all know from any town on a Saturday night full of drunks. Well, put a group of the most dangerous people in the country in a small area full of illegal hooch, and I don't need to tell you the outcome. We found loads of hooch, placed prisoners on report and governors used to slap their wrist and send them back to the wing. At one point we found a large amount of hooch in the cell of a notoriously violent prisoner and my senior manager told me to tell the officers to take most of it but leave him some to keep him quiet. I had a massive argument behind closed doors with this manager and all he could do was threaten me with my career. I nearly told him where to stick his career, the weak-kneed tosser.

At one point we had Charlie Bronson on the wing. When he had his OK head on, he was alright, but it did not take him long to change his head by taking people hostage, always civilians, to putting a bucket of cleaning water over a Governor's head and many incidents of threats of violence. Both prisoners and staff had to be very cautious around Charlie as he was so unpredictable. Eventually even the weak management had had enough of him and put him in the Segregation Unit. This was after he put a bucket of dirty water over one of the senior managers' heads. We did have a bit of a chuckle with Charlie over this.

I was on duty day when there was a lot of disgruntlement from a decision to remove an influential prisoner to the Segregation Unit. Throughout the day there were small incidents of confrontation and prisoners pressing alarm bells to disrupt the wing and test the response of staff. Meal times were an obvious place to create a further confrontation, getting other prisoners to join in and generally creating a bad feeling. This continued throughout the day and we asked the senior managers to leave the prisoners locked up after tea to give the staff a breather and let the prisoners calm down. Prisoners had association in the evening up to 8pm when they were locked up for the night. The senior managers decided against the wing staff's advice and ordered that the prisoners should have association as normal. As the night went on, it was obvious a certain element of the major players on the wing were determined to bring this to a head. At about 7pm I was patrolling the wing to gauge the feeling and try to give the officers some encouragement and guidance when a notorious IRA prisoner came up to me with a huge pair of scissors in his hand and said to me, "You have 10 minutes to get off the wing mister before you get these in your chest," meaning the scissors. I tried to reason with him but realised he had been drinking hooch and I became rather concerned at this stage. About five minutes later one of my colleagues phoned me and said do not come round to the main office as a large group of prisoners were threatening to take them hostage and to get ready to leave the wing. This was a horrible feeling that we were losing control of the wing and a few of my colleagues were in serious danger and there was nothing I could do about it. About five minutes later we saw a group of prisoners running towards us in a very angry way with weapons in their hands so we locked the office and escaped through the emergency exit in to the grounds. This was a sickening feeling and I felt like a coward that I had left my colleagues in there with these people. At around midnight the situation calmed down, the prisoners were given a few assurances by senior managers and the staff being held were released unharmed if not a bit shocked. After everything calmed down and the prisoners were locked up, we had a de-brief with the Governor and Deputy Governor where the Deputy Governor said, "Well, that was a bit of fun, wasn't it?" We just looked at him with disgust and the Governor to his credit told him to go home and apologised for him. I have come across some clowns wearing suits in this service but he was the only one that came to work with a red nose, face paint and big feet.

At one point in the year the prisoners just got to the point where it was like a game to see how far they could push us, and for about a week we had prisoners using the food as an excuse to cause as much disruption and confrontation as possible. Prisoners would come for their meal and purposely find something wrong with it, then encourage others to join in. We had prison orderlies who collect and serve the food but during this period they refused to do this as they came under pressure from other prisoners, which then caused the staff a problem as we had to use additional staff to serve the meals. One prisoner in particular had an issue with his diet. He was a small Jamaican who, when he got excited, you had no idea what he was saying which made him even harder to deal with. His usual answer to his frustration was to come down for his meal, find some excuse to complain about his meal then throw something in all the other meals, thus disrupting the whole meal, meaning we had to go for more food from the kitchen. Another of his tricks was to grab a tray or two of food and throw it all over the floor and walls. Even the weak-kneed senior managers eventually got fed up with him and moved him to another prison. I used to get so pissed off at meal times when prisoners complained about perfectly good food I used to take the plate from them, sit down and eat the whole plate full saying how nice it was and thank you for their meal. It usually worked and it saved me money as I did not have to buy any food. Humour is often the best way to deal with situations in prison, even in scary ones.

Giving prisoners telephones on the wing from a point of view of contact with family was a positive, however as usual with this type of prisoner, and in particular the way Full Sutton was going, it created more problems than it resolved. They were not happy with the amount of time they were allowed on the phone so once again pushed the boundaries. We had a task in the wing called Social Work In Prison (SWIP) which was where an officer assisted prisoners with welfare issues. Some of this work involved phoning people up on the prisoner's behalf but soon ended up with the prisoner being able to use the office phone for personal calls. Prisoners eventually started asking to use the office phone in an evening for so-called emergency reasons. They were allowed this on exceptional reasons and had to be sanctioned by a manager, however as time went by the weak-kneed senior managers gave in to prisoners' aggressive demands to use the office phone, and this more or less became the norm in the evening. This meant more confrontation as prisoners would not come off the phone when asked and unlike the prisoner wing phones you could not switch them off remotely so you had to insist they finish the call, which created yet more confrontation and often meant prisoners were late to be locked up and staff regularly late off duty.

Throughout the year prisoners were getting more and more confident that they could do as they pleased, and wing staff more and more stressed and fed up with the constant pressure of threats, violence and total lack of backing from senior managers. This manifested itself in senior managers virtually bunkering themselves in the administration and avoiding prisoner contact as much as possible. In fact one of them turned up for work one day, sat in his car for about an hour then disappeared. He turned up some time later doing a cushy training job somewhere as we later found out he could not cope with the pressure. He should have tried being on the coalface putting up with crap day after day with no help from people like him.

Each wing at this time had a senior manager or Governor 5 in overall charge, and the one we had was nicknamed 'Just off to admin'. The reason he got this name was because he used to arrive on the wing at about 9.30am, saying he was doing work in the admin. Prisoners went off the wing to work and education etc. at 9am. He would come to the office about 11am to say, he was just off to admin, just in time to miss prisoners coming back from work, then return to the wing about 2pm, you guessed it, when prisoners had gone back to work after lunch, then again in the afternoon he would 'just go to admin' before they returned in the afternoon and we would see no more of him until the following morning around 9.30am. Leadership of the highest quality, don't you think? This man went on to be the Governing Governor of a prison in years to come.

Anyway back to the horror show. I recall once sitting in the wing office when a prisoner, who was normally a decent prisoner, kept coming to me saying if I did not do something about the conditions on this wing he was going to take the law into his own hands. He was a rather large man with a bald head and muscles where I didn't think you should have them. I tried to reason with him and asked him to sit down and we could sort his problem out. I got the impression he had gone past this point, as he started to gather all the TVs from the common room and dump them in the wing office. By the time he had finished I had about eight rather large TVs in the office and a still-angry monster in front of me threatening to use my head as a football. I tried joking with him that if he kicks like a Man U centre forward I would be OK. Humour often works well, but not in this case. Maybe he was a Man U fan? I eventually got to the bottom of his problem, which was that on two weeks running the canteen had forgotten to get his favourite breakfast cereal. I sorted this out for him and we were best mates after, and he even returned all the TVs. I bet not many of you will actually believe this but it was true. This man was serving 19 years for a brutal robbery. I assure you I could not make this up. Sugar Puffs have something to answer for.

Humour and talking about football are generally the two things that get you through a day in a prison, as most prisoners can relate to one or both. One day I was asked to go talk to a rather belligerent prisoner who was being particularly unhelpful in his behaviour and making all kinds of threats. I walked round to his cell where he was remonstrating with two officers who were trying to search his cell. It was something we had to do to each cell at least once a month. He was objecting to the officers touching his personal things and accusing them of making a mess. I asked him what the problem was and he said, "These two muppets are being disrespectful to me." Having spent many years in prison he knew that this had to be done and the officers were doing their job in a professional manner, but once again he was pushing the boundaries so we would back off and leave him alone. During our conversation where I was explaining the search was going to happen and he should just make it easier on everyone by complying he picked up a knife he had got from the kitchen, put it under my throat and said, "What would you do if I stuck this in you?" I just spontaneously said, "I would bleed all over your cell, these two would ring the alarm bell, a load of men in uniform would beat the s—t out of you, and you would get another ten years in prison." At that he just laughed, said, "You're fucking mad you are," then let the officers search his cell. I walked away with a grin on my face, arse going ten to the dozen and knees shaking but a certain satisfaction that even in adversity humour can come through.

I was lucky enough to have Christmas Day off and I did a night shift on New Year's Day so I could celebrate New Year.

1992

1992 continued in the same way as 1991 with prisoners pushing the boundaries, officers getting stressed, sick levels going up and senior managers doing nothing to stem the rising tide of inevitability that a serious incident would take place sooner rather than later.

In my case this came in April of this year when I was on duty at the weekend. You can always tell in a prison when things are not going right, as the atmosphere changes. Prisoners stop talking to you, some more reasonable ones don't come out of their cells to stay out of the way and little incidents take place, like prisoners pressing alarm bells, having confrontations with staff over the smallest thing etc. This weekend two of our London guests who thought they were gangsters were particularly noticeably stirring things up and being rather obnoxious. I did find out that one of them (who was a bit nutty at the best of times) had had a problem with his visits. This is one thing that can really be a flashpoint as you are affecting their time with their families. I tried my best to deal with this but found his visitors had been turned away for not having a visiting order and they had come all the way from London on a Sunday. They said they had been told it would be OK. I did not believe this but tried to arrange an alternative, i.e. a phone call. He was really not happy about this and spent the rest of the day festering and generally being a dickhead. The evening got worse and it culminated in me and my Principal Officer being held in one of the small TV rooms with him and his equally loony mate threatening to kill both of us. This went on for about one hour, where they would calm down and we were chatting normally, and all of a sudden they would be shouting, threatening and being totally out of control. Both these prisoners were serving life for murder so you can imagine what was going through my mind (or maybe you can't?) as they were waving table legs around threatening to put our skulls in with them. My Principal Officer was a woman of about 5' 2", very slim and soft spoken. She was brilliant in the way she kept very calm, at least on the outside, and eventually talked them round to letting us go. I am not sure if being a woman helped but I owe her a debt of gratitude that I will never forget, but probably never pay back as I eventually lost touch with her over the years.

When we came out and the two prisoners were taken to the segregation unit, the Duty Governor in charge of the prison that evening was an absolute disgrace as he phoned me up and started laying into me about not following procedures and how I had put other staff in jeopardy. He never once asked how I was feeling or what actually happened. My reply to him was, "Fuck you and fuck your prison and if you had the balls to say this to my face I would put you in hospital." This is not my normal way of reacting but I had just spent an hour fearing for my life, the last 18 months putting up with crap from prisoners, getting no assistance from people like him in his ivory tower, and finally to be spoken to like this put me over the edge. I told him I was going off duty, stuff his de-brief and he could take whatever action he wanted against me as I had gone past caring. I drove all the way home in a complete daze, walked in the house, sat down and burst out crying with my wife in a bit of shock wondering what the hell was going on, as I had never reacted to anything like this before. I am a pretty tough person emotionally, or was up to this point, and I just broke down having no control over my emotions. I have never felt like this before or after, but I guess I was near to a breakdown and this evening was the tipping point.

I went to the doctor the following day and he signed me off work for two weeks. He was also a police doctor so fully understood where I was coming from. During this two weeks nobody in a senior role came to see me to ask if I was OK or if I needed any help, and nothing ever came from the incident as far as a disciplinary report against me. What does that tell you about the senior managers at this time? At this point I would gladly have left the Prison Service and in fact, after obtaining my degree I very nearly did leave. I returned to work after two weeks full of anger, resentment and other emotions both towards prisoners and senior managers, but it made me appreciate the great professionalism many of the young officers showed on a daily basis and how supportive they were to me and each other. A pity the people who should show these qualities were sadly lacking. I vowed at this point if I ever became a senior manager in a prison I would not conduct myself like these people did at this time.

Not long after I returned to work I realised not a lot had changed as I was called to an incident on the exercise yard. As I arrived at the doorway I was met by a ring of around 80 prisoners who were refusing to let the officers get to two prisoners who were fighting like Muhammad Ali and Joe Frazier. The two prisoners were lifers, one a Libyan national and the other a traveller. This was obviously a planned fight and the other prisoners would not let us anywhere near them to stop this. Once the fight was at its conclusion the prisoners in the ring parted and let us take the two fighters away. This was a strange experience, as both prisoners shook hands and gave us no problem and the other prisoners just dispersed and that was the end of it. The worrying issue here was one of these prisoners could have been badly hurt and there was nothing we could do about it. As it happens both prisoners were generally pretty decent who just got on with their sentence with little fuss and were usually respectful to staff. I was really enjoying my job at this time. Can you feel the sarcasm in my words?

In September of this year I moved to the security department. I must admit this was such a relief to get away from the day-to-day hassle of aggression, confrontation, and no support from senior managers. The security department in a high security prison is an important and very interesting role. The role involves collating/analysing intelligence, carrying out intelligence-led searching, advising staff and senior managers on security matters, liaising with the police and as the senior officer you were in charge of escorting Category A prisoners to court, and transferring to other prisons in the Category A van. This was a specially equipped vehicle that was secure inside where the prisoner was handcuffed to an officer; another officer sat at the back of the van and the senior officer sat facing the prisoner. The driver was an officer specially trained to drive to a high level and alongside the driver was a navigation officer who obviously navigated and was in constant radio contact with local police in the area we were in at the time.

My first Category A escort was to HMP Belmarsh in South London. To be honest I was a little bit excited to be doing this. The prisoner was quite a notorious one who spent the whole journey not saying a word to us, which made the long journey a little bit uncomfortable but at least he caused no problem either. We used to stop off at HMP Leicester, as this was about halfway, for a toilet and lunch stop. We felt a bit like royalty as when we arrived we were given special treatment because of the type of person we were escorting; the prison was virtually closed down until we had our prisoner secure in a cell in reception. We all had a bit of lunch then went on our way down the M1 to South London. Belmarsh was a relatively new high security prison with even more electronic gizmos than Full Sutton. This prison also had a special unit which was bigger than Full Sutton's and it held some pretty notorious and infamous people. It was also a local prison so it held prisoners on remand. Many of the prisoners at this time were IRA. We stayed overnight in the police station house in Greenwich and had a nice evening out before going back in to Belmarsh in the morning to pick up a prisoner to take to Full Sutton.

I did another Category A escort on the 16th December. This was taking a life sentence prisoner by the name of Frank McGhee to HMP Whitemoor. The reason I have named this prisoner will become clear soon. He was a cold-blooded police killer serving a minimum 25 years. HMP Whitemoor is in Cambridgeshire and it was about a four hour drive. The journey was largely uneventful until we were almost at the prison then all hell broke loose. McGhee suddenly went berserk he tried to stab the officer handcuffed to him in the eye, he then started spraying tear gas in our eyes and generally being extremely violent towards the three of us in the back of the van with the intention of trying to escape. We eventually overpowered him and pinned him to the floor for the rest of the journey while the two officers in the front radioed for police assistance. The police were quickly with us and escorted us the rest of the way to Whitemoor. There was a greeting party waiting for us at Whitemoor who took charge of McGhee and escorted him to the segregation unit. We were all examined by the medic and Jim, one of the officers with me, had a nasty cut just above his eye and could easily have lost his eye had McGhee done what he had intended. The tear gas was horrible making your eyes sting, but the effects soon wore off with some water. We were shown what McGhee had access to in the van and it was quite shocking. There was the tear gas canister, a spike, money and a set of keys. This must have been on the van as McGhee was strip searched before the escort. The van was also searched, but we think the items were hidden inside the seat. We were briefly interviewed by the police and allowed to travel back to Full Sutton. On the way back we discussed how that could have happened and as much as we did not want to contemplate it we had to come to the conclusion that the items were planted there but by whom, I do not know. McGhee was charged with five offences from possession of a firearm to assault – the firearm was the teargas canister – and his trial took place in 1995 which I will cover later in the book.

I had to work the morning of Christmas Day and a late shift on New Year's Day which was not too bad as I was home for lunchtime on Christmas Day and did not have to go to work until lunchtime on New Year's Day.

1993

I continued my education in security, and in a prison of this nature this was a very important and interesting job and gave me quite a bit of exposure to the Governor and Deputy Governor and other senior managers. You might ask why I would want this after my opinion of senior managers at this time. Unfortunately if you wanted a career, i.e. promotion you had to get these people on your side; sickly I know but that is the system I was in. My direct manager, the security Principal Officer, was a man called Tom Matheson. Tom was one of the best people I worked under in the whole time I was in the Prison Service. He was very much old school in that he was out and about in the prison supporting wing staff and others, putting himself about with prisoners so they gained his trust, and he gained valuable intelligence in this way. He had a great way of mentoring you by being supportive, non-judgemental and offering advice rather than just giving you a bollocking.

He was a big tough Scotsman who did not mince his words but at heart was a big softie. I learnt so much from Tom that held me in good stead for my future years, in particular how to manage people and most importantly how to manage your managers.

In March of this year I did a category A escort to HMP Liverpool. The prisoner we took was a sex offender who had committed quite a serious and nasty offence of rape. We arrived at Liverpool reception and the staff there were very unprofessional in the way they treated the prisoner we brought, which I suspected was because of his offence. We were taking another sex offender back to Full Sutton with us so we had some lunch while the Liverpool staff brought our new prisoner to reception. When we arrived back at reception we asked for the property and paperwork for our prisoner. We were given a bag of property that was in a loose bag. All property for prisoners should be in a sealed bag with a numbered seal. I enquired about this and the reaction I got was, "He is only a nonce, what are you bothered for?" The term nonce is a slang prison term for a sex offender. I tried to explain it makes no difference what or who he is, we should treat all prisoners with professionalism and within the rules. This went down like a lead balloon. As we were searching the prisoner we were taking back to Full Sutton, the Liverpool staff stood in the background making all kinds of childish remarks. I told them to move away and let us do our job, to which they made silly childish remarks again. I was so glad to get out of this prison and the disgraceful unprofessionalism they showed. When I got back to Full Sutton I made a complaint to my Deputy Governor about the conduct of the staff at Liverpool. He wrote to the Deputy Governor at Liverpool, who apparently had words with the reception staff. I was told by other Full Sutton staff who went to Liverpool after me that there was a sign up in their reception saying 'SO Ward from Full Sutton is not welcome here'. Very professional and says a lot of the type of city Liverpool was at that time. Remember the dockers! Thankfully I never went back to that place again.

In June of this year I was given the opportunity to go on a two week security course. This was very welcome, even though I had been doing the role for ten months. The course was pretty good and I gained some valuable knowledge to help me in my role and ideas to develop when I got back to Full Sutton. I must have been impressing some people as I was temporary promoted to Principal Officer for three months. At this time this was quite an achievement to be a security PO in a high security prison with only two years' experience as a manager, albeit on a temporary basis. It showed the senior managers had confidence in my ability. I was not about to let them down.

About a month in to my stint as PO we started to get some intelligence that was potentially very serious. It was very much a judgement call when to act on intelligence and whether the intelligence is good. There is a system in place to assess intelligence to know whether it is good, bad or indifferent. This intelligence was about three category A prisoners devising an escape plan. The prisoners were located on one of the two new wings that had just been built on half of the massive sports field. These wings were much better designed than the original four, as they were built on a gallery style on two floors but they were open so supervision was much better. However we were still going through a tough time with prisoners testing staff all the time. These three prisoners took advantage of the intimidation of staff to create an effective no-go area at the end of the wing, and they had manipulated a situation where they were located in cells next to each other.

We acted on the intelligence one evening when the prisoners were locked up for their tea. We searched all three cells at the same time to avoid warning them and what we found was a treasure trove of escape equipment. It was ingenious how they had hidden the equipment, although helped by intimidating staff when they had done previous searches. Built in to the cell furniture we found tools, ropes, maps, weapons and a set of ladders that were brilliant in that they were in pieces in each cell with holes drilled in them, all marked up so it was easy to fit them together. The three prisoners were very cool while we were searching, not particularly saying anything and more or less accepting they had been rumbled.

We had to leave the wing locked up all evening due to the amount of equipment and the fact we had to ensure it was all logged and a chain of custody had to be maintained in case criminal proceedings followed. So everything was logged, bagged and tagged and taken to the security office to be locked up until the following morning. The following day was going to be a very busy but interesting one. I got to work early the following day to start the process of analysing what we had and writing lots of reports. It was soon obvious this was a very serious and clever attempt to escape from a high security prison. It was also obvious that some members of staff had assisted these prisoners, as some of the tools we found had to have been brought in by staff. That was worrying and quite hard to accept. We put the ladder together and a few days later put it up against the wall and sent a 15-stone officer up it. It not only reached to the top of the wall, it easily held the officer's weight. We also found some very serious looking spikes which we later found out were to be used against the dogs patrolling the perimeter. We realised we had prevented what would have been a very embarrassing and newsworthy escape, not to say there would have been three very dangerous criminals back on the streets. A good job all round and very satisfying for me personally.

In late November the Governor asked if any managers wanted to do an exchange with a prison in Groningen in Holland. I fancied this so applied and was successful. As ever, my long suffering wife was very supportive of me doing this. So off I went to Holland with another colleague. We went on the ferry from Hull and caught the train up to the north of Holland. It was bitterly cold when we arrived in Groningen. We were met by the two prison staff who were going to put us up in their house and taken to the prison. The prison was an old one and it would not have been out of place in England with its design. It was also quite strange how the attitudes of their prison officers were very similar to ours, including the type of humour.

During this week we were taken to different types of prisons. One was a large segregation prison where the most disruptive prisoners were sent. This was a very strict prison where the staff were all volunteers and specially picked. By the look of many of them they were picked for their size, as most officers I came across were all built like rugby players. We were taken to a room where there was what could only be described as a doctor's examining table with about four straps on it. We were told this was called the bike and was used for the most violent and disruptive prisoners as they were laid on this and the four straps held them down. The prisoner stayed on this until the staff were confident they had calmed down. We were told it was used mainly for junkies and the majority of them were foreign prisoners, predominantly from the Eastern Bloc countries.

Another prison we visited was the complete opposite in that there was about eight small units that looked like large cottages. There was only a small fence round the perimeter and the prisoners were given lots of freedom within the units. We looked in to a cell where the prisoner had a phone on the wall which he could use anytime, he had a fridge, TV and other mod cons. Prisoners were given access to excellent educational facilities, they went out to work at local offices, shops etc. It really was home from home but the authorities assured us they had great success at rehabilitating criminals back into decent law abiding citizens. This was more like a holiday camp than a prison, but I guess if it worked for them, fair play.

We had a very interesting day when we visited a drug clinic in the centre of Groningen. The front of it was like a shop and was in the middle of other shops, which we were told did not go down too well with some people as there were always junkies hanging around. The doctor who ran the clinic was a bit of a character, but a very down to earth pragmatic man. The front of the clinic was a bit like a pizza takeaway with a high counter. Addicts came in to the clinic with their ID and if they were entitled to it they were given a shot of methadone. They had quite a good relationship with the police in that by and large the police left them to it, but had posters everywhere asking people to contact the police privately if they had anything to report and the clinic ensured this was done tactfully.

The doctor explained to us how the clinic operated and he showed a real passion for his work and was certainly very forward thinking, which was not always accepted by the more conservative Groningen population. I always thought the Dutch were very liberal minded people, but there are very many of them who are just like the British middle ground that have little tolerance for people taking drugs and the criminal consequences of this. He took us around Groningen and was particularly interested in showing us their famous cafes. He said if you just want a cup of coffee and a cake go to a bar, but if you want a cup of coffee, cake and a joint go to a café. We went in one and it looked like any café in the world apart from the sweet smell and the two counters. One counter for your coffee and cakes and the other for your fix. There was a price list on a board with about 20 different types of marijuana. The doctor did offer to buy me some to try, which I politely declined. Once again he said the police were very tolerant of these cafes but would immediately shut them down if they sold anything other than marijuana. This seemed to be accepted by both sides and it was more or less self-policed. Maybe a lesson for us? I personally have no time for illegal drugs as I have seen the effects of them over the years, but I guess some people will always take them so maybe we tolerate the softer drugs a bit more and have a degree of control and compliance? We were then asked if we wanted to go out in the methadone bus. This intrigued me and I was definitely not going to say no. This was a big vehicle that was identical to the ones you see in the UK going to small villages as a mobile library. We drove out to the outskirts of Groningen, parked up at the kerb side. The two ladies in the vehicle pulled down a counter inside the van, which was a dispensing area. All of a sudden a load of people came from all over to board the vehicle for their tot of methadone. This was certainly an eye opener for me and I kept a very open mind about it.

The Dutch are lovely people and our guests made us feel really at home, taking us out to the local hostelries and restaurants. I really enjoyed this week and it was a great eye opener for me to see different ways and attitudes towards criminals and how they viewed drug use, but at the same time some attitudes were just like ours. I came away with loads of ideas in my head but not sure the English and Welsh Prison Service was ready for some of the more controversial ways the Dutch were trying. When I get to my time at Brixton you will see there are some different thinkers in senior positions in our service, but they were eventually removed by the bureaucrats. More of that later. After I came back from my experience in Holland I went back to my own rank of senior officer. I had Christmas Day off and was on nights over New Year so not too bad.

1994

Working in the security department was a great place to know what was going on in the whole prison, by having access to all the intelligence coming in and sitting in the security committee meetings analysing this, and listening to senior managers dealing with this and the way they make decisions. It is also a good feeling when they ask you your opinion and sometimes act on that.

Having this information we could see that the prison was still dangerously close to a very serious situation happening and there was genuine fear someone could possibly lose their life, be that a member of staff or another prisoner. The one thing I have not mentioned with all this difficulty with prisoners pushing the boundaries is that there was many prisoners who were equally as afraid, as they had to live among this violence and intimidation more than the staff. All most of them wanted to do was get on with their sentence in as easy a way as possible, some genuinely wanting to better themselves and be released to a normal law abiding life. Most prisoners in my experience just want to get on with their sentence with as little fuss as possible, stay safe, behave in a decent way and leave and get on with their lives whether that is further crime or leading a decent law abiding life.

Early in the year we got a new Deputy Governor. He was a very tall thin Irishman who I knew nothing about. He initially came across as rather a brusque, bordering on rude man but I came to like and respect him for what he did. Within about three weeks of him arriving at Full Sutton, that major incident I mentioned above happened. We had created a lifer wing on C Wing which by its name had all life sentence prisoners on there. To be fair it was a reasonable thing to do on paper, as many lifers are very good prisoners due to the fact they know this is their life for a very long time and want to make it as easy as possible; also one thing lifers do not like are silly little junior gangers serving sentences of five to seven years who see prison as a bit of a game and are trying to be the big time Joes. These prisoners are like children in a tough man's world running around doing stupid childish acts and the more mature prisoners, many serving life, find these people a nuisance and an irritant they could live without. Lifers also find it quite hard when other prisoners are being discharged, so if they are all together in one place this is not as big an issue. So to create a lifer wing was done for the correct reasons and I think if the prison had been more stable when we created this wing I believe it would have been more of a success.

We kept having small incidents on the lifer wing and bits of intelligence coming in to suggest there was an underlying issue. It was proving very difficult to pinpoint what the problem was but often signs of impending trouble is when the more decent prisoners start asking to be moved or hint at officers there are issues. As it happened it would appear a disturbance was planned when the prisoners were unlocked one morning; there was a shout of, "Chapel!" from a prisoner and all hell broke loose. The shout of chapel referred to the Strangeways riot where prisoners totally wrecked the prison a few years earlier, and this started in the chapel. Officers eventually had to leave the wing due to the intensity of the violence from prisoners. The wing was smashed to bits and set on fire. Thankfully no staff were hurt and after a couple of days the last of the prisoners was removed from the wing and the investigation could start. I remember the new Deputy Governor saying, "From today we take control of this prison." This was music to our ears that finally someone in a high position was taking charge. I was told by a friend who was a lower grade Governor that the Deputy Governor got all the senior managers in the boardroom and gave them the biggest dressing down he had ever been party to, telling them to get out there and show some leadership and give the uniform staff the backing they deserve when making tough decisions under very stressful conditions. He went on to say: get in the faces of prisoners, set the agenda, take no crap but at the same time ensure the rules were followed, decent prisoners should feel safe and an atmosphere of safety and security along with decency was the way forward. To his credit, he took the lead by going to each wing to address prisoners, telling them everybody had had enough of this prison being a place to feel scared and things would change, and those who did not accept this would not be tolerated and would be dealt with in a severe way within the rules. He did get some angry prisoners trying to intimidate him, but to his credit he stood his ground and most of them did back down and those that didn't were transferred or taken to the segregation unit and he vowed he would disrupt their lives if they did not want to be part of a better prison. It took about 12 months of hard work, but this man was as true as his word and the prison was unrecognisable after this time. There are not many like him around, more is the pity. He did get on in his career, making it nearly to the top which shows you can be tough and make unpopular decisions and still get to the top if you have self-belief what you are doing is best for the whole and not just one little career within that.

In May of this year I had to attend the trial of McGhee at Leicester Crown Court, the prisoner who attempted to escape from the category A escort back in December of 1992 I described earlier. The five of us who were in the van, the two officers in the back with me and the driver and navigator, travelled down the night before and were booked in to a hotel. The following morning we met the prosecution barrister; this was the first time we had spoken to him. The first day was mostly taken up with legal arguments and senior prison people explaining the way prison works to the jury. There was armed police around the court as McGhee was a very dangerous person and had connections to serious criminal people.

My two colleagues were the first up the following day to give their evidence. They were both given a hard time as was to be expected, being accused of all sorts of things from assault to abuse and anything in between. The defence barrister did his best to discredit the two officers by bringing up all sorts of garbage that McGhee had told them and questioning their integrity. Albeit the jury obviously knew McGhee was a prisoner they had no idea he was a cold blooded murderer of a police officer and a career criminal.

The following day it was my turn to go in to the witness stand. It was noticeable that the court building was like a fortress with armed police everywhere, which seemed to be a bit over the top and I wondered what was going on. I did not realise at the beginning of the day, but at the end I realised why the heavy armed police presence and I will explain that now.

I went in to the witness stand and took the oath, the one where I do not have to swear to God as I am a non-believer. McGhee was sat opposite me with a stupid grin on his face. The prosecution barrister was the first up to ask me questions, so it was a pretty easy start as he just asked me to go through what happened without any aggressive questions or doubting what I was saying. As the prosecution barrister finished I noticed a bit more tension in the court and the appearance of more armed police. I was handed over to the defence barrister who stood up looking all pompous and pleased with himself.

He started fairly easily by getting me to tell him a bit about my career, how long I had been in the service, had I ever had any disciplinary actions against me etc. He then started to ask me questions about the procedure for escorting a category A prisoner, from the start of collecting him from his cell, how we search him, right through to getting in the van and the journey. Out of the blue he said to me, I put it to you that you had an arrangement with McGhee (he called him Mr but I would not dignify him doing this) that he paid you £1000 to allow him to escape and that you planted the escape material in the van and that you reneged on this deal. At first I did not know how to reply to this, but remembered our barrister telling us to keep the answers short so I just said as calmly as I could, no, that is not true. He continued with this point and I just said this was not true. He then asked me if the van was searched before McGhee got on it and I affirmed this was the case, so he then said if that is the case how could the escape equipment get on the van. I could not really answer that. He said he could and the answer was that I put it there. I again just said that was not true. He started asking me if I had any debts, to which I replied only the normal ones of mortgage, car loan etc. which I could pay without a problem. He then started saying that we all like the nicer things in life and this was an easy way to do it. As much as I wanted to say, "Do you really think I would risk everything for a pitiful £1000?" I just said yes, I like the nice things in life but I like my family more. The barrister said thank you, please remain there, as he called the next witness.

I began to realise why there was such a big police presence when the next witness who was a big London gangster proceeded to suggest to the jury that I regularly brought in alcoholic drink for prisoners when I was the Senior Officer on D Wing. Again I just said this was not true. Next witness was another London gangster who said I was regularly bringing in drugs on demand and that I was good to work with. Once again the reply was, not true. The third and final witness was yet another London gangster who carried on the same theme that I was regularly bringing contraband in to Full Sutton. I was in the witness stand for about three hours and at the end of this time I felt absolutely drained mentally and very angry that I had been ambushed with all this nonsense.

Worse was to come the following day when the court reconvened and the jury were sent out to deliberate. They came back after a couple of hours to find McGee not guilty of all the offences. I could not believe this and the grin on McGhee's face was almost unbearable, but what was worse was the fact the jury must have believed all these serious and dangerous criminals, as opposed to a hard-working loyal Crown Servant who did a dangerous job keeping these people behind bars on their behalf. So much for the jury system.

Prison guards deny helping in escape plot

EP 26-5-94

FULL Sutton guards have been accused of helping a maximum security prisoner's alleged escape bid.

Police killer Charlie McGhee, on trial accused of attempting to escape lawful custody, has claimed in court that he paid £1,000 to three guards in return for being allowed to break out of a van transferring him from Full Sutton to another prison.

Prison officers James Fowler and Shaun McCarthy and senior prison officer Paul Ward have all strenuously denied being party to an escape plot or receiving a share of a £1,000 pay off.

McGhee, 36, denies the attempted escape charge but claims he is only guilty of conspiring with guards at Full Sutton Prison.

He alleged three guards in the van on the journey from Full Sutton to White Moor Jail, Cambridgeshire, backed out of the deal at the last minute after taking his money.

In 1989 McGhee was jailed for life, with a recommendation he serve at least 25 years, for shooting dead an off-duty policeman during a robbery in Hemel Hempstead in 1988.

McGhee, of Luton, Bedfordshire, told a jury at Leicester Crown Court one of his co-defendants during that original trial had escaped from prison in similar circumstances.

He claimed he knew of "many" cases of inmates escaping by paying off prison staff and said a Full Sutton inmate suggested he buy his freedom after news of his transfer came through.

McGhee told the court: "I was put on to a certain prison officer by the same friend. I had a talk with him, and we came to an agreement for a bit of money.

"The agreement was that somewhere along the route I would go through the motions of trying to escape and I would be let loose. It cost me £1,000.

"I was given an address where to send the money in Yorkshire, and I arranged for someone on the outside to send the money.

"The whole thing was discussed in the corridor of the prison. It was no secret place, and it lasted five or ten minutes. I dealt with the one officer, but I knew there would be more involved."

McGhee said he was strip-searched at Full Sutton on the day of his transfer but found when he was handed his jacket back the pockets contained a number of weapons.

He found himself armed with a CS gas cannister, a blade and a small sharpened radio aerial, the court heard.

McGhee told the jury: "It was obvious they came to be there because of the agreement I had made. I was meant to drop them on leaving the van.

"All I had to do now was to go through the motions of trying to escape and they would let me go. But when I went through the motions they jumped on me."

Earlier the prison officers told the court they were set upon in the back of the van by McGhee towards the end of the three-hour journey to White Moor.

Mr Fowler suffered scratches, bruising and soreness to his eyes, and Mr McCarthy suffered eye soreness when McGhee discharged the CS gas in his bid to escape, the court heard.

The officers managed to restrain him before the van reached White Moor, where he was being transferred so he could be near his family after the death of his mother.

McGhee denies attempting to escape lawful custody, having a firearm with intent, common assault and two offences of causing actual bodily harm to his guards.

The trial continues.

An article from the York Evening Post.

When I got back to Full Sutton and had time to think about this, I asked to see the Governor as I wanted the police to investigate me so that I could prove this was a load of rubbish. The Governor was extremely supportive of me and arranged for a police inspector to speak to me. The inspector said if the judge felt I was guilty of these lies then he would have asked for an investigation, but the fact he didn't meant he did not believe the witnesses. A pity the jury didn't feel the same. The police did investigate it and I was exonerated, however much of the damage had been done as this was reported in many papers, including local ones, but the police investigation went unnoticed by most people. To be fair I was given fantastic support from everybody at Full Sutton, even some prisoners showed some support towards me. One of the prisoners who was a witness was still located at Full Sutton and when he saw me he said, "No hard feelings Guv, but you know how it works." I just said, "No I don't know how it works, but I do know you people lie for a living and are the scum of the earth." He just smirked and walked away.

Due to the tremendous support I received I quickly put this behind me, accepted it was part of the job and moved on with my career. The jury might not know justice when it smacks them in the face but there is justice coming from somewhere as McGhee dropped dead not long after this, so it was me who had a smirk on my face having the last laugh. Good riddance, you murdering bastard.

Later in the year I got back on the bike and did another category A escort to Parkhurst, taking a Jordanian man who shot the Israeli Ambassador to London. It was also the first time I had been to the Isle of Wight since I was 11 years old. This escort passed off without any problem at all. One thing to point out is that since the McGhee incident we double cuffed the prisoner, in that we put a set of handcuffs on each wrist of the prisoner, then another handcuff on the prisoner, then on to the officer. This made it very difficult for the prisoner to assault the officer as he has no hands free. There were a number of other changes as well, but for security reasons I had better not say. I guess by now procedures will have changed again.

I had to work this Christmas Day. I just worked in the morning so was home by lunchtime to see my children opening their presents and have our Christmas dinner.

Chapter 5

1995 to 1998

1995

By the beginning of 1995 we were starting to see a big improvement in the atmosphere in the prison. The Deputy Governor was as good as his word and carried on bit by bit chipping away at changing procedures, giving uniform staff confidence to make decisions and actually say no to a prisoner and be backed up by senior managers. He was ruthless with the senior managers in making sure they were visible and backing uniform staff. As strange as it may seem to people who do not understand the way prisons work, most of the prisoners actually prefer it when we are in charge instead of the thugs and bullies, and they were relieved we were taking control as this was their home and they wanted to feel safe and secure in it.

By comparison to last year this year was pretty tame, but it gave me the opportunity to concentrate a bit on my career as I felt I was now ready for the next level of management, that of Principal Officer. I applied for my first Principal Officer board in August and sat the board in September at HMP Lindholme, and then I did a few more at other establishments as well as Full Sutton. I did OK with most of these interviews and was convincing enough on the Full Sutton one for them to promote me. As is the way with the Prison Service, they keep you waiting and it was January 1996 before I was officially promoted. I must say one thing, the type of questions I was asked compared to some of the ridiculous questions I was asked for my Senior Officer board were actually relevant to the work I would be doing as a manager at this level.

The Prison Service itself was getting more professional in the way it operated and I spent some time at our training school in the Midlands doing workshops on devising a drug strategy. This was a comprehensive strategy, dealing with the prevention of drugs coming in to a prison to helping prisoners with drug treatment. This meant a lot more co-operation between different disciplines within a prison, such as the Psychology Department. We also started to invest in computer software that allowed us to analyse intelligence information in a much more scientific way, working closely with the police who had been doing this for years.

Throughout all of my trials (no pun intended) and tribulations, not to mention having a young family over the last few years, I continued to study for my Open University degree. I took my final exams in the summer of this year and when I got my results I had got the six units I needed for a Honours degree. Apart from getting married and having my children, this was one of the most proud moments of my life. My school years were not my finest time, apart from the sport, and if any of my teachers knew I was about to be a BA (Hons) they would not believe it. I had my degree ceremony at Harrogate conference centre in December of this year and to walk on that stage in my cap and gown to receive my degree with my family watching was almost too much to take, and I had a bit of a tear in my eye.

After getting my degree and still remembering the past few years where I started to hate this job, I decided to try using my new-found education and move out of the Prison Service. I looked for other positions in various types of management. I did feel at this time my skills in the Prison Service were not transferable to other management roles, but that was my typical lack of confidence in my own ability. I decided to go to an agency that specialised in getting you interviews for degree level management roles. They wanted £400 to join their agency and my mind-set at this time was, I am not paying that; it stopped me looking any further and I decided to stay in the Prison Service and try to advance further in what I knew best. The fact that Full Sutton was getting a better place to work also swayed my mind. Another big issue was the pension the Prison Service offered, which in my case was an index-linked one which I doubled up the years after 20 years and could retire at 55 years old. This again was a product of my upbringing of, go to school, get a job, retire and that's your lot until they put you in a box. But things changed later in my life.

1996

In January of this year I was officially promoted to Principal Officer. This was a big deal as this was the highest uniform grade and one at this time that was a well-respected rank if you did a good job. I was given the role of Security Principal Officer which in a high security prison is a role that usually goes to an experienced person, so I was rather chuffed that I was trusted to take this role as a relatively inexperienced PO.

The interesting thing about this level of management was you had your core role but you also did what was called Oscar 1, which was basically where you controlled the operational centre of the prison and was very much a great experience on decision making in day-to-day management of the whole prison. I really enjoyed this role, as part of your job was to get all around the prison to ensure all was well and everybody was doing what they should be doing. Also you were the focal point for many operational decisions and your personal radio was always going for decisions to be made. This was a massive learning curve for me and I felt good motivating staff and listening to the issues and sorting out a way to deal with problems that arose.

Another role of the Principal Officer was to be in charge of the prison at night. Because there were a number of POs, we did not do nights too often so my first set of nights was in May of this year. I must admit to having a few nerves as it is quite a responsibility to be in total charge of such a place, and particularly as was usual with the Prison Service we got next to no training for this role.

My first set of nights was a bit of a baptism of fire. They were going quite well until the third night when I got a call from an officer on A Wing who suggested I come and speak to a prisoner. A Wing was a Rule 43(a) wing which is a rule that allows prisoners to apply for protection from the main stream type prisoner, usually because they are a sex offender or in fear of their safety on main wings for other reasons, such as being in debt or informing on other prisoners. I made my way to the wing and to the cell in question. When I got there the occupant of the cell was in tears and threatening to harm himself. We only open cell doors in an emergency at night, so I spoke to this prisoner through the door and saw him through the spyhole in the door. He was holding a razor blade and threatening to cut himself. I decided to go in to the cell to take the razor blade off him and make sure he was OK. He gave the blade up and eventually told me he was OK now. About an hour later I got an emergency call on the radio to attend A Wing. The same prisoner had another razor blade and when I arrived at his cell he had cut himself and was bleeding quite badly. When we entered the cell I found the prisoner had cut his scrotum very badly and realised he needed medical attention rather quickly. The good thing about a place like Full Sutton was there were medically trained staff on at night. The prisoner had committed some horrendous sexual offences, and said he could no longer live with the guilt of what he had done so wanted to take his life and felt he had to suffer so cutting the part of his body that caused the crime was his way of equalising things. Due to the serious nature of his cuts we had to call an ambulance. Opening a prison up at night is a very vulnerable thing to do and particularly at a high security prison. It got worse when the ambulance crew arrived as they said he needed to be hospitalised. Thankfully I had read the procedures for this and was confident I had covered all the angles. Sometimes it is good to have things like this happen early in your promotion, as it stops complacency creeping in and gives you confidence to deal with issues that may arise. Off he went to have his balls put back in place. I would have stitched them to his ears for the offences he had committed.

I had been a member of the Lions Organisation for a number of years. The Lions are a charitable organisation where every penny raised goes to a cause, as we as members pay our own administration. It is also a great organisation for socialising and meeting people. In September our club paid for a 'grant a wish' for a disabled person. The person who won this award was a young man called John who was severely disabled and his wish was to go across water, so we decided to pay for him to travel to Dublin. I volunteered to take him with another member. This was a very humbling experience watching John try to do things able-bodied people take for granted. I shared a room with him, and watching him get up in the morning and dress himself made such an impression on me that I try never to complain about stupid little things. It also brought it home to me how difficult it is for disabled people in wheelchairs to get around and how many places are inaccessible. Dublin Lions looked after us for the weekend and we had a fantastic time, but it was so rewarding to see John with a smile on his face all weekend. I never heard John complain once all weekend about anything, yet I go to work every day listening to people who have committed the most horrendous crimes moaning and complaining about food, conditions, what they can and cannot have and everything in between. The liberal chattering classes have something to answer for by treating these people better than less fortunate people in our society who have committed no offenses.

Throughout the year we kept improving the atmosphere in the prison and taking more and more control; the more decent prisoners became more confident to offer information on the disruptive element. The disruptive element was getting smaller and smaller and being marginalised to the point they had no option than to go along with the positive flow and direction the prison was going in. Don't get me wrong, this was still a prison full of very dangerous people who need to be treated with caution, and any prison is operated with the co-operation of the population.

Because I had worked in security as a Senior Officer and now a Principal Officer I felt I needed to gain some time managing a residential wing so I asked to move. I was asked by the Deputy Governor if I would go on A Wing, as he was not too happy about the way it was being run. A Wing, as described before, was a sex offenders' wing where they applied for R43 (a) which is a prison rule where prisoners can apply to be protected from other prisoners. This was not my ideal place to work but said I would do it for a short period if I could be moved to a 'main' wing at a later date.

The main issue on the wing was that the manager on there was not very good with people and he had lost the co-operation of the staff, which was affecting the general running of it. He was one of these who managed by bullying and abdicating instead of delegating. For those of you who don't know the difference, abdication is where you tell someone to do something without any kind of direction or knowledge as to whether they can do it, and often the person doing the telling has no idea how to do it themselves. Delegating is what a good manager does in that you ensure the person you are asking to perform a task/project has the necessary skills, you give them guidance as to what you want to see as an outcome, ensure they feel comfortable what they have to do and ensure you get them to feedback to you what it is they are doing to ensure understanding, and finally you are capable of doing the task yourself. That is my opinion at least.

I started off by getting my Senior Officers in to get their opinion on what the issues were and ask them what they felt we should do to improve things. It is at times like this you find how many people are promoted beyond their competence and who is not ready, as many of them just look at you and think, well you're the manager, you tell us what to do. I did have two good ones, however, who gave me their opinion. I then held meetings with the officers to gain their views and finally I spoke to a number of prisoners to ask them what their experience was of the regime and what they felt was making their lives difficult. I then had a look at the type and number of request/complaints, adjudications etc. to gauge the mood.

Without blowing my own trumpet (go on then, I will), it did not take a brain surgeon to put things right. I started by ensuring there was more communication between wing staff and prisoners, between wing staff and wing managers. I told the Senior Officers to get out of their offices and patrol the wing, talk to staff and prisoners, be a presence and equally ensured I was around as often as I could. Whenever possible I ensured I stood at the servery when a meal was being served as every prisoner on the wing passed by to collect a meal. Many staff told me not to do this as I was delaying the serving of meals, as prisoners were constantly asking me questions. I refused to do this and said when the wing is running properly, prisoners will not need to complain to me as the wing would be running smoothly and they would be confident their issues would be dealt with. This is exactly what happened as after a few weeks I got few complaints standing here and plenty of hellos and other passing comments.

Sex offenders in a high security prison will use the written form of complaint and be a bit more litigious than the main population, who will use a more Neanderthal approach first and use threats of violence. I found this a really good learning process as I had to be more switched on to the Rules and Regulations and I taught the staff to ensure they had an audit trail for everything they did, as you never knew when you would need that to be able to answer a complaint or legal issue.

I had a number of very litigious prisoners on the wing at this time and one took me to the civil court on three occasions, but because I had ensured I had audit trails for everything I did he ended up being made a vexatious litigant. This is when a person makes so may spurious litigations the judge stops them from doing multiple applications so he had to have one answered before he could make another. He continued to do them but it took him a long time and never won one of them. He was a silly old git who had nothing better to do with his time, but I found it all quite amusing and enjoyed the challenge.

Another prisoner who was slightly in a different league was an infamous prisoner who was an ex-police officer for a short time who killed and cut up some homosexual men. His case was high profile at the time and he felt he was a bit above everybody else because he had a good education and the notoriety of his crime gave him quite a bit of news coverage. Once again he was always threatening to take me to court for one reason or another. I said the same to him as all the others: feel free, get on with it as I have nothing to fear. He never did take me to court but we had many an interesting discussion in my office where he acted like some jumped up lawyer and I always remained very calm listening to his complaint and ensuring I documented everything and if he did have a genuine grievance I ensured it was dealt with. He was possibly the most pompous prisoner I have ever come across, but I think I got the better of the duel.

One of the most bizarre situations I dealt with was when a trio of prisoners had a bit of a love tryst and they came to me to sort it out. One prisoner accused another of stealing his boyfriend and the other said he had not as he was his boyfriend. When I got the person in the office who was 'the boyfriend' he said he was really mixed up as he loved both of them and could not end the relationship with either one. There was a serious side to this as the two who were each laying claim to be the boyfriend were getting to the point that they could use physical violence against each other, and they were both serious offenders serving a long time for serious sexual offences with high levels of violence. I eventually got all three of them in my office. At first I thought I had made a bit of a mistake as the two boyfriends started getting a bit heated and threatening so I just stood up and shouted, "Enough, if you cannot sit and discuss this like sensible adults I will separate you by sending you to different prisons." That worked as they pleaded with me not to do that. I turned to the one they were fighting over and said he had to make a choice of one or the other or learn to live with both of them and share the relationship. A bit odd I know, but we eventually came to a compromise where he spent equal time with them both. I was dying to say, why don't you just have a threesome and then everybody is happy. Having a homosexual relationship was illegal in prison at this time, but I would defy anybody to stop it so I took the pragmatic view and thought, as long as everybody is happy, nobody gets hurt, what's the problem. Let's face it, you tell me how you stop it? One thing that did come out of this is I take my hat off to marriage guidance counsellors, because I couldn't do that for a living.

I had to work on the morning of Christmas Day but was home in good time to enjoy most of the day and my children were used to opening their presents later.

1997

I started to think about my next promotion which was to 'Governor 5' as it was called then. This was quite a big step up, as it was more of a strategic than operational position and much more responsibility and also you came out of uniform and in to a suit. In April I applied for a promotion board at HMP Haverigg in Cumbria and was granted one. On the 21st April I made my way to Haverigg. This prison is in the middle of nowhere but also very close to the beautiful Lake District. As usual I sat in front of three people who asked me my opinion on this and that mixed with a few operational/strategic questions, how would you deal with this situation, that situation etc. I have to admit I was not the best in an interview situation, which I found such a false environment. I did not get this promotion and to be honest I was not too disappointed as I did not really want to take my family away from York as the children were happy at school, so this was a good practice for future boards.

In June I moved to B Wing as the wing manager. B Wing was very similar to D Wing in the type of prisoners that were located there but it was very noticeable the difference in atmosphere. Prisoners were being generally polite and respectful, they were going to work, education etc. and it was actually quite a pleasant place to go to work, within reason. As opposed to my last time on the wings, I was actually allowed to manage. It felt good to be in charge of the wing and be able to influence the way I feel a wing should be run. There was a wing Governor but I made it clear from an operational point of view I was in charge and he was there to support me and represent us at board level. I had some great staff that were prepared to go along with the vision I had for the wing. That vision was to treat prisoners with respect and help them to get through their sentence in a positive way but at the same time ensure that respect was given to the officers, and those that did not want to go along with this ethos would be dealt with in a robust but fair way. I really enjoyed this challenge and I think by and large I succeeded with the comments I got from prisoners and the buy-in from officers. I like to think I treat people in the way I like to be treated myself and I have found that is the easiest way to get the best from people and encourage them to act the same. Many managers in the service seem to think being a bully is the way to manage, taking the view: this is a disciplined service so they should do as they are told. I find these people lack so many skills and miss the point of managing people. Some of the young people who I manage today are the managers of the future.

One role I really enjoyed was chairing sentence plan boards. A sentence plan was a way of managing a prisoner through his sentence from the point of view of what he needed to address his offending behaviour, dealing with other issues such as drug dependency, anger management, family issues etc. The sentence plan board was the time all this comes together and decisions are made on whether the prisoner is heading in the right direction or if not, what we feel he needs to do to get on the right path. The prisoner himself has the right to attend the board and is encouraged to do so as it is important in my opinion that he is part of the process and contributes fully. It is so easy for professional people to think they know what is better for an individual than that individual themselves. The board was made up of the prisoner, probation officer, education officer, employment manager, and the prisoner's personal officer from his wing and sometimes an external probation officer.

In August of this year I moved to the secretariat. This was a new department and I was quite proud to be chosen to be one of the pioneers of this project. There were three of us in the team. I was the only operational person as my boss was an administration person and the other person was an Executive Officer. The role of the secretariat was to support the Governor with policy documents, dealing with Treasury Solicitor casework, dealing with questions from MPs, drafting Governors Orders, managing the Standards Audits, contingency planning. So for three of us you can see this was a very busy and important role, as well as a very interesting one. As well as doing this I still had to do the generic Principal Officer role.

In December I spent a week at a prison in Middlesbrough (Holme House) with the external audit team to learn how a full audit of a prison was conducted. This was a very interesting week as the audit team allowed me to witness everything. I did find certain things a bit off-putting in that the auditors, who were all operational people seconded to this unit, were trying their hardest to find things wrong. I felt to a certain extent they were trying to justify their job, as Holme House was a very well run prison and some members of the audit team seemed to think it was a challenge to find things to criticise. Talk about giving people confidence who were doing a difficult job very well. The thing is, these same people could be back in a prison at any time on the other end of the audit and I am sure they would want to be treated professionally and with some understanding of how difficult a job prison staff do. As they say those that can do it do it, those that cannot teach it, or in this case audit it.

1998

The secretariat work gave me great exposure to the senior managers, including the Governor, and as I was now actively seeking my next promotion it would do me no harm. This miffed some of my fellow Principal Officers as they felt I was getting an unfair advantage. Was I bothered, nah! The one thing about me was I had very few friends in the Prison Service so I did not care what people thought of me. I never went out of my way to antagonise anyone but neither did I care if I did. If they are that shallow why should I worry?

One of my roles was to review the contingency plans and to ensure the Command Centre was always ready to use. The Command Centre was a room where if there was a major incident taking place, the person in charge of the prison at the time would go to this room and take charge of the incident. The room had screens with views of the prison, all the contingency plans, phones to HQ, radio contact, maps of the prison etc. There was up to around six or eight people in the room depending on the time of day/night, all with specific roles. There could be two people in there for a time if the incident happened in the evening or night. Reviewing the contingency plans was a very time-consuming job, but it taught me so much about the whole prison and beyond it was invaluable. We had to do so many contingency plan exercises a year. Most of these were desktop exercises but we had to do a live hostage exercise once a year. This meant opening the control room and effectively running a hostage exercise as if it was actually happening. We always had a de-brief after an incident and I ensured they were conducted in a constructive way without blame but a learning way. The prat that was in charge when I was taken hostage on D Wing could learn a lot from this.

I loved dealing with Parliamentary questions. You had to make sure you researched these spot on because what you replied to HQ was likely to be a reply that an MP or even the Prime Minister gave to a question in the Houses of Parliament. Equally I enjoyed answering solicitors' letters. Some solicitors can be really pompous in how they write letters and often threatening in a legal way. I tended to reply to the initial letter with as little information as possible so they had to write back asking for more, then you gave them a bit more and it became a bit of a game. To be honest the solicitors couldn't really give a monkey's as they got paid and couldn't really care about some prisoner locked up for years.

I had to draft replies to prisoner complaints on behalf of the Governor. Again I enjoyed doing these, researching the issues and forming an answer to the prisoner. Many of these complaints had no foundation, and I enjoyed it when I could give a comprehensive answer where the prisoner had no choice than to accept it. On the other hand I was fair if a prisoner had a genuine complaint. Many prisoners in this type of establishment knew the system and were very good at putting in complaints and many were serial complainers knowing they could potentially clog up the system, therefore there was a good chance they would have their complaint upheld because it was easier to pay out than fight. One instance of this was a South African prisoner who was serving life for a horrendous murder. He was a very keen artist and had through his long sentence collected quite a bit of artist materials, even though most of it was obtained through the education department. He was an obnoxious person who complained at anything and everything. He was given a cell search one day and got a bit angry with the officers searching his cell. He decided to try to prevent the officers touching certain of his art things, to which they told him to mind his business as they could search whatever they liked and would take care with his property. He would not accept this and he physically tried to stop one of the officers, which was an assault, so the officers attempted to restrain him which turned into a bit of a fracas in his cell where things were broken. He was later moved to another prison and accused staff of damaging his artwork and losing some of it. We proved most of his property was given to him by the education department and because it was not his property, it was not recorded, but this ended with his solicitor. Managers above me finally made the decision to pay this prisoner around £2000 in compensation, saying it was sometimes better to use discretion. As much as I understand the politics it is, in my opinion, sometimes better to spend a bit of money fighting something you know is right to save in the long term. Doing this just encouraged more prisoners to make spurious financial claims. Once again an example of weak-kneed managers taking the easy way out.

During this year I applied for two Governor 5 promotion boards at Highpoint in Suffolk and Sudbury in Derbyshire. I was unsuccessful in both. Full Sutton held an Assessment Centre for promotion to Governor 5. This was a bit of a trial for how future promotions were to be done. I will explain this later. This assessment was a written test first, which cut the number of people in half. The second part was a mix of exercises such as discussion in a group and other psychological-type scenarios. I got through to the second bit but was not successful at the second.

I also applied for a sideways move to Holme House, the prison in Middlesbrough I did the audit visit. I felt after over ten years at Full Sutton I needed to broaden my skills and felt this move would be good for me. I got a letter in October telling me I had been successful. This would mean a move of house, which Jenny once again accepted if it was to further my career. Again she was very supportive and I was always appreciative of this, even though I may not have said it at the time. We looked at places to live and as much as Middlesbrough is a dump, there are some lovely towns and villages around and beautiful countryside. We eventually settled on a place called Stokesley. We put our house on the market and viewed many houses. I also had to consider the children who were at school and had friends in York, but I got them to accept it. In March 1999 I got a letter from the Governor of Holme House telling me due to a dramatic change in direction, there was no longer a vacancy for me. They waited six months to tell me this and we as a family were all ready for the upheaval of moving to another area. To say I was angry is an understatement and to be fair to my Governor, he was very angry with Holme House and told them this was no way to treat me, let alone my family. As ever you cannot beat the system so I had to put this behind me and get on with it.

The good thing about working in the secretariat was I got Christmas and Boxing Day off.

Chapter 6

1999 - 2002

1999

During 1998 the Prison Service was developing a new process for promoting people to Governor 5. This was called a Job Simulation Assessment Centre (JSAC). It was developed by a group of psychologists at HQ. I believe this process originally came from the USA or Canada but they scrapped it as it was found not to work. Typical of the Prison Service to take this on, call me an old cynic but it did create a lot of jobs for psychologists.

The JSAC was a long-winded expensive process which in my opinion was designed to promote automatons and which took no account of personal character and true ability. I did fail a couple of these things, so many might say it was just bitterness on my part but I would disagree as I will explain later how I was temporary promoted to Governor 5 for a long time and was doing it very successfully in the real world. Can I also add the private sector Prison Service did not promote their senior managers by such a robotic system, but one based more on ability in the real world. The JSAC was in two parts: the first part was a written test of about three hours, and if you got through this you were invited to a specially prepared site that was set up for the simulation exercises.

The first stage of the JSAC is a written test that lasts about 3 hr 45 min. This is broken down in to 3 topics.

1. Data analysis:

   You are given the background information describing a prison and specific monitoring information, such as the prison population by age, by sentence, the type and number of complaints, drug testing results, adjudications and prisoner applications. From this we are required to list all our observations, identify trends, predict possible outcomes, give conclusions and make recommendations.

   The exercise is designed to test how you appraise statistical data, select relevant data, predict possible outcomes, think logically, plan practically and write with accuracy, brevity and clarity.

2. Drafting:

   We are provided with a situation such as a complaint and then required to write a written response, identify and address all issues then conclude the matter without the need for further correspondence. The exercise is designed to test how you appraise written information, represent the organisation outside the service, treat delicate issues with sensitivity and discretion, address issues in a positive manner and again write with accuracy, brevity and clarity.

3. Written appreciation:

   We are given three prison-related topics where you choose one then describe what the operational effects would be if this became policy. We were required to produce an executive summary/overview, provide a bullet point list of the issues, complete an analysis of the issues, and give our conclusion. The exercise is designed to test how we appraise the issues, address issues in the broader context, address issues in a positive manner, make appropriate plans, generate different topics, identify risks in options and once again write with accuracy, brevity and clarity.

   The second part of the JSAC is a simulation exercise. We had to go to Birmingham prison for this, where there was a building set up for this purpose. It was set up with a number of offices that have a camera in the corner. You are allocated to an office which has a desk, telephone and an in-tray full of paperwork relating to the exercises that are coming. You are allowed about 20 minutes to read the papers to prepare yourself for a series of meetings with various fictitious staff who all have different problems that you are expected to resolve. The cameras are there so a number of people in a control room can mark your performance as you go along. They are

- Motivation and commitment
- Organising and empowering
- Team building and liaison
- Problem solving and continuous improvement
- Leadership and decision making

All the people taking part in the JSAC are prison staff taken out of prisons. The JSACs went on for weeks so you can see how expensive they are to put on, in addition to the fact prisons have to reduce their staffing for weeks to accommodate them. But no worries, it is you the taxpayer that pays for this. JSACs are carried out for promotion to Senior Officer, Governor 5 and to senior manager. Wow how much does all that cost and how many empires of psychologists did it create?

I thought I had done OK with my interviews but when I got the results I had failed miserably. When I got my feedback it took me all on to bite my tongue as what they were expecting from us was ridiculous. We were expected to ask a multitude of open-ended questions in such a way that the actor gave you specific information in return until you eventually got what you thought was an answer. In my humble opinion these exercises were designed to create a load of senior managers acting like automatons, taking any personality or difference in character away, thus leaving the service with managers in senior positions who were not original thinkers but ones who were promoted by following a system which can be learnt, therefore producing less and less creative managers with ideas to take the service forward.

Around April of this year I was moved from the secretariat and asked to become the 'lifer' manager. There were around 100 life sentence prisoners at Full Sutton at this time, and this was a very important position. Most life sentence prisoners were the best type of prisoner to deal with as they generally accepted their lot and knew they had to make the most of their time in prison, as they were there for a long time and fighting the system was futile. There were those who did want to fight the system but I think the only thing they were fighting was themselves and their guilt.

Life sentence prisoners had a lifer plan which was the way to manage their sentence, helping them to hopefully be released as a better citizen at some point in the future, and my role was to ensure all the lifers had reports done on time, that they were moved to other prisons when necessary to gain the correct offending behaviour programme, and I was a point of contact for any concerns they had. At this time we were trialling a new programme called OASyS. This was a system devised by psychologists to analyse a prisoner, from what makes him tick to what he needs to make him tick in a different way and become a better citizen. I know this is not a very intellectual way to put an intellectual piece of work, but you get my drift I guess. At this stage it was a paper version but in time it became computerised and improved along the way. I know I have had a bit of a go at psychologists, but to be fair to them this was a good piece of work that took a lot of putting together and like anything in life it was not perfect but much better than what we had. I will relate a story I personally found amusing in the early days of this project. One of the senior psychologists had interviewed a life sentence prisoner, filling out this rather lengthy document based on answers he had given to the questions. This prisoner was a pretty tough Glaswegian aged 45 and he had spent the vast majority of his adult life in prison and his childhood in homes of some kind or another. He was as tough as they come and generally a decent prisoner. The psychologist, prisoner and I sat in my office to discuss the outcome of his OASyS report. The psychologist explained fully what we were doing and how the report had been put together, which the prisoner was OK with. The bit I found comical was when the psychologist said to him he was suffering from a level of mental illness. At this the prisoner started getting a bit agitated as in his world calling someone mental was effectively calling him a nut job, as he put it. The psychologist tried to explain this was due to him answering in the positive when she asked him if he felt depressed sometimes and that depression was a mental illness. He just came out with, "I have just been sentenced to life imprisonment with a recommendation I serve 20 years and I will be nearly 70 yrs old when I get out so how the fuck do you think I feel?" He turned to me and said, "Mr Ward, will you get this crazy cow out of here so me and you can have a sensible conversation about my sentence." I had to be professional and try to calm him and play down the terminology of the report by explaining it does not mean he is a nut job, but depression is a form of mental illness. We were not saying he was crazy and accepted it was normal to feel like he did. He accepted this and left, turning to me and winking at me. Sometimes the job had its good times as this made me smile. I had a chat with him later in the day and had a good laugh and reminisced about times gone by when everybody knew where they stood and life was much simpler. This said, I did embrace progressive methods of helping prisoners to understand there is a better way to get through life and how to make better choices. I also had a chat with the psychologist to explain to her how to be a bit more diplomatic and try to understand the mentality of the people she was dealing with. To be fair to her, she was appreciative of the advice and went on to be a very useful person to have around as she also gave me a lot of advice.

One very satisfying moment I had as the lifer manager was with a prisoner who I had when I was on A Wing. He had spent 20 years in prison and all this time he had denied his offence. His offence was a horrendous sexual attack on a woman where excessive amounts of violence were used, leaving the woman scarred for life both physically and mentally. He was a very ugly little man for whom I could understand why he found it hard to have a relationship with a member of the opposite sex without forcing himself upon them. This prisoner was actually a decent prisoner, in that he did not cause any problems for the prison authorities, but he was going to spend the rest of his life in prison unless he addressed his offending behaviour and because he would not accept he had committed the offence he would not be allowed to do an offending behaviour course that he needed as he had to accept his offence. Catch 22. The offending behaviour course he needed was the Sex Offender Treatment Programme (SOTP). To do this you had to accept your guilt, as part of the course was to talk about what you did and the consequences etc. I will explain a bit more about this in a short time.

I had quite a good working relationship with this prisoner so felt it was worth a go getting him in the office and working through his issues. I explained to him there was a course he could do which was not offence related but based around thinking skills. It was designed to make prisoners think about their actions and that there is a consequence for most actions, whether that is good or bad. Many prisoners have spent their lives committing crime, being selfish, having children to multiple partners etc. without any thought for the people they committed the crime against, feeling sorry for themselves when they get caught, taking no responsibility for children, just enjoying the making of them but with no consideration for their welfare and generally being immune to responsibility. I asked him if he would do me and him a favour and give it a go. I asked him what he had to lose. One thing that came out of this meeting was that he could not read or write and he was embarrassed about this, thinking these courses required the ability to read and write. To be fair there was an element of reading and writing but we could get round it. I spoke to the education department who arranged to do a one-to-one with him for basic reading and writing before he did the thinking skills. He agreed to both the one-to-one and taking the thinking skills course. After about two months this prisoner came to see me and explained he had admitted his offence and broke down in tears thanking me for persuading him to go on this course, as it had made him question himself and he told me the reason he had not admitted this offence was because he could not accept what he had done to his victim. He said he felt a massive weight had been taken off him and felt he could now try to move forward. As much as I abhor what he did to this woman it was a good feeling that I had, in some small way, helped both the prisoner to come to terms with his life and move on and possibly his victim, who may eventually try to move on too knowing he admitted what he did to her.

In November of this year I was temporary promoted to Governor 5 so I had to spend some money on suits, shirts and shoes as I had always had these provided for me being in uniform. I never put a uniform back on again, as I acted up for some time and then eventually got through one of these ridiculous JSACs to be promoted in my own right. I was no different a person, or any more skilled when I passed the JSAC than when I failed, I just learnt how to get through the JSAC process. In other words, give them what they want and then get on with the day job.

Once again I was more or less just left to get on with it with little formal training, however my immediate boss was really helpful and a constant source of guidance. The role of a Governor grade was very much different than a uniform manager. For one it was much more strategic than operational, you had a greater responsibility and people looked to you much more for decision making. The Prison Service hierarchy had a propaganda saying that, 'people are our best asset', then they invested next to nothing in developing people to become the future managers, or when they obtained promotion, guide them through the initial stages to ensure the people we promoted were ready for the move up. That is unless you were on the accelerated promotion merry-go-round, and then money was thrown at this. To be fair there were some very good people who came through this process, however there were many who were just not cut out for it and ended up in high positions, often governing prisons when they shouldn't be left in charge of themselves. Another great saying was 'the Prison Service is great at promoting people to a level of incompetence'. Not in all cases but more than you would like to think.

One of the duties of a Governor grade was to be the duty governor. This is where you carry a two way radio from the opening of the prison to the locking up and then you are on call until the following morning. As I said before, the Orderly Officer O/O (Principal Officer) is in charge operationally of the prison and the duty governor is there to back the O/O up and be the ultimate decision maker. In the evening when all other managerial staff have gone home, the duty governor is in charge of the prison, so quite a responsibility. The first duty governor I did, I was unusually a bit nervous, but to be fair I had plenty of good people to refer to if I needed to get advice and even in the evening when I was on my own I knew advice was only a phone call away. As it happened the day went by pretty uneventfully. I liked doing a duty governor because you had to visit all parts of the prison, which was good because I met many people who I did not generally come across and learnt much more about the whole prison. One of the duties was to go to the kitchen and test the meal and I can say what I tasted in prison kitchens was by and large good food, well cooked and nutritional even though one of the biggest complaints of prisoners was food. I bet 99% of them did not eat as well as this when they were outside, and they did not pay for it either. Complaining for complaining's sake I would say. The problem is the politically correct people would never say to prisoners, there is nothing wrong with this just get on with it. On many occasions when I came across prisoners complaining about food, as I explained earlier I would take their plate off them and eat their meal in front of them and say, "Thanks for that, it was delicious," and generally it was. I used to do about one duty governor a week and even though they were long days, and potentially long nights if you were phoned from the prison, I always enjoyed this part of my duties as I got to walk around the prison meeting lots of people and getting to know so much about what was going on.

As there were only two Governor grades on at Christmas I was lucky to have the day off.

2000

I continued to work with the life sentence prisoners as the lifer governor for a short time before I moved to prisoner services which included the library, workshops, employment of prisoners, gym, kitchen and education; so very much areas of a prison I was not too familiar with, but it gave me great experience in contract management as the education and library were managed by external agencies.

One thing about being a Governor grade was that you sat in on more policy/strategic meetings, often with the Governor and Deputy Governor in attendance which gave me access to how they managed and how decisions were made, the thoughts of people at a high position and how they conducted themselves. It was also satisfying when they asked my opinion, which made me feel quite valued for once. It is a pity you have to get to this stage to feel like this, and was one lesson I took away for my later times in the service when I made it an important part of my management style to take opinions from everybody regardless of their position in the service. Let's face it, who knows more about what goes on at floor level than a prison officer working day in day out on wings, talking and listening to prisoners' concerns, opinions and often information that they have? It is equally important to listen to support staff who often have good ideas how to improve systems that make it better for prisoners and make a prison officer's life better, not to mention sometimes there were financial saving ideas.

One thing a Governor grade has to do on a rota basis is a night visit. This was originally done by the Governor in years gone by so the Governor could have access to night staff and they could speak to him. As years went by it became a task for a lower grade governor to do this task and was designed to ensure everything was in order, but also gave night staff the chance to put any questions to a senior manager. They were a bit of a farce really from the point of view of ensuring all was in order at night, as you had to give prior warning to the Night Orderly Officer you were coming, therefore they could put the TVs away, hide the made up bed and be dressed properly with all documentation ready for signing.

The Governor grade visiting could do the visit either at night or early morning but it had to be when the prison was in lockdown mode. I cannot obviously tell you exactly how this operated for security reasons but in a nutshell the Governor grade had to phone the control room and be put through to the Night Orderly Officer, where you said a certain thing to him regarding coming for a visit. If you said the wrong thing the control room would call the police and the police would be at the prison gate to meet you to ensure you were OK and nobody was with you. The police also visited your house to ensure your family was OK, as they could be being held hostage while you went to the prison at the most vulnerable time. The first one I did was an absolute disaster and very embarrassing. I thought I had said the correct thing to the Night Orderly Officer but I later found out I got it slightly wrong. The police were at the gate waiting for me and asked me loads of questions until they were satisfied everything was OK. I got a call from my wife later in the morning in a hissy fit asking me what was going on and was I alright, as she had a police officer knocking on the door at 4.30am asking if she was OK. She did not have a clue what was going on and said she was but thought something had happened to me, but the police officer just said everything was fine. He did not ask to go in and check the house, which he should have as there could have been people in the house threatening my children so my wife would say everything was OK. Although this was actually a great training exercise for me, the night staff and the police. It took me a long time to live it down and you can imagine the ribbing I got from everybody (that is after the Deputy Governor gave me a pretty decent bollocking). I can tell you I got it perfect the next time I did one and every other time since.

One of the things I had to do fairly quickly in my new role was to renegotiate the education contract. I had never done anything like this before so it was a very steep learning curve but thankfully my boss was used to doing this as he used to be head of training in a previous life so had done this on many occasions, and was a great source of advice to me during this time. One good thing about the Prison Service is all prisons do the same things so there are always people in other prisons to phone up to ask their advice or find out who is doing best practice and ask them to send their version. Most people were happy to help and happy to send their versions. It always helped if you stroked their egos a little bit as everybody likes to be appreciated.

This was a fairly long process as you had to go out to tender and there was loads of paperwork to go through, interviews of contractors, legal issues etc. I must admit reading through contract documents is not the most exciting thing I have done in life but it was good to look at ways we could improve the education delivery and try to get the best for the least cost which proved invaluable skills for some of my later jobs. We eventually chose Manchester College as we found them to be quite innovative, experienced in prison education needs and most importantly the best value.

One area I was in charge of was the gymnasium. This was good for me as I was a bit of a gym bunny myself. It is a bit of a stereotype within prisons that Physical Education Instructors (PEI) are not always the brightest buttons in the box but can lift weights. Some of the PEIs I had did follow this stereotype but the majority were willing to embrace the changes that were happening all over the service. One of the changes was that teaching education can be done anywhere, and what better place to teach education than in the gym where many prisoners want to go? Prison gyms have always been a place where the big boys go to get bigger so we had to look at a way to make better use of the gym. I asked the manager in the gym to liaise with education about how we could make better use of the gym in relation to sentence planning, education and encourage other types of prisoner to take part in exercise than the bully boys lifting weights. Having said that, many of the bully boys were educationally challenged but it was not seen as the thing to do in prison to 'go to school' so many of them would not do conventional education. What a perfect place to get them to better themselves in other ways.

As I said many of the PEIs welcomed the opportunity to embrace change by helping prisoners in other ways and actually gaining skills and qualifications themselves. It is said around 75% of prisoners are at an education level below an 11 year old in Maths and English, so even something as simple as showing a prisoner how to use the machines and to measure calories, speed, weight was teaching them a basic level of maths. We looked at other types of education from health management, nutrition and leadership to social skills.

Many prisoners in prison are or have been drug users, some heavy. Learning about health and how the body works is a great way to see what harm drugs are doing and nutrition shows them how the right food alongside exercise works with the body. We had prisoners taking refereeing courses, thus teaching them leadership, discipline and the need to have and abide by rules. We had a big changing room which the PEIs suggested we cut in half and use one half as a classroom. I thought this was a great idea and so we obtained half the funding for this through the City of Manchester College and it proved to be a great success. One other really good thing this did was get prison staff and education staff working together and better understanding each other's work and how it all ties in together around the prisoners' life. It was amazing to see some of these big macho body builders going to the gym to sit in a classroom as well as lift weights. The other good thing about all this was we involved the prisoners in the whole process, because after all it was for their benefit and this way they had buy in, and therefore it was not something we dictated to them.

The workshops at Full Sutton were much different to what I had been used to at Manchester where they were predominantly 'noddy shops' where a prisoner did not have to think. Some workshops were 'noddy shops' at Full Sutton but many of them were more skill-based such as building, painting and decorating, plumbing through to repairing motorcycles to fashion.

One of the workshops was sponsored by a fashion company called Red or Dead. The workshop was set up the same as a conventional company in that it had a manager, an accountant, salespeople, machinists etc. who were all prisoners and they were mentored by someone from the company. The quality of the clothes they were making was good enough to be sold in the open market, and I visited a Red or Dead shop in Leeds where the denim jackets and jeans made at Full Sutton were being sold for around £60. One of the prisoners working in this workshop asked if it was possible to arrange a fashion show. We gave this some thought and came to the conclusion, why not? Obviously as well as the organisational side we had to consider the security side. The buy-in to put this on by the prisoners was very positive to the extent that they didn't complain about any of the security constraints imposed by the security department. The show was to take place in the visits room where there was a stage erected and the family of the prisoners were invited to attend along with members of the press and staff from Red or Dead. The show went off without any security issues and everybody respected what was happening so it was a great success and Full Sutton received some good publicity, which pleased the Governor. As is the case some members of the public complained about the money spent and the fact prisoners were taking jobs from decent law abiding citizens. The workshop was actually self-financing, and as for taking jobs from other people, well, you make your own mind up.

Another workshop that was excellent was the motorcycle repair workshop. There were only about eight prisoners in here at any one time but the quality of work was top class. One of the prisoners working in here was a Dutch drug dealer who was serving 20 years. He built a motorbike that would not have been out of place in any serious motorbike museum. The detail that prisoners put in to their work and the application to learn was something many college students could learn from. Prisoners worked towards genuine qualifications and again they showed total respect towards the whole concept of what was on offer here. I often wondered if the prisoners had taken this kind of opportunity in their earlier lives whether they would have ended up in the situation in which they found themselves now. I guess that is a whole discussion in itself and another discussion about our education system.

Another very successful workshop was one where prisoners learnt to translate books into braille. This was a very popular area of work for prisoners. Again it surprised me how people who had by and large spent most of their lives committing crime or generally making no use of their life spending hours learning how to do such a wonderful and rewarding thing. It was interesting to see how such a workshop made the general life of a prisoner much better and how they reacted to their sentence as a whole and how their attitude towards staff changed to a more positive one. Having witnessed how people who society have given up on react to a positive chance in life, it makes me ask the question why these people end up doing what they do to end up in a place like Full Sutton. I guess it is the nature and nurture argument, and I am a big believer in the environment in which you are brought up in. It is easy to be a successful, law abiding citizen if you are the child of a professional couple living in a nice neighbourhood and attending a school of like-minded people as opposed to someone brought up on a rough council estate, going to an inner city comprehensive, possibly brought up by a single parent, usually a mother and associating with people who are on the fringe of crime or in it full time. As much as I believe the correct type of education is very important, you also need the correct environment as well to ensure people end up on the better side of life.

I was finding this year a really interesting and progressive year in that I was learning some really valuable experience in relation to managing contracts, working with other agencies and the way they operated and how to manage them as well as developing strategic skills in managing prisons and the wider political ways of the service. I quickly realised I had to think and deal with people in a different way. I had to be much more cautious in the way I spoke to people, and generally what I said as the slightest mistake was pounced on by uniform staff and in particular the Prison Officers' Association (POA). A big learning curve for me but one I thoroughly enjoyed and took to with vigour. The Prison Service was becoming much more politically correct and the new staff coming in to the service were very much different to the people in the service back in 1980. It was a mixture really of good and bad. The good bit was that people coming in at this time were not prepared to put up with being treated in a disrespectful way and expected to be spoken to with respect, but the bad part was in a disciplined service sometimes you had to just do as you were told and question it later. I also found some new younger staff were much more needy and softer than days gone by and would go sick at the drop of a hat.

At the end of the year I was given the opportunity to join a small team putting together a bid on behalf of the public sector Prison Service to manage the first ever private prison that was coming to the end of its ten year contract.

The prison was The Wolds in East Yorkshire. This was a fantastic opportunity to further extend my learning in a more business environment, learning how to put together contracts, financial management at a service level and working with external contractors as well as putting a tender document together. I spoke to the leader of the bid team and must have impressed her as she offered me a position, and I liked her straight away and felt I could work with her so accepted. After over 13 years at Full Sutton it was definitely time to move on, if nothing else to re-charge my enthusiasm with a change of scenery.

2001

I started 2001 in a really upbeat mood and was raring to get going in my new role which was completely different to anything I had done before. This was going to be a serious learning curve for me, but one I was relishing to start. The mere fact this had got me out of Full Sutton was enough to get me jumping for joy. The bid process was a massive task where we had to put together a progressive and full regime at a very competitive cost. This was kind of alien to us, as being public sector we have not been trained in a way where we had to run the service like a business. Luckily we did have a couple of previous public sector bid teams to consult who had been through this process, and one going through the process at a more advanced stage. One of them, Buckley Hall, had won their bid and the prison was back in the public sector.

For the first six weeks we were to be based in London in an office in Westminster with our hotel about 30 metres away, as we were having an office prepared in the training suite at Lindholme prison in South Yorkshire. I travelled down to London on the 2nd January. I met my boss Jacqui at the office and she said the other members of the team would be joining at different times during the week. The first person I met was Mandy. Mandy was on the team to deal with the non-operational aspects of the bid. She is a lovely lady and we were to be joined later by her partner Clif. Mandy & Clif have remained great friends ever since this time and even though they now live in London, I try to stay in touch and meet with them as much as possible. Next it was Keith who was the accountant. Keith was in the office when Mandy and I came back from lunch. We introduced ourselves and had a bit of a chat. A bit later in the day, Mandy and I looked at Keith and he was fast asleep in the chair. We both looked at each other thinking: if he is the accountant, we have a problem. Keith turned out to be a very switched on guy and one of the nicest people you could ever meet, except he came from the wrong side of the Pennines. Keith sadly lost his life in the tsunami in Thailand on Boxing Day 2004 along with his son and daughter. RIP Keith. The rest of the team was Steve, who was someone I knew when he was at Full Sutton, who was the facilities guy; Dave, who was brought on board for his knowledge and contacts with the POA; and Norman, who was Jacqui's deputy. Norman was alright at first but he turned out to be a bit of a dick in the end. Our paths cross later in the book towards the end of my career. For the next six weeks we spent a lot of time in each other's company both at work and in the evenings at the hotel so it was great that we all got on really well, although Norman found it hard to chill out and it was obvious he was more bothered about his personal career than being part of a close team.

We received our specification document which was split into different areas such as education, facilities, security etc. We split the various areas between the team, taking into account all our different skill levels and experience, so this first six weeks was very much the planning phase where we project managed the coming 12 months. One thing Jacqui arranged was a few days at Newbold Revel, the Prison Service College, where we did a team building programme. There was a serious side to this but equally it was great fun doing all sorts of activities and a bit of drinking as well.

By the end of February our offices were ready at Lindholme which meant we could be home every evening and we could set our stall out in our own place. As well as this being a great job I was also making a bit of extra money as well, as I was on detached duty which meant I got a mileage allowance, subsistence and other expenses. I travelled up and down in an old Nissan which had been round the block a few times, but never let me down and cost me nothing.

We visited the Governor and staff at Buckley Hall in Rochdale. Buckley Hall had gone back to the public sector after their bid was successful. It was a bit of an eye opener however as firstly the Governor said they had to cut the finances to the bone to win the bid, which had left him with a thankless task trying to deliver the regime on a shoestring budget. He did say at one point he wondered whether it was worth winning. When we spoke to some of the staff on the residential wings we were surprised to find many of them who had joined the prison when it was private did not like being in the public sector as they, particularly the officers, said they felt they were just turnkeys in the public sector as opposed to the private sector, where they felt they had more authority to make decisions. Maybe it was a bit of arrogance that we in the public sector think we are the best at running prisons, as for a lot of years the public sector have been the only people running them. We do have this strange faith in this country that Governments can run businesses and other agencies, as many people want to re-nationalise lots of the industries that were privatised and are working fine. I remember the 1970s when nationalised industries were in full swing from the car industry to prisons. Look what happened to the car, motorbike, engineering and many other industries that were run under nationalisation? Constant strikes, poor workmanship, bad management, strong politically motivated unions. Why anyone would want to go back to that beats me. I guess many young people who didn't live through this see some romantic notion that a nationalised workforce will get treated better and have more equality. The dreams of youth?

We were allowed under the rules to visit The Wolds prison for a half day and could speak to whomever we wanted. So we visited early in the year. I was very impressed with the cleanliness of the prison and the professionalism of the staff. The facilities were pretty impressive, although to be fair the prison had only been built for ten years. We were treated with respect by the staff and they appeared to be fairly honest with their views. There was a mix of views, with some saying they were happy with their present employer and others who wanted us to win the bid and come over to the public sector. A theme that did come through from most people was the lack of staff. This we did witness as I went on to one of the residential units. The custody officer let me on to the wing but did not follow me on; he just said go where you like. The only member of staff I saw the whole 40 minutes I was on the unit was an education officer taking a class in the middle of the unit. When I say he was taking a class, the prisoners were more or less doing what they wanted. I had a chat with an old boy who had a brush in his hand. He was an old lag who had served a lot of prison in his time. I asked him what he thought of the prison. He said it was great as the staff just left you alone and the wages were really good. He winked at me and said, "You never see the officers and they keep us all sweet by paying good wages so we don't cause any bother." Very interesting but it appeared to be true. One thing we did find out was how good the private sector was at massaging the Key Performance Indicator (KPI) figures.

We also visited the public sector bid team who were putting together the bid for a prison in the Midlands called Blakenhurst. This was also a private prison at this time. The Blakenhurst team were about five months in front of

111

us so we had a lot to learn from them. The team down there were very helpful making the visit really worthwhile. We stayed over in a nice hotel and all went out in the evening for a nice meal and a few drinks. A few of us decided to make a night of it and by the end of the night I was a bit worse for the alcohol. As I made my way back to my room I could not get the key to unlock the room, so tried the door to see if it was unlocked, still no success. I eventually realised I was trying to get in to the wrong room. The following morning at breakfast my boss Jacqui said, someone was trying my door handle last night at about one in the morning. I asked what room was she in and when she told me I realised it was the room I was trying to get in. I had a bit of a smile on my face and enquired if she was maybe imagining it. She didn't think so but it didn't seem to bother her too much. I never did tell her it was me.

Clif and I were given responsibility for putting together the regime's specification which included all the residential, workshops, education, offender management, gymnasium etc. We spent a lot of the beginning of the year meeting with all kinds of interesting people, from the Chamber of Commerce to gym providers, in our pursuit of the best practice within both public and private sector in delivery of education, offender management, employment training, health and many others. It taught me such a great amount about both running a prison regime and how private industry works.

We got to the point of interviewing lots of potential suppliers of regime services. We chose a company called Aqumen who were going to provide a one-stop service of facility management, education, workshops and employment training. We offered them the contract for all these services and were confident they would provide a great service as they were a very experienced company. We encouraged all our potential partners to be innovative in areas like prisoner resettlement, work experience based on future work patterns, health and welfare education based on a holistic view from exercise to healthy eating. We really had a vision that we were going to be the leaders in offender management delivering a modern and positive experience designed to give prisoners a chance to see there is a better way in life than crime.

We began to put our final bid together towards the end of the year in preparation for presenting to a panel of the great and good of the Prison Service hierarchy. In the beginning of December we all went to a posh hotel in London to present our bid. Jacqui presented the overview of the bid and we all had a bit to say about our part of the bid. We were then questioned on how we would deliver the bid and how confident we could do this within the budget we set. We felt we gave a good account at the end and now it was just a case of wait and see. Towards the end of December the decision of the panel was given and it was decided to award the contract to the present contractor. We were bitterly disappointed and felt really deflated after 12 months of hard work dedicated to winning the bid. There was only one thing for it, go out and have a good drink to celebrate a great effort. One of the great things to come from this 12 months was the friendship I got, and most of all from Mandy & Clif who remain great friends to this day.

Because I was technically on detached duty from Full Sutton, my option at this point was to go back there. I really did not want to do this as I felt I had moved on and this would be a backward step for me. Jacqui was very supportive of all the team and she knew I did not want to return to Full Sutton. She made a few enquiries on my behalf and asked if I fancied a position on the team who were replacing the old computer system LIDS to a new more modern system named Quantum throughout all the public sector prisons. This appeared to be another great opportunity working on a project where I would again be working with the private sector and learning about managing big projects.

I had a great Christmas break this time with nearly two weeks off.

2002

I spent the first two weeks of 2002 closing the office down at Lindholme before travelling to Prison Service HQ to meet my new boss and team on Quantum. The team of people I would be working with were a mix of operational and non-operational prison staff, and various people from our partners Electronic Data Systems (EDS) who were supplying all the equipment and skills to import the data across to the new system. This was a huge project that involved a lot of co-ordination between EDS and the Prison Service. The pure logistics of replacing all the IT equipment and infrastructure in every prison, HQ and all outlying offices was huge, not to mention the training of all the staff and the security risk of sending lots of engineers, analysts and others in to all areas of a prison and all types of prisons.

I was allocated a number of prisons I was to be responsible for in helping them implement the new IT. These were fairly spread out across the country, so it was going to involve a lot of travelling. I met with the EDS team and had to quickly learn a bit about the technology to understand what was involved and be able to talk to the staff in prisons in a way they would understand. Every second Tuesday we had to go to Telford to the EDS HQ for a project progress meeting. This was a very long day as it took me three hours to drive there; the meeting went on until about 5pm and then drive back. These meetings were very interesting to see the dynamics of how EDS operated between each other and how they then interacted with the prison staff, and also how a large project like this was managed and more importantly controlled, as it was a massive financial undertaking. They were very demanding of their own staff, but then again it was a massive project for them as well as us and the costs for us and profits for them were not something either of us could take lightly.

I had a contact at each of my prisons who I basically had to talk through the process, and met with all the Governors so they understood what was involved. Without the prison's co-operation this project would be very difficult. I spent the next few weeks getting to know my contacts at the various prisons which involved a lot of travelling and hotels. I did not particularly enjoy staying away from home but I loved the variety of travelling, meeting lots of different people and visiting different prisons. I came to realise there was a lot of people making some serious money on the back of this project. My boss and his boss were self-employed consultants previously from the civil service who had cleverly seen a niche in the market to go on their own. They were earning around £1000 a day and moaned about having to pay their own expenses out of that. They were actually really good guys but not sure what they were doing warranted that kind of money from the good old taxpayer ⊠ but hey ho, who can blame them. To be fair they often dug in to their pockets when we were staying over in London, buying all of us drinks.

Having seen a bit of the private sector Prison Service and now seeing how the private sector worked with EDS, I liked the professionalism and positive way the people went about their business so applied for a position of Assistant Director at Dovegate prison near Uttoxeter. This was run by Premier Prisons and was a state-of-the-art new prison. I was granted an interview and went down early so I could have a tour of the prison. The one thing I did not like was the Americanisation of this prison, in that there were a lot of electronic sliding glass doors on the wings and this meant because the wings were so secure there was little interaction between staff and prisoners, with staff sitting in offices like glass bubbles operating doors and supervising prisoners from a safe distance. There was some interaction but I thought if we go down this road, then all we are doing is containment. I knew the reason for this was financial as you need fewer staff, which is your biggest cost in any prison. But what is the cost of the re-offending rate if you are just throwing these people back on the street worse than when they came in? To be fair there was a therapeutic part of the prison, but that was more for mentally ill prisoners.

So on to the interview. One of my interviewers was an ex-Governor from Full Sutton who I did not particularly like, and him and me had had a bit of a falling out when we were at Full Sutton. When I walked in to the room he looked at me and to be fair to him, he was very professional saying hello and nice to see me again, probably really thinking something different. The interview was much different to interviews I had experienced in the public sector as the questions were much more about managing systems, finance, people, how to delegate and get the best from people around you. For the first time ever I actually started to enjoy an interview, as it was much more about the work than the politics. The last question however stumped me a bit when the Personnel Director asked me what salary I was looking to achieve. Being in the public sector, your salary is a given, so this threw me for a second but just said £50,000+ and they didn't bat an eyelid, so I wished I had said more.

They interviewed four people, two of their own, me and a young chap from the public sector who had just qualified under the accelerated promotion scheme and was presently at Full Sutton. They chose the young man from Full Sutton and apparently I came a close second, according to the chair of the board. Not sure if he was just making me feel better or not. Anyway I found out the young man who was successful was sacked after about four months because he could not take the pressure, and went back to the public sector. Such is life, who knows where I would have ended up if they had made the right decision in the first place.

So back to my computers and travelling round the country getting lots of mileage allowance, subsistence etc. I really enjoyed the pre-meetings at prisons where you met the staff there and explained to the Governors what was going to happen. Some Governors were a bit put out by someone like me coming along and saying we need access here, there, given sets of keys and basically disrupting their prisons. Some even said no to certain things that had to be done and it was great that I just escalated this up the ladder and the Governor was generally told to wind their necks in and get on with it. To be fair, the vast majority were very helpful and understanding. The year flew by and I had a really steep learning curve about project management on a large scale, organisational and logistical skills and even a bit of technological knowledge. I did work very hard and for long hours but the fact I enjoyed it so much meant it was not a major issue.

Towards the end of the year I was asked if I would speak to someone at HQ about a different position. With the roll out of new computers and IT, the next step was to start looking at updating the software to a much more modern system of offender management. I met with Brian who was a real gentleman. He was an ex-senior probation officer who had come over to the Prison Service via some other scheme that was going around at that time. He explained that we were about to embark on another huge project, even bigger than Quantum and would I be part of a small team, initially, putting together a feasibility study. We were to partner with EDS on this project and my initial role was to work with their business analysts as an advisor on how our systems, processes, rules and regulations work so they could translate that into computer speak. What the service was looking at was to computerise what we had previously done on paper, from the reception process through to offender management and everything in between.

Chapter 7

2003 to 2005

2003

2003 started with yet another change. After spending all those years in one place at Full Sutton it seemed strange to be changing jobs almost every year but it made life much more interesting.

The Prison Service team at this stage was me, my boss Brian and Mick who was a colleague and friend from my Full Sutton days. Mick was also a fellow citizen of Leeds so we made a great team. We were to do the initial scoping exercise, looking at other systems that were already in place and working with the business analysts from EDS in compiling an 'as is and to be' document. That is, what we had in place then and what we would be looking to have in place in the new system. We started by researching the various offender management systems already out there around the world and talking to lots of people.

Mick and I visited Magilligan prison in Northern Ireland where we were told they had been looking at updating their management systems. We flew out to Belfast from Leeds/Bradford Airport early in the morning. This was the first time I had ever been to Belfast so was really looking forward to the visit. To be honest, I did not really see much of the city as we jumped straight in to a taxi to drive to the prison. The prison is quite a notorious one from the days of the troubles in Northern Ireland, and it still held many of the Republican and Loyalist prisoners, however it was a while since those days and the political process was taking over. The prison was in the middle of lovely countryside as I recall, however the prison itself was a pretty ugly looking place. We entered the first bit through a turnstile-like entrance before reaching the main gate. We had a walk round the prison, which was pretty clean and seemed to be fairly orderly. As it turned out the system they were looking at was not quite what we were expecting, and was not much better than what we already had. We did however have a good day and we were looked after very well by everybody at the prison. Our flight home was about 6pm so I got home about 10pm that evening.

This job was largely based at our HQ in London so I spent a lot of time living out of a suitcase lodging in a hotel in Pimlico. Once again, my very understanding wife accepted this and never once complained. This made my life much easier as I could concentrate on my work without having any added pressure. I could not be luckier having this wonderful lady to be my best mate and life partner, not to say great mother to our children.

A lot of people in HQ tended to turn up for work around 9 or 10 in the morning and often leave about 4 in the afternoon. Many of them made the excuse it was the amount of travelling they had to do and they had to get certain trains. In some cases I would accept that, but many people just used it as an excuse and the managers by and large let it go as they were just as bad. I was nearly always the first in the office and last out. I did like to go out at lunchtime and have a walk round Westminster and get a bite of lunch.

In the evenings I would often go for a run along the Thames and through various parks, which I really enjoyed. Quite often in the summer months I would have a walk out or take the tube to other parts of London. By this time Mandy & Clif were working at Wormwood Scrubs and were renting a flat just off Kensington High Street, so I would sometimes go stay with them and have a nice meal and a catch up. They were living the London life renting a flat in a posh part of town, enjoying the restaurants and sites. One night I had a walk out to Sloane Street as Jenny wanted a certain Louis Vuitton handbag. For those of you who don't know, this is a pretty posh and expensive handbag shop and Sloane Street is full of designer shops and designer people with some very expensive cars. I went in to the shop and found I was the only person in there, so was given instant attention by very efficient looking assistants with their little bags strapped to them. I knew which bag I wanted so went straight to it and asked the assistant for it. She got all excited and off she went behind some curtains. She came out a little bit later and two very posh looking women walked in to the shop while I was waiting. The assistants were all over these women so I assumed they were regulars, or just very rich.

After some time of watching this bit of a show I was kind of wondering what was happening with my purchase. After about ten minutes, I approached the assistant who was looking after me and asked her where my handbag was. She looked at me quite shocked and said, "Oh my gosh, I have forgotten about it." She dashed off behind the curtain and came out with a swanky bag with my handbag in and another box which she said was four silk handkerchiefs as a way of apologising. I thanked her and left the shop with a wry smile on my face. I often wondered who those two women were. One thing they were obviously more important than me, or more the case, a damn sight richer.

I continued with visits around the country talking to lots of people in various different disciplines. I also met extensively with the EDS business analysts talking about how prisons are managed so they could equate that to computer speak. I really enjoyed our conversations as we had a mutual respect for our knowledge and learnt a lot from each other. They were fascinated by how prisons work, and I was fascinated by how they transformed our processes into an analytical process.

I continued to put together my 'as is and to be' document. This was very much about blue sky thinking and at this stage my brief was to put everything in that we would want in a offender management system, even though we knew it would probably be too costly to put everything in. It is easier to take things out later than not put them in for consideration. One thing that I felt was important to put in was for officers to be able to use PDA handsets on the landings. I cannot remember what PDA stands for, but basically it is a tool that would allow an officer on the landing to have all the information at his/her fingertips. Prisoners are always asking questions about their wages, canteen, applications etc. At present the officer has to either go away and ask somebody else or tell the prisoner to put a paper application in that could take days to come back. This all takes time and money and may frustrate the prisoner leading to a potential conflict. What could be better for positive relationships and saving time and resources than to be able to give the prisoner an instant answer? We also put in this document things like being able to count prisoners off wings and in to education/workshops so we could track prisoners at all times electronically. This was to be done by having sensors which worked by wireless technology, and each prisoner would have a wristband attached on reception which would be used to track their whereabouts.

As the year went on we sourced a number of off-the-shelf systems that were out there being used by a number of offender management services around the world, as well as companies who would do a bespoke system. We got the options down to four, two off the shelf and two bespoke. We hired a room in a posh hotel in London for the four potential tenders to present their systems to us. After a very long day we eliminated two and had a close contest between the other two, so we asked for another presentation the following day after we had formulated some more questions. We eventually went for a Canadian system called Syscon which was already working effectively in Canadian prisons and a lot of Australian and USA prisons.

I felt this system was pretty much ready to go apart from adapting it to our rules, laws and legislation, so in my opinion I thought it would not take a lot to have this system working in our prisons. I was very wrong and will explain later. The guy who was to work with us in explaining the system and helping us to transfer it to our offender management was a man called Randy Feduik, who was an ex-prison officer from the Canadian Prison Service. He was very interested in computer technology so when Syscon put this in to the Canadian prisons Randy showed a lot of interest and was very knowledgeable so Syscon asked him to join them. He accepted and never looked back.

Working with HQ-type people was much more frustrating than operational people. If there was a way to complicate something or an excuse to have endless meetings then they would do it. Decision making was largely by committee and even then that took ages to get a decision. The amount of high ranking people earning pretty good salaries all creating roles for themselves was there for all to see, except the top people who couldn't see it, or if it was easier not to see it, then they did not have to challenge and change it. An example of the Civil Service mentality was when I was sat at my desk on my computer and I received an email from Brian. I looked over my shoulder where Brian was sat literally two feet away from me and said, Brian, you have just sent me an email telling me about a meeting that you have just arranged. He said, yes, what is wrong with that? Well I am nearly sat on your knee, why didn't you just tell me? He said, if I put it in an email then nobody can say I didn't tell you about it. I just looked at him and shook my head and I think it was at that moment I was beginning to realise this kind of environment was not for me. All I can say is if this was a profit making company it would have gone bust years ago with the entrenched bureaucratic attitude, over-promoted people, over-staffed, no urgency, creating-jobs-for-the-boys environment. How many years have Government ministers been saying they will rid the public sector and other areas of red tape? Well, as I write this book in 2016/17 I am still waiting for that to happen, even after eight years of austerity. So I go back to the point I made above about the Syscon system being easily adaptable to ours. It took around another four years and goodness knows how many millions of pounds over budget before we finally got a system in place, and when it was put in it was a very poor relation to the one I saw being presented to us as a virtual off-the-shelf package, and so far from the blue sky thinking document Mick and I initially put together. I know this might sound like I am a bit bitter and twisted but that is not the case, I am just letting people know what I saw, and feel it is in the public interest to let people know how their hard earned tax is being spent. Look at other IT projects Government agencies have tried to implement. The Inland Revenue and the NHS to name but two. Use the Freedom of Information Act to obtain costs for these projects and how unsuccessful they have been if you do not want to take my word for it. Our precious NHS is scandalous in the amount of money it wastes through bad management, over-bureaucratic and over-managed, yet we think it is wonderful. I have utmost respect for the nursing staff, junior doctors and many lower administrative people working in the NHS, but look at the amount of senior managers doing what? Look at the arrogance of senior medical people who only want to work when it is convenient for them, not for the patient. Just don't get ill at the weekend.

Have you tried contacting someone at the Inland Revenue to sort out a problem? If you actually managed to speak to someone, let me know how you did it. Try writing to them and you may get an answer two months later if you are really lucky. My brother worked for the Inland Revenue for 40 years and he told me they have big sacks where the outgoing mail goes in but they do not send it until the bag is full. If your letter goes in the bag first you may receive it in about three months. Take a look at local Government and see how inefficient they are. I guess by now you have surmised I am not an admirer of the way Government agencies are run. I stayed for 33 years in one and as I will allude to later in this book, it is one of my biggest regrets I did not leave and develop the mindset and courage of an entrepreneur in my younger life. As I explained at the beginning of this book the entrepreneur has always been in me, I just lacked the support, courage and environment, as well as the wrong mindset at that time to leave. It was easier to get a job like everybody around me and it was how I had been brought up to think.

I decided to leave HQ at the end of the year but I kept in touch with people from the project from time to time, and it just kept on growing and growing, with people making careers out of it getting promoted beyond their capabilities, making themselves hard to employ back in the operational field because they were too inexperienced for an operation role at their inflated status. My boss Brian ended up with a title like Project Director by the time he decided to retire on some over-inflated salary. In the three to four years he was doing this, he shot up the promotion ladder much quicker than he ever would in an operational role. To be fair I am not having a go at Brian as he was a very capable person but at the system that allowed these situations to happen. I sometimes wonder where I would have ended up if I had stayed. I could have given myself the title 'executive director of the empire'. It was not just the Prison Service team that grew to a ridiculous size, but EDS staff came from everywhere with their flashy titles and expensive accounts. Oh, if only the taxpayer knew where their money was going.

Towards the end of the year a vacancy came up at HMP Brixton for a Governor 5. I really fancied this and asked Jenny if she was willing to move to London for a time. She said she would, so I applied for the position and got it. Not long after, Jenny said she did not want to make this move but if I really wanted to do it carry on. This was the first time in all the years I had been in the service Jenny had done this, and I totally respected her position as she was really happy living where we were and a move to London was a step too far for her. All the years she has put up with following me with my career I had no right to be annoyed or feel she was being unfair, but I felt I needed this move so we agreed I would go there on my own for a short time and hopefully get a move north later. As you will find out, I was there for three years, which was much longer than I had anticipated. I had to ask the Governor of Brixton if I could come on long-term detached duty terms, which he agreed to do. This meant I could get my accommodation and travelling once a week paid for. Because I was due to start at Brixton in early January and HQ more or less shut down for two weeks I had a really good break over Christmas and New Year.

2004

After a welcome break it was another year another job and another exciting challenge. I had arranged to stay temporarily with the mother of an ex-colleague from HQ. She lived in Camberwell which is not the most salubrious part of London, but her house was a lovely three storey Victorian one and I had a large bedroom on the top floor where I could see across the rooftops of London. She was a lovely lady who made me feel really welcome and let me come and go as I pleased. I travelled down on the Sunday so I could take my clothes etc. and have a night to get ready to start at Brixton. I had to walk through a pretty dodgy area to get to the bus stop on Brixton Road. It was a bit scary at first coming back after a duty governor about 10pm, but to be fair nobody ever bothered me and I just did what all Londoners do, head down and walk on minding my own business.

I got up bright and early on the Monday to catch my bus in to Brixton. Brixton Prison is at the top of Brixton Hill and the bus stopped right outside the road entrance to the prison. The prison is on Jebb Avenue and there are some flats just outside the prison wall which used to be prison quarters for single officers in days gone by, but are now private. I am certainly glad I was not living in accommodation looking at a prison wing with prisoners shouting obscenities out of the window all day. The prison has not changed much over the years and is not the most welcoming of places to look at. I turned up at the gate and went in to a small area where there is a window looking in to the gate lodge with prison staff all milling around. I stood there for a little while being ignored. I thought I would wait to see how long the officers would ignore me. I got to the point that I decided to make my presence known. As I tapped on the window I got a rather sullen officer came over to the window who pleasantly said, "What do you want?" not, "Can I help you, sir?" I explained who I was and got a kind of apology and they opened the door for me. My first thoughts were I hope I will be responsible for this area of the prison, as I would be changing the gate staff attitude or changing them. This is one of the most important parts of a prison in my opinion, as it is the first impression a member of the public or visitor gets of the prison and if this is not right then it gives a bad reflection of the prison generally.

I was taken up to meet the Deputy Governor. John was somebody who I knew from meeting at various training events and other meetings. We always got on pretty well so I was happy to meet him again. We then went on to meet the Governor who was another John. The Governor was a fascinating character and someone I came to have a lot of respect for, and found him and the other John to be great mentors. The Governor John was very much a man who had a bit of an issue with the mainstream establishment, which was right down my street. He was eventually removed from Brixton and sent to the punishment wing of HQ, but there is many a story in between now and then.

I was told I would be Deputy Head of Operations which included security, visits, reception and would you believe, the gate. I spent about two days getting around different parts of the prison to get to know the geography of the prison and meet lots of different people. Going round the residential wings was like going back in time to my Manchester days. The wings were all Victorian style open gallery, and one thing that hit me was the noise and buzz around the wings compared to the more orderly and quiet wings of Full Sutton. Brixton at this time was a local prison which housed both convicted and remand prisoners waiting to go to court for trial. There was also a full wing designated to foreign prisoners, which was full of many nationalities with many from East Europe, particularly Polish, Latvians, Russians as well as Arabic and African. This was a very interesting and at times very difficult place to work. There was not a lot of workshop or education space, so giving prisoners productive work to do was not easy. I would say around 60% of Brixton prison population excluding the foreign national wing was black and minority ethnic in its makeup, so a bit different to what I was used to. On top of this, the makeup of staff was around 25% black and minority ethnic.

The healthcare at Brixton was a bit of a strange mix as it had a modern purpose built building where they had the offices and consulting rooms, then there was another building that had cells on two floors, which was a disgraceful place that was filthy and full of various types of prisoner suffering from mainly mental health type illnesses. This unit was nicknamed 'Fraggle Rock'. Not a very complimentary name but after visiting it, it was an apt name.

I then went to reception and found this almost exactly the same as when I came here about 20 years ago. It was a very cramped space where the staff had to process prisoners both coming in and going out, and keeping them separate was not easy. Storage space was very tight and all sorts of property used to go missing. The staff working in here albeit had a good old moan, but by and large got on with the job with good humour and resolve. I then visited the security department where I was to have my office and concentrate much of my effort. Compared to the resources, equipment and staff mindset of Full Sutton I felt I had gone back 20 years in my life. It suddenly dawned on me what a massive task I had ahead of me. The positive part of this was the Governor recognised this prison was operating in a different era, and he was transferring senior managers in who could move this prison forward and getting rid of those who were stuck in the time warp. I was chuffed he saw me as someone who could be part of the team moving it forward.

After my first day I left to catch the bus back home to my digs. By this time it was dark and I was a bit nervous walking from the bus stop to my digs. The main road was OK as it was pretty busy but I had to walk about quarter of a mile to my digs through a pretty dodgy area. Maybe I was being a bit paranoid as all the time I was there nobody bothered me. While I was in my room there was a constant noise of sirens and once I heard a bit of a commotion outside on the street about 11.30 at night. Looking out of my window I saw a man in the street staggering around and a police car turned up. Two police officers got out of the car and spoke to the man, who obviously said the wrong thing as one of the officers took out his baton and clobbered the man then just left him lying in the street. Not the type of action you expect to see from one of the Met's finest? You might ask what I did about this. Well, I watched for a while until the man got up and wandered off so knew he was OK. Maybe a bit cowardly but I had no intention of reporting the police officers as I had enough on my plate.

My first week was really about getting to know the geography of the prison, the people, my colleagues and immediate manager as well as chats with the Governor and Deputy to understand the vision and direction they wanted the prison to go. I was impressed with the enthusiasm of many of the staff, but not impressed with the lack of vision from them, particularly some of the senior and principal officers who seemed stuck in this old fashioned way of prison life. To be fair the majority of the 'old school' were those who had been at Brixton since Spartacus was a lad. Again the Governor was wise enough to see this and was bringing in managers who were prepared to buy in to his culture. The Governor was very clear that he would not tolerate any kind of intolerance to race, religion, or beliefs of any kind and he took that out in to the community by making himself available to various groups and being very outspoken in this area. He may not have done things in a particularly conventional way and sometimes, me being responsible for security in the prison, I had a few discussions where I had to advise him against certain things. Sometimes he listened to me and pulled back, but other times he said, "Just do it," so I did, but made sure I had something in writing that I had advised against it. Cover arse time is important in this litigious world. Besides the sometimes off the wall things he wanted to do, I loved his attitude to the hierarchy who were themselves stuck in the mud as far as being innovative. He effectively put two fingers up to them and ran his prison his way, which by and large was successful and quite fun to be a part of.

By the end of the week my head was spinning a bit and I was ready for the train home to my lovely wife and kids. The Deputy Governor was really good with me and said I could go whenever I wanted on a Friday if there were no important meetings. I did not abuse this and usually left about 3pm to catch the 4pm train from Kings Cross to York. I usually caught the bus down the hill to the centre of Brixton, but sometimes left ten minutes early and walked if it was a nice day. The centre of Brixton is a buzz of activity with all sorts of people walking around. On many occasions over the next three years I would see ex-prisoners on the street corners and they always said hello and often offered me, "Something for the weekend, Sir," if you know what I mean. I politely declined and wished them a nice weekend. My trip back home was OK usually. The underground is a great system and the journey from Brixton to Kings Cross took about 20 minutes, and then a two hour journey from Kings Cross to York where I caught up on some reading or dropped off to sleep.

Back on the Monday and I was to do my first duty governor. This was an experience to say the least. Doing duty governor at Full Sutton was by and large generally an easy time, with the Orderly Officer dealing with most day to day operational decisions with the occasional referral to the duty governor for the odd decision or to ask your advice. This first duty governor at Brixton was non-stop. The radio never stopped asking for Victor 1. Victor 1 was the duty governor call sign on the radio. All day it was can you call here, call there. Mostly when I called it was a pretty mundane question and I asked the person why they were referring this to me and not making the decision themselves, asking their direct manager or finally the orderly officer. The answer I got mostly was, "We always call the duty governor." Well, this was going to change as far as I was concerned. I approached the deputy governor about this matter to see what other Governor grades did, as we needed to be sending a consistent message. John just laughed and put his arm round me and said, welcome to Brixton! Then we had a serious discussion and as ever he was well aware of this and fully backed my view. I talk a lot about mindset, or certainly will do when I get to my new life as an entrepreneur, as this is often a very difficult thing to change in people who are set in their ways or have been conditioned to think in a certain way. Often in the Prison Service that mindset is a negative one based on frustration with bureaucracy, political correctness gone mad, constant bad management, lack of communication as to why decisions are made or changes are made, lack of consultation and a general feeling that the people at the top don't care and all they are interested in are their careers. To add to this, it is hard to be innovative when you are driven by a hierarchical monolith where free thinking is not encouraged, leading to people just going through the motions and feeling totally isolated from the decision-making process.

Anyway the new management starting to emerge was determined to change this and ensure decision making was taken at the right level and give people the confidence and authority to make decisions, but be aware when decisions need to be escalated upward. This was hard work and took quite a long time to change but by the time I left Brixton the duty governor was getting about a quarter of the calls than when I did my first one. Many of the better managers appreciated and understood what we were trying to achieve and embraced it, but there was always going to be those who resisted it and a big reason for this was they were promoted beyond their capability, and to be fair a lack of investment in management training.

On to my day job which was predominantly security, but I had to have knowledge of reception, visits, the gate and control room for when my boss was not around. My boss was a Mancunian who had spent the majority of his career in London where it was easier to climb the promotion ladder, and it did frustrate me a bit to work under someone who was not capable of managing at that level. He was OK as a person although we had a few clashes over the things he wanted to do, and the way he went about them was not to my liking. The security department was that in name only as the systems and processes they had in place were either non-existent or from a different time. They were still using paper systems to collate information and the analysis of the information was as bad as the West Yorkshire police in the days of the Yorkshire Ripper. I quickly began to realise this prison was a massive challenge but one I was going to relish, even if at times it would drive me nuts.

There were more illegal drugs in Brixton prison than in a Colombian drug dealer's hideaway and more mobile phones than Phones 4U. The security team were very willing and wanted to do a good job but had just lacked leadership and a strategic way to go about their work. Many items of contraband were coming in over the prison wall; as Brixton was an inner city prison, the public had access around most of the wall. The people throwing the items over the wall timed it for exercise where they could reach the exercise yard with up to 250 prisoners out there supervised by maybe three officers, or when the outside cleaning party cleaned up on the inside of the wall and picked up the parcels before the supervising officer saw what was happening. Other methods were in parcels to the prison and as much as it pained me, from prison staff bringing illegal items in for a price. They could get up to £250 for a mobile phone, so it was quite a temptation for an officer on a relatively low salary living in London to virtually double that with little chance of getting caught.

We did catch one officer bringing large quantities of drugs and mobiles into the prison. A prisoner stopped me one day and said he knew one of the officers on his wing, and where he knew him from was serving a prison sentence in Rikers Island prison in New York. I had to be very careful with this information as at first I thought it was a bit fanciful, but the prisoner who told me gave me a lot more information that was quite feasible. I took this to the police liaison officer, who made enquiries with other agencies including Interpol. We kept a close eye on this officer while enquiries were being made but could never catch him in the act. We did eventually find where he was holding the illicit items before being distributed around the prison, but could not find enough evidence to prosecute him. This officer was an African and he had about three addresses and lots of different names, but eventually the police tracked his history and found he had spent time in Rikers Island on drugs offences. We could not prosecute him for trafficking as we had no evidence, but he was charged with obtaining money by pecuniary advantage. This was that he lied about his past to get a job in the English Prison Service and obtain a salary for a number of years. He ended up with 18 months in prison and obviously was sacked. So as much as we would have loved to see him get ten years for trafficking, at least he was out of harm's way for now and would never be working in a prison again.

We eventually persuaded the Prison Service to come up with some money to erect netting between the wall and some of the wings where it was the easiest to throw items over the wall. The first week we did this we collected from the netting around 100 mobiles, enough drugs to retire on if sold on the street, and many other items. One of the most comical ones was a McDonald's meal neatly wrapped inside a box and tied so none of the contents came out. It was a bit cold in the morning when we retrieved it. The attraction of McDonald's eh? This put a slight dent in the supply of illicit goods coming in to the prison, but as ever desperate people will always find ways round everything and prisoners always have the upper hand as they have two things in their favour. The element of surprise and they do not have to abide by the law/rules like prison staff do. One of the most troubling ways we found prisoners were getting illicit items in the prison was a lady officer who came to our attention through a prisoner informant, who said she had joined the service for the sole purpose to traffic goods in to prison. This was very hard to prove and quite hard to believe. We asked the police to do some background checks on this lady and there was nothing to suggest she was involved in any crime and had no record with the police. The only thing we had was she previously worked for Serco working at the courts and transporting prisoners to and from prison and court. They had suspected her of wrongdoing, but she resigned before investigations could find any crime being committed. She was suspected of giving prisoners illicit items at court and passing things between the prisoner and people outside. We gathered intelligence on her, did staff searches at times we thought she was bringing items in and built up a picture of her movements etc. At some point she became aware we were looking in to her, which was of concern because we kept this between a small group of people. She came to see me to question why we were investigating her. I told her that she was not being accused of anything but we had information that she was possibly bringing items in to the prison and I asked her outright if this was the case. She obviously denied it and I asked her why she thought this information was coming to us. She said she had no idea and was a very good liar as she remained very cool and composed, whereas in my experience if you were totally innocent you would be pretty shaken up and a little bit angry at being accused of something. I certainly would. Eventually as more information came in, it was brought to my attention from the police that she was associated from her younger days with a group of known criminals. She was questioned about this and once again denied any involvement with these people, remaining very calm at all times. Not long after this she resigned from the service. Although we could never prove anything to put her in a court of law, I think her actions spoke for themselves. We and the police were convinced she joined the service with the sole purpose of working with this gang of criminals. This was a worrying development due to its sophistication and planning. I first heard about this type of thing from the days of the IRA, where they had people who kept clear of crime all their lives and had a good education becoming solicitors and police officers etc. for the sole purpose of working for the IRA. That was one thing about working at Brixton: there was never a dull moment.

Earlier in the book I told you about the time I worked on the bid team tendering for the Wolds prison. We had chosen a company called Aqumen (Carillion) to do our facilities management. At the same time we were doing that bid, Brixton was going through the same exercise, however no private company bid for it but Brixton still had to go through the expensive process of putting a tender document together (it could only happen with a Government agency). They also asked Aqumen to bid for the facilities management and they won this bid, which meant for the first time a private company would be delivering facilities management within a public sector prison. This caused many issues with the unions and POA, and many straw heads saw this as the demise of the public sector and the end of the world, or at least the end of their world of constant tea breaks, shoddy work, being virtually unable to be sacked and generally an easy life. All I can say is, as the security manager and a senior manager in the prison, Aqumen were a breath of fresh air. I worked closely with the contract manager and his staff as repairs to the prison have a big influence on security. I found the attitude they took towards their role was very professional and a massive improvement on what we have always had. They brought a private sector attitude to the work, which meant doing a quality job in a timely fashion and treating the Governor and his team as customers. An example was something as simple as a broken toilet seat in a cell. The public sector staff did not see this as an important job as it was only for a prisoner, so it could take weeks to do a job like this, where Aqumen realised it was an important repair and would do it the same day the damage was reported. The difference this kind of attitude made was that prisoners did not feel they were being treated disrespectfully and this had a positive knock on effect in other dealings with prison staff, making the prison a better place to work for everybody. Not that I want to see people lose their job but Aqumen did not tolerate any poor work or breaches to the security of the prison, so they would sack people who did not come up to a high standard. It would take about three years and many appeal processes to sack an incompetent person from the Prison Service.

One of the big issues we had, and a growing problem, was the Muslim service on a Friday. There were many prisoners who were genuine Muslims who went to the Friday service for the right reasons but equally there was a sizeable minority who were there to do their dealings and try to stir up problems. During my time at Brixton this service grew in popularity and many prisoners jumped on the bandwagon of the religion and in particular the violent part of the religion that was growing due to the issues in Iraq and other parts of the Middle East. If you asked many of the converts in the prison to quote from the Koran, most of them probably would not even know what the Koran was. This in my view was very cynical and an insult to the Islamic religion. The amount of drug dealing that went on in the service was again an insult to the people who were at the service for the right reasons. In saying that, the imam was not particularly helpful in working with us to ensure the people at his service were there for religious reasons, and in fact at times we felt he was scared of the people who were there as plastic Muslims. In saying that, the genuine Muslims at the service did not give much away either as we got very little good intelligence about the plastic Muslims' nefarious actions.

There was one particular person who was a regular prisoner coming in and out throughout the years and in the past had shown no religious leanings, yet all of a sudden on this present sentence he became a devout Muslim, wearing all the clothes, headgear, walking around with the Koran etc. He was a big influential man who many other prisoners feared and we had a lot of intelligence to suggest he was a big player in the drug scene in the prison and was using the Friday prayers to distribute his drugs. This information did not come from the Muslims who must have known it was going on, so make of that what you will. He knew full well we had to be sensitive around the service as we did not want to be accused of racism or seen to be offending their religion, so he felt pretty safe to carry on his actions. He was cynically using the present sensitivities around the Muslim religion to carry on his criminal activity. I had a bit of a love hate relationship with him as he was always very polite with me and was mostly pleasant, but both of us knew he was toying with us and no doubt laughing inside. Sometimes needs must, so I manufactured enough intelligence on this individual to justify getting him moved away from Brixton and disrupt his operation as much as possible. Not particularly professional, but the rules are all in favour of the criminal both inside and outside of prison so sometimes you have to even things up a bit. We have to play by the rules; criminals don't, so they are always one step ahead of the people who have to uphold the law. I am not advocating people in positions of authority should flout the law but would ask the lawmakers to take a look at how we make the job of law enforcers very difficult and the criminal's life much easier. Unfortunately most of our lawmakers have no real concept of the real world, living in a bubble of Westminster with many brought up in comfortable middle class worlds. If they would only ask the many decent people who live in areas where crime is rife how they feel about the laws of this land they may look at things differently – or maybe not.

I mentioned above about being accused of racism. Every member of staff had to do a yearly awareness training on matters around the PC world we live in (not the one that sells computers). The guy who was in charge of political correctness at Brixton – not his correct title – had made a career for himself around the world of race relations and other -isms. One day he was taking the senior management for this refresher training when he came out with a statement that we should not be using the word 'nitty gritty' due to the fact this was an offensive saying as it referred to the detritus that was at the bottom of slave ships. I didn't think much more about this until I read an article in the paper about a police officer challenging this. He was a bit of an amateur historian and looked this up. He found out that the phrase 'nitty gritty' pre-dated the slave ships by a lot of years, therefore this term had nothing to do with racism and there was no reason for it to be offensive to anybody. I spoke to our guy at Brixton about this and showed him the article and his reply was, "It doesn't matter as it is in people's minds now as having a racist connotation." I just shook my head and laughed at him, telling him it is people like him that create racism rather than helping to eradicate it. I have no racist bone in my body and feel I am tolerant of people who may think and act differently to me, but in my opinion people who are going around making things up purely to further their own careers and self-interest are as bad if not worse than those who act in a racist or homophobic way and actually do harm to race relations instead of good.

Staying on the theme of racism, towards the end of the year I was accused of being racist by a black officer, who accused me of bullying him because he was black. This stemmed from the fact he was one of the laziest and most useless officers I had ever come across and I challenged him in a way nobody else had done before, possibly due to the fact he was black and they were afraid to challenge him. He knew this and therefore decided to use the race card against me so he could carry on picking his salary up for doing nothing. I was not suspended, which kind of hinted the Governor was not convinced there was anything in this, but as is right and proper it was investigated by an independent person. While this was hanging over me I had a number of black officers come to my office to offer me their support and said they would gladly speak up for me against their colleague as they were glad somebody was challenging his laziness and incompetence as it affected them more than me. This investigation petered out when the officer withdrew his allegation. Apparently a number of black officers had a chat with him about the actions he was taking, and how making spurious allegations of this nature took away how genuine ones would be investigated in the future. I had mixed emotions after this as I was relieved the truth came out, however mud sticks as they say and there will always be people who doubt my integrity. The number of black officers who came to see me to say sorry for this and how embarrassed they were restored my faith in people, however the person who should be apologising to me, the person who accused me, never said another word to me. He was sacked about 12 months later, which gave me no satisfaction but was another positive for me as it proved me right. The race relations industry does a lot of great work highlighting the wrongs that some bigoted people do, but it also does a lot of harm by being very one-sided and creating an atmosphere where people are afraid to discuss matters of race in fear they will be accused of being racist.

My first year at Brixton came to an end on a bit of a sour note. It was to get much worse at the end of December. I received a phone call from one of my brothers to say his daughter, my niece, had been involved in a car accident. She was in intensive care and was not expected to live. I got the call to say she had died and my heart sank. I phoned Jenny and I could not speak for crying and felt so helpless for my brother and sister-in law. My niece was like a daughter to me as our children had all grown up together. She was 22 years of age, three months older than my son and I tried to imagine if this had been one of our children and could not get anywhere near to how her parents must be feeling as it was so painful for me, and to this day it still is. My colleagues were very good to me over the Christmas period, allowing me to take a good bit of the holiday period off, which was very welcome having spent 12 months away from my family apart from weekends. It was a good feeling to be catching the train home for the last time in 2004. It was great to get home but this was one of the worst Christmas I have ever had. The emptiness and grief of losing someone so young and close to you was just unbearable.

2005

After a welcome break I caught the train back to London; even though my thoughts were far from work, I had to get on with it. The funeral of my niece was in early January so we all drove down to Shropshire where my brother lived. I am non-religious and do not believe in any kind of afterlife, so death to me is pretty final and for someone to die before they have had any kind of life hits me hard. This was one of the longest days of my life and I was so glad to see the back of it. My niece was buried in the churchyard and I have only been back to the grave once, as I cannot get my head around such a beautiful person being in the ground at such a tender age. We do visit her grave regularly when I visit my brother but I stay in the car when Jenny goes to the grave as I hate to think she is under the ground so prefer to remember her as she was. RIP you lovely girl.

Early in the New Year I was moved to be deputy head of performance management. This was a new role to me as it was about measuring, recording and improving performance of the prison through Key Performance Indicators (KPIs). This was the tick box culture that politicians of all persuasions love. As long as you tick enough boxes everybody is happy, and don't worry about quality because they don't want or know how to measure that. My boss was a master at ensuring the performance figures we entered each month made us look good even though they were manipulated along the way, and I was about to learn how all this was done. As a manager of other departments, I was well aware of the importance of meeting and if possible exceeding our targets. One of the easiest ones to manipulate was the searching figures. You had to ensure cells and other areas were searched so many times each year. If you felt you were not going to meet these, you just got officers to sign to say they had been searched, or just do a cursory search of a cell and sign the form. Any prison that failed this target had to be pretty stupid. As far as the politicians were concerned this particular target was being met by the whole service. Nobody asked the question about the quality of the search or what, if anything had been found. I would estimate around 2% of illicit articles found in a cell were found on a routine cell search, the rest was found on target-led searches where we had specific intelligence. These types of searches were not a performance measurement, so the quality side of the job was totally ignored in favour of figures. My boss and I used to hold a performance meeting once a month with the functional heads and at this meeting we used to monitor that month's figures to ensure they were on target or find out why they were not on target and what they were doing about it. Often we would take the functional head to one side and help them to meet the target, if you know what I mean. I did not really enjoy this part of the job as I found it all so false and a complete waste of resources. If we put some of these resources into actually doing the job we would have gained more quality instead of lies, damn lies and statistics. I accept there has to be a measurement of performance but the way many government agencies do them is purely a tick box system that tells the public nothing about how well taxpayer's money is being spent. Look at the NHS. How many people do they employ to gather statistics that are generally fudged but tell the taxpayer nothing about the quality of care people receive?

Luckily for me, early on in 2005 there was a promotion board at Brixton for a functional heads role. I spoke to Jenny about this as it would mean me having to stay at Brixton a bit longer if I got it, and as ever she was very supportive of me and gave me her blessing to go for it. I had my interview with the Governor and one other and I must have impressed them as I was offered the promotion. This promotion was a very significant one for me as it was as high as I could go to keep my reserved rights to retire at 55 years of age. As I joined the job prior to September 1987 when Fresh Start came in, I was entitled to what they called reserved rights. These allowed me to double up on my pension after 20 years and retire at 55 years if I wanted. So when I was told I had passed the promotion board it was like a sack of spuds being taken off my back, as I was free from any more promotion boards which meant nobody had any leverage over me anymore and I could start to say what I thought instead of toeing the party line all the time. Don't get me wrong, I was very professional at all times and very loyal to the Governor and deputy, but it meant behind closed doors and at the senior management meetings I could say my piece without it affecting my career progression as I no longer had one. How many people in the world are suppressed as to what they feel they are comfortable saying without it affecting their careers? This is probably more so in the public sector than the private, as the private sector generally thrives on people being free to express their thoughts and ideas where the public sector is very political and hierarchical, which in my opinion holds back and frustrates a lot of good people in these jobs from developing. I always tried to get the officers and senior officers to express their views and ideas, but the culture they all grew up in makes them feel it is pointless as no matter what they say they are not listened to and decisions will be dictated to them higher up. Younger people coming in to the service over the last eight to ten years before I left were better at expressing an opinion, as most of them did not come from a service background where you obeyed orders come what may. When I joined the job in 1980, 75% of officers had come from a service background where that had been the reverse by this time.

Anyway I was now on cloud nine as I felt like a free man with no more stupid JSACs to sit through, no more interviews with people judging your whole career on a 30-minute interview; I was free to get on with my job as a professional manager without the shackles of any more promotions to bother about. I was asked to be the Head of Operations which as discussed earlier involved security, visits, reception, gate and control room. As the head of security I was party to a lot of sensitive information and I was the advisor to the governor on these matters. As I said earlier, the governor was like no other governor I had worked for before. His idea of security was very much about treating people with respect, trust and giving them the time of day and he believed you got that respect back. This worked to a point, but we don't always deal with people who show respect to other human beings or authority so there has to be a helping hand for these people. Don't get me wrong, the governor was one of the most experienced in the country and he fully understood how prisons worked, but he was a bit of a pioneer of his time. Unfortunately for him the people at the top of the service were not ready for his style of leadership and he clashed on a regular basis. Halfway through the year he clashed once too often and was removed to the naughty floor at HQ. I was genuinely disappointed in seeing him leave as I loved his style of leadership, and he certainly left Brixton in a better position than it was when he came.

The governor was very much into letting all sorts of people come to the prison to try their brand of rehabilitation with prisoners, and he did enjoy the limelight that came with these various outside groups. He was very much into unconventional ways and was willing to try many innovative ways to help prisoners look at alternative lifestyles to the cycle of crime. Music was a big way he felt you could reach out to prisoners, and to be fair he had some success with prisoners who took part in these schemes. He got me in the office one day and told me he was going to allow Richard Ashcroft, the rock singer, to shoot a video for his new album in the prison. This was going to be a security nightmare with all the people, equipment etc. that had to be accommodated. Thankfully a lot of it was to be done in an area outside the wall, but he also needed to film in the prison at times. I worked very closely with the guy in charge, and for an arty sort he was very co-operative. Richard Ashcroft himself was a bit more arrogant and less patient and understanding of his surroundings but I guess these peoples' egos are inflated by today's fascination with fame, flamed by the constant media hype. Anyway it all went off pretty well and I got a signed CD at the end of it. The CD was actually OK and Jenny and I went to see him live at Newcastle some time later.

The new governor was a totally different person who was very much in the old style mode of following orders, ensuring everything was done to the book as dictated from above, ensuring he took no risks that would affect his beloved career and generally toeing the boring party line so Brixton became like any other prison, a place where there is little innovation and do as you are told from the top. I guess the words 'company man' could best describe him. To be fair he had a very difficult job following the previous governor, and by the time I left Brixton I quite warmed to him. He was a very demanding boss in that he had exceptionally high standards and was a much more organised person. I did think at times he was unreasonable in his expectation of his senior managers but I guess he did push you out of your comfort zone which is not a bad thing.

One thing the new governor did was stop a lot of the external people coming to the prison, and nearly all requests to do things like Richard Ashcroft were a no-no. He was more interested in meeting targets, passing inspections, getting good audit results. As this was what the prison was measured on and our core business was running a prison as effective and efficiently as possible, with the minimum media attention for wacky things and maximum for being effective and efficient, nobody could blame him. It made my job as security chief a lot easier but also much more boring and mundane. I guess all good things come to an end eventually.

The governor set about dismantling much of what the previous governor had done which caused a bit of a rift between him and the deputy to the point the two of them just could not work together. I think the deputy was so close and loyal to the previous governor it was hard for him to see all the good work he had done being removed to be replaced by boring old convention and robotic ways designed to pass audits, inspections etc. rather than innovate and inspire prisoners to find a different way out of the spiral of crime.

As I explained earlier one of the massive problems for Brixton was the number of drugs and mobile phones that was coming in to the prison. I used some of my budget to improve the intelligence gathering systems we had by purchasing new computers and software, sending staff on training courses to analyse intelligence and generally trying to change the mindset of officers to think in a smarter way. It was not just security staff that needed educating but everybody working within the prison. Information was gathered and analysed by use of Security Information Reports (SIRs). These were reports that anybody in the prison could fill out to inform the security department of information they felt was relevant. The number of these reports was very low and when we surveyed why this was, a lot of people did not understand the importance of writing down information that they thought was insignificant, and they were concerned that they would be seen to be ridiculed. It took a lot to change this attitude but we eventually started to get across that intelligence was like a jigsaw where lots of tiny bits of information can eventually make a big picture. The amount of SIRs being submitted at the end of the year was nearly double at the beginning due to a concerted effort to educate staff.

I must just relate a rather comical incident about mobile phones. We had some good intelligence that a prisoner was carrying a mobile phone around with him. The officers approached him on the wing and he ran off but he was quickly stopped and although he put up a bit of a fight, he was pinned down on the floor ready to be taken to the segregation unit to be strip searched. While he was pinned down on the floor a mobile phone started to ring. Everybody was looking around to see where it was coming from when one of the officers said, "It's coming from his arse." Everybody burst out laughing and someone said, "Well, that's some ring tone." Just in case you did not get this, a crude word for a backside is 'ring piece'. I bet many of you reading this book find it hard to believe you can hide a mobile phone in the cheeks of your backside and walk around normally. Well, you would be surprised what prisoners will keep there. The reason they hide illicit items in places like this is because prison staff cannot search in intimate areas without good intelligence and a doctor has to do it, so it very rarely happens. We can strip search a prisoner and get him to squat so hopefully anything up there will drop out, but even doing this it does not always drop out. Desperate people take desperate measures. Women visitors often put drugs, mobiles etc. in similar parts of the anatomy then pass them to the prisoner. Drugs are then often swallowed in a condom and retrieved when they go to the toilet. I have never taken drugs but if people go to this length to take them maybe I should see what I have been missing. But I only want to try them if they have been in a vagina, then in my stomach in a condom, out of my backside with everything else then fished around with my hands for the condom. I apologise for the crudeness of this, but I guess you get the point I am making. What chance are these people giving themselves in life? You can blame society, bad luck, nature, nurture, whatever you like but nobody forces drugs inside anyone, so all you do-good middle class lefties, stop feeling sorry for these people and that the world is against them, because they do nothing to help themselves.

There had been a terrible terrorist act on the underground and on a London bus by some Asian men from Yorkshire on the 7th July 2005. This left London in a state of nervousness, especially on the transport system. And as I travelled on the bus and underground on a regular basis, it made me think a bit about my vulnerability to people who have no regard for their own life, yet alone others'. About two weeks after this the police liaison officer at Brixton came to my office to say there had been another incident where a terrorist had been shot on the underground and he was really pleased that his colleagues had prevented another potential terrorist act on the streets of London. It turned out that the police had mistaken a Brazilian man, Jean Charles de Menezes, for a terrorist and shot him around seven times, killing him. The order to shoot Mr De Menezes was given by the officer in charge of the incident, Cressida Dick. She managed this incident from her car where she was given details of the incident as it was happening and her decision making was made on the information she was given. It is easy to criticise her but unless you are put in that position, I do not think you can really comment. The one thing this very switched on police commander did was log everything she was told, by whom and at what time. When this incident got to the courts she was actually praised for her actions as she made the correct decisions based on the information she was given, and I believe not long after she was promoted. The reason I am relating this is due to the actions of Cressida Dick, this changed the way we in the Prison Service dealt with incident management. To protect yourself when you were in charge of an incident, you now had to keep a log of every piece of information you were told and more importantly log your decision and the reason for that decision (which was largely based on the intelligence/information you received). Basically it was 'cover your arse time'. That just about summed up this job. There was no tolerance of genuine mistakes or human error, something I will touch on later in the book.

I explained earlier what an adjudication is and at Brixton we used to do on average around 12 a day. These were allocated for the morning only so you can imagine how much of a sausage machine they were, and I know many Governor grades felt every prisoner was guilty so did not take much time over the evidence and others took it very seriously, as they should, and often ended up going on in to the afternoon. A lot of prison officers did not quite understand the process of law and expected the governor to find the prisoner guilty just because they had placed him on report. Some did not understand that the adjudicating governor had to follow the rule of the law and a finding of guilt was based on evidence and not just the officers' evidence. Some officers often did not fill out the paperwork properly by either making the wrong charge, giving the prisoner the wrong instruction or no instruction at all, and many other mistakes. I always tried to give the prisoner a fair hearing and based my finding on the evidence on both sides. I often had to find a prisoner not guilty for various reasons and I always tried to speak to the officer afterwards to explain why I made the decision I did. Some officers would accept this and thank me for explaining, however many were angry and not prepared to listen as they thought I did not believe them but believed the prisoner. Prison officers can be very stubborn people who have very fixed views about justice. They cannot seem to accept that even if the adjudicating governor might agree with their anger at the system, the system is what it is and we have to abide by this. I bet not one of those officers ever wrote to their MP to have the law changed. I would also like to think the law would protect me if it was ever needed to.

I used to enjoy doing adjudications as I found them a good challenge when you came up against the odd brighter prisoner who could put up a good argument, but even then they tended to read the bits of prison rules they wanted and not look at the whole picture. I have come across some, particularly in places like Full Sutton, who were very switched on and made a point of reading up on prison law. This was good because it taught you a lot and made you read more of the law yourself so you could deal with most situations with confidence. By and large in a place like Brixton, prisoners either pleaded guilty or accepted the finding of guilt as they were just trying it on. I used to have quite a bit of fun with many prisoners as they often saw the process as a bit of a game and a break from their mundane lives. As much as there is a lot of anger in prisons, there is also a lot of humour between prison staff and prisoners. I would say humour and talking about things like football are two of the biggest ice breakers for good relationships between officers and prisoners. I do recall one adjudication where a rather obnoxious prisoner was in front of me. He was very un-cooperative and an angry man who had a long history of assaults on prison staff. I set about the adjudication as always, asking the prisoner if he was feeling OK and other pleasantries, but got few pleasantries back so knew this was going to be a bit of a challenge. As the adjudication went on he was getting more and more animated so I sent him back to his cell for ten minutes to calm down and compose himself. After ten minutes we reconvened and I asked him if he had calmed down and was prepared to carry on in a reasonable manner. He replied that he was, however as soon as I asked him to explain his actions he picked the table up in front of him and threw it in my direction. Thankfully the desk I was sat at was quite a big one and his table hit the desk, leaving a big gouge in it. At that point the officers restrained him and removed him as I extricated myself from the desk totally unhurt. He was found guilty in his absence, and was further charged for throwing the table at me and was found guilty of that by another governor. I would say he was a bit of a loser in life and was destined to spend many years of his sorry life in a small cell. Once again as with the drugs, for you middle class leftie do-gooders, it was his choice to take the actions he did as he was of sound mind and chose to be a violent thug instead of a decent member of society.

The Governor and his management team continued the good work of the previous governor in improving conditions and involving prisoners in this process as much as possible but in a more mechanical way. We had committees for almost everything, which prisoners took an active part in, and by and large this was a good way to ensure the changes we made were both sensible and sustainable as well as for the right reasons. The one area we found very hard to deal with was the hospital wing where the more difficult patients were kept. These were predominantly prisoners who were mentally ill. The building was a major part of the problem as it was dark and dirty, and because of the design there was little we could do to improve this. As explained previously the hospital was nicknamed Fraggle Rock and any prisoner who was in there for any time was stigmatised and labelled by both staff and prisoners as a Fraggle. The governor had no choice other than to have the building condemned and closed. I must admit it made our job a lot easier closing this down as we had on a daily basis serious issues in there from assaults on staff to assaults on other prisoners, prisoners cutting themselves and at least two suicides in a short space of time. It was a depressing place to visit and even worse to work there so what it must have been like to live there I cannot imagine. It is not often I felt sorry for prisoners but I had some sympathy for the prisoners held in this awful place.

This brings me to another point that I think people should be aware of, and that is the number of mentally ill people that are locked up in a 'normal' prison instead of a special hospital. As I explained earlier it is only those with a treatable illness that go to a special hospital. I think it is about time we looked at creating a prison/unit for people with non-treatable mental issues where the staff are trained to deal with this type of person. I know we have places like Broadmoor, but these places are for seriously damaged people. There are a lot of prisoners with mental issues in the mainstream prison system that are being made worse because they are getting little treatment and by and large being dealt with by prison officers, who are not trained to deal with mentally ill people. This is not right for the prisoner with a mental illness and it is not right to put untrained prison staff in the position of looking after them. Many of these prisoners end up in segregation units where their condition is made far worse as prison staff tend to treat them as bad rather than mad. I do not profess to have any qualifications in this area but what I do have is many years of working with prisoners and witnessing more and more cases of mental illness through the years. Whether that is from years of drug taking or other reasons, the reality is this type of illness has increased and the powers that be have appeared to put their heads in the sand. Maybe it is down to cost but you have to weigh that up against the cost of these people committing further crime. Or it could be they just don't know what to do about it as, in my opinion, we put too much faith in the people who govern and lead us and do not question them often enough to hold them to account. Ask yourself a question: when did you last write to your MP to question a situation you are not happy with? If not then I would say, put up or shut up. For those of you who say, what is the point, I would say, there is every point and I am a big believer in people power used properly. Politicians desire power, so if enough people write to an MP expressing their concern or asking the MP to go in a certain direction, they have to take note even if it is for the selfish reason of getting re-elected. How do you think minority lobby groups often get changes? How often do we question a doctor, solicitor? We just accept they are educated people and allegedly know what they are doing. Look at the bankers, they knew what they were doing, didn't they? Look at world leaders, religious leaders who lead us into wars and other man-made disasters.

As I explained earlier Brixton had a full wing of foreign national prisoners made up of many nationalities. Many of these did not speak English very well and brought different problems for prison staff and yet another challenge. I must say the staff who worked on this wing were very dedicated to ensuring everybody was looked after and catered for as best as they could. With so many different nationalities in one place, there was from time to time tensions, as you would have differing East European drug gangs, from Russians to Poles, Latvians and more. You then we had people of different religions who were fighting each other in their home countries and often hated each other for no other reason than they were a different religion. There would be fights break out and often there was no reasoning with them, particularly if it was on religious or ethnic grounds. It certainly made me appreciate how tolerant the British are in comparison. Another issue was language and their understanding of the British judicial system. This came at a cost as to employ a translator was very expensive. It also cost a fortune to get information translated into a number of languages. Dealing with so many different cultures did have its interesting points, as many of the prisoners had interesting stories to tell and often they were very polite towards prison staff. Some of the worst foreign prisoners were the East Europeans. They were generally into the drug or organised crime scene and often a bit thuggish. As much as I think having people from other cultures coming to live and work in Britain is very healthy, when some of these same people decide to show disrespect for our country and come here to commit crime they should, in my opinion, be automatically removed from the country without an appeal. This is one area in which allowing anybody in the EU to go to other EU countries regardless of their background has to be unacceptable.

We continued to look to improve the conditions in the prison and two areas that desperately needed updating was reception and visits. The visits room was a very old-fashioned long table just like Strangeways over 20 years ago, where the visitor sat on one side and the prisoner on the other with little privacy from other visiting parties. Although it was a logistical nightmare as we could not close down the visits for a month to six weeks, we could not leave them in this time warp, so had to look for a way to update them causing as little disruption as possible. We came up with a solution and the money to do the changes. One thing I am very big on in life and work is communication. I think if you communicate with people it makes it a lot easier to manage any change. We had to have fewer visits each day while the work was going on, so we communicated regularly with the prisoners, letting them know what was happening and showing them what the end product was. The vast majority of prisoners appreciated what we were doing making things better for them and their visitors; however there are always those who will use something like this to try to cause a problem or an excuse to have a confrontation. Thankfully the majority were reasonable and often other prisoners dealt with the ones who wanted to make an issue out of it by telling them to wind their necks in. We transformed the visits area with individual tables so the visit was much more comfortable and private. We put pictures on the wall that prisoners had painted in the education department, and made the room a brighter place creating a much better atmosphere.

The one thing I never managed to improve was the reception area. I explained earlier in the book what Brixton reception was like 20 years ago. It had not changed one bit from when I visited all those years ago. There was little privacy to strip search prisoners; the staff had nowhere to store anything, very few facilities to enjoy a break. It was quite a depressing area for someone coming in to prison for the first time, but the officers working in there were generally excellent in their attitude, making the best of very poor conditions. I understand there has since been some extensive building work carried out at Brixton in the years after I left. It was also converted in to a category C prison, which would mean much less movement through reception.

Once again my colleagues were great with me allowing me to have most of the Christmas break off.

Chapter 8

2006 – 2009

2006 started as 2005 ended, with the management team continually looking to improve the prison environment and the relationships between staff and prisoners. Over the holiday period Jenny and I had a chat about the situation of me trying to get back to Yorkshire during this year. We were OK, but it was time to move back home and I felt had given enough to Brixton and with the previous governor leaving I felt I did not owe the present governor the same loyalty. To be fair, the governor appreciated my position and said he would do all he could to help me. This did not stop me giving my all to the cause of continual improvement of the conditions for both prisoners and staff at Brixton. I really felt I had connected with this prison and the people, but for once I had to think of myself and more importantly my family.

One major issue for prisoners and their relatives and friends was being able to book visits. There were so many people trying to get through to book visits and the line was constantly engaged. The governor was very keen for me to get this right to the extent he became quite unreasonable about it. Much of it was down to resources. All we had was one person staffing a phone, so you can imagine how hard it was to get through to book a visit when remand prisoners could have a visit every day. I spoke to a few other prisons to see what they were doing and I got a few ideas. I decided to use a text and email system so people could book 24 hours a day. I re-arranged the staffing so I had two staff for two hours per morning each, one booking the visits from the text and the other booking from the emails and we could reply by the same media. This was not perfect, but it did improve the situation and the visitors and prisoners generally appreciated what we were doing on their behalf. The governor was still not happy and I felt he was pushing me for some reason, so I suggested the only sure way to improve this problem was to invest in technology or more staff, or both. He was not prepared to do this so we had a few frank discussions over the coming weeks. You cannot get blood out of a stone. This was becoming a little like abdication management on the governor's part, as he was telling me to sort it but had no ideas himself. Power does go to some people's heads sometimes.

I had a few interviews for positions in Yorkshire prisons with little success and started to get a bit concerned I would struggle to get a move. I had an interview at a particular prison and I knew the deputy governor there. I phoned him to ask if he could give me a few pointers regarding the prison and the way the governor thought. I was not looking for any advantage, just a bit of help from someone I thought was a friend. He suggested we have a game of golf and we could chat about the prison and where the governor saw the direction it was going so I could do some research and thoughts about how I could help that to happen. We had the game of golf and all the way round talked about everything but the reason we were there. At the end of the game I asked why we had not discussed what we came here to discuss, and he said, "I didn't want to give you an unfair advantage." I felt like wrapping my golf club round his neck. This person shall remain nameless but the Prison Service was full of people like this, people who you thought were your friends but all they were interested in was their own little precious careers. That is why I have very few real friends from the Prison Service after more than 30 years working in it. The other reason is most of them have nothing to talk about other than work, and I didn't like the job that much to talk about it in my social life. To be fair, the interview I gave at this prison was not very good at all and I did not deserve the job based on that. I had a couple of other interviews which were OK but I was not successful.

The deputy governor asked me to move away from the Head of Operations under a management restructure. I was to do a much softer role with a title which I cannot quite remember, but it was concentrating on community services. It involved developing relationships with external agencies who assisted prisoners with rehabilitation both inside and outside the prison, looking at different ways to help prisoners see a better way in life than crime. I was also the Governor grade responsible for the chaplaincy, which for an atheist was a bit strange.

We invited a group of musicians in to the prison who worked on rather strange instruments which were, apparently, very easy to learn to play. The idea behind this was to give people confidence, discipline and teamwork; all good attributes to have in a working environment and a good foundation to be a decent member of society. I am not sure how this actually worked with prisoners after they were released, but it had a positive effect on them while they were in prison. We did not choose the prisoners to do this because they were already decent prisoners, but allowed some prisoners with difficult attitudes and not great track records for behaviour. There was a very surprising improvement in some of the more difficult prisoners' behaviour. I asked one of these prisoners what had been the reason for his change and he said it was the first time anybody had taken time with him and gave him a level of trust. He also said for the first time in his life he felt important that other people relied on him as part of the group of musicians. That made me think how we would harness that to reflect our society outside. Think about this one, you policy makers out there.

The chaplaincy was quite a challenge. The first meeting I had with them was like a lamb going to slaughter. You would think a group of Bible and Koran bashers would be pussycats, but that turned out to be anything but. I would rather face a group of angry prisoners any time. They were a very demanding bunch and what made it worse was each member of the respective religions wanted different things. The imam was the most demanding and the most unreasonable of them all. I got the impression he felt he was in the driving seat due to the fact the biggest attenders at services were the Muslims. The fact half of them who attended were there to do their dealings or because Islam was becoming fashionable seemed to pass him by. I was at my most diplomatic best at these meetings, playing the game as the governor would expect. I know the majority of people within the chaplaincy, regardless of religious persuasion, are well meaning but were equally naïve in their trust of the average prisoner. The CofE chaplain was a bit of a nut job which was fairly consistent with many prison chaplains I have come across over the years. It could be that they end up practising in prison because they are too barmy to be let loose on the general public. I must admit this is one area of my work at Brixton I was not too successful with. I certainly know why there are so many religious wars if this lot were anything to go by.

The governor had a chat with me about a possible move. It was technically based at HQ in London but I could work from home. It was subject to the governor accepting a swap with a lady who wanted to be back in a prison and she lived in South London. The governor said he would do everything he could to get me this move, but he had to be sure the person who was coming in my place was suitable for Brixton. As ever, the governor was the consummate professional and he was more concerned about what was best for the prison than my personal circumstances. I had to grudgingly admire this and accept what will be will be. As it happened, he was happy that this lady was suitable for Brixton and so the swap was going to take place at the end of the year. My new role was to be working within a new group that was responsible for managing change within the service. I was to be part of a small team managing the upcoming massive building programme to cope with the projected increase in prison population and replace some of the run down infrastructure.

It seems strange that I seem to keep finishing jobs at the end of the year and starting another one in January.

2007

Once again I had a decent time off over Christmas before starting my new role. I was to be part of a small team working with the contractors and project team, who were increasing the size of the prison estate due to the projected increase in prison population. I met my new boss who was to turn out to be one of the nicest and most intelligent people I worked for in the service. He was a great mentor and inspiration. The team was to be five of us in total to cover the biggest prison building programme in many years. Our role was to be the eyes and ears for the Prison Service to ensure we were getting the best deal at the most efficient cost.

This was a massive learning curve for all of us as this type of role had never been done before, so we were effectively making up the rules as we went along. The programme of work was a huge one and spread throughout the estate, from the far north of the country to the far south. We split the prisons we were to cover so we had to travel as equally as possible. I ended up with prisons from the Isle of Sheppey to the North East. I really enjoyed travelling around the country meeting lots of people and visiting different types of prisons. It was also interesting to work with the contractors who were doing the building work. I did not know this at the time but working with building companies, from project managers to quantity surveyors, was to give me great experience for my future life after the Prison Service.

I was also to learn skills that would help me in my new life after the service. One of the most important was to take project management qualifications. This was very expensive training and I qualified in PRINCE2 project management. I also learnt about putting together costing analysis and many other parts of the building industry. Another great skill I was to learn was negotiating. One of our roles was to put together the bids for the amount of staff that would be required and the equipment and resources to go with it. Governors obviously wanted to get as much as they could and it was our job to ensure they did this but not an excessive amount, so negotiation was a major part of our role. When you are dealing with intelligent people who are used to getting their own way and outrank you, it is quite a skill to learn to persuade them they will have to reduce their bids. Most governors were reasonable and understood we had to get best value, however there were some difficult and sometimes very arrogant ones who were hard to deal with and at times I had to go up the chain of command to make them see sense.

An interesting part of this job was the large project meetings we did with all the various contractors, as it was great to see how such a big build programme was put together with the various different professions from architects to quantity surveyors. Part of our job was to offer the operational knowledge to the project. Architects are very good at designing buildings, but designing a prison building is different in that people have to live there in a safe and secure way so sight lines are vital, no hidden corners where naughty things can happen, and trying to make it secure but at the same time create an atmosphere that is not oppressive. We were also there to try to get best value for money. Experienced contractors used to doing work in prisons always try to make a bit of extra money (or a lot) as they know it is very difficult to do building work due to all the security issues and the additional time it takes. They add on loads of extras as they can only work for a certain length of time, they have to be escorted everywhere and try to make up all sorts of things. The contractors will say due to all the issues I just mentioned it costs them time and money, so it becomes a bit of a game. When you go to the car park with them the only people getting in to the expensive German cars were the contractors.

I spent a lot of time on the road throughout this year and slept in quite a few hotels. I liked the travelling as I love seeing different places and being on the open road or on trains. I have always loved trains and as a young man was an avid train spotter, so whenever I got the chance to go by train I did. I accept I am a big kid at heart with trains. It was even better as I got to travel first class. I must confess the amount of money we spent on train tickets was a bit obscene and all first class travel was stopped not long after all the scandal blew up about MPs expenses. I had moved on by then so I had the best of it. One of the best journeys I did was from Derby to London Liverpool Street. I cannot remember the name of the train company, but I sat in a first class carriage to find I was the only person there. This train company was one that provided a meal as part of the service. It also provided a complementary glass of wine. Because I was the only one in the carriage, the attendant was obviously a bit bored as she kept coming and chatting and asking if I wanted some more wine. She said you might as well, it's free and there is nobody else to have any. I ended up getting off the train feeling a little bit tipsy having drunk a full bottle of wine. Thankfully I was going to my hotel and travelling on the underground as my meeting was not until the next day.

I was developing some really great skills that would help me in my future life as a property entrepreneur. One of those was in project management. As explained earlier, the service paid for me to take qualifications in this. It was a very expensive course we did and then an exam so we became qualified in PRINCE2 project management. This was the project management system recognised by government agencies. It was a very intensive week of study and quite a difficult exam, but I really enjoyed it and for one of the first times in my life I actually felt OK taking an exam. As this was a massive building programme I also learnt about programme management, managing risk through risk registers, systems analysis and many others. Another very useful skill that I use in my life after the Prison Service is negotiating. I had to negotiate with the prisons that were having the work done regarding additional resources; we had to negotiate with the contractors, with other Prison Service departments who argued they need additional resources and many others. Obviously the respective governors wanted to get as much extra resource as they could. Most of them wanted more staff resource than we were prepared to accept. Staff are the major resource in a prison and the major expense, so this is the obvious way of making economies of scale. Most of our negotiating was done with good humour and a degree of compromise as we on the team all had a lot of operational experience and understood the pressure on governors to deliver ever more services with fewer resources, but at the same time we had the pressure of delivering more prison places and obtaining a degree of economy of scale. We generally reached a good compromise with the majority of governors.

As I explained earlier, we were allocated prisons spread out all over the country so I had to visit them all to do start-up meetings to explain what the process was and help the prison teams to put together a bid, what the build process would be and who was who within the programme team. I started off at Featherstone near Wolverhampton where they were having a new wing built, then on to Highpoint to the south of London. They were having almost a new prison built within the present grounds, so this was a real challenge and the governor here was a real difficult person as he was adamant he needed much more resources than the target budget for this site. He was a very switched on governor and well connected with the higher echelons of the service, but at the same time he was very professional in the respect that he was trying to get the best for his prison by hard negotiation but was also fairly realistic as to the need to be financially efficient.

My next prison was the Mount, just to the north of London. We were building a new wing here. The governor was a young man who was very ambitious and because of that he wanted to be seen to be doing the right thing and keeping his additional costs down to the lowest he could. One of the major issues with the South East prisons was recruiting officers. Because in the South East, and particularly near to London, it was fairly easy to get a decent paying job, the Prison Service was not an attractive career option here as it was in the North and Midlands. Talking about the Midlands, my next prison was at Brinsford which was virtually next door to Featherstone. This prison was having a new wing but was a slightly different challenge because it was a young person's prison, which meant a different regime that would require extra resources which the governor tried to exploit. Once again it was through some tough negotiations and compromise we eventually came to a suitable bid. We not only had to negotiate the resources to staff the new building at each prison but also the number of staff to manage the building process in relation to escorting building workers, additional security measures and the disruption to the present regime.

In July of this year I attended a two day risk register training. This has to be on a par with Health and Safety training for excitement, but it was something we had to understand and contribute towards. At the time of doing this I really had to keep motivated but as it turned out it was a really useful skill for my future life as a property developer. I could not get my head round how people actually did this sort of work for a living. A risk register for a programme of this size was quite a sophisticated document, and essential to ensure the programme ran as smoothly and efficiently as possible.

The next prison was Ranby near Retford. This was already a very big sprawling prison that sat in large grounds. We were to build another unit of three wings here. This one was to be quite a long project due to the complicated nature of the prison to start with. My next prison was Lewes which was about 12 miles from Brighton. This again was a difficult prison, as it was a very old prison and the security issues working in a very tight area were a challenge as well as the governor who was a lovely man but a bit of a crackpot and at times very unreasonable. Lewes was a lovely place and I spent a few nights over the year staying in hotels here and discovering the town. It was an old town with lovely buildings and an interesting history. The next prison was Nottingham. This again was a very big build, where the prison was being extended by about half its present size. To do this we had to demolish a very old wing to rebuild the new. The logistics and security for this build were probably the most challenging, being a major city centre prison and a local prison where they served the courts, so the movement in and out on a daily basis was very busy. The project team here were a pleasure to work with, as they listened to all the advice we gave them and they worked very closely with us and were very reasonable in their bidding process.

Towards the end of the year I went down to Rochester and on to Swaleside on the Isle of Sheppey to meet their teams and go through the process with them. Once again both these prisons had very big builds that would be major projects going into the next year.

One of my roles was to co-ordinate the recruitment of staff and ensure as best we could this matched up with the timing of the build work. We no longer had central recruitment so each prison had to recruit their own staff locally. This was a logistical nightmare as we had to match this up with the training school that had to train the staff as well as the normal recruitment. With all the changes in conditions for employment of prison officers over the years and in particular recent to these times joining the Prison Service was becoming a less attractive place to work than it used to. I was lucky to join the service at the time I did, as I had a pretty good pension and the great prospect of retiring at 55 provided I stuck to the present grade I was at. When I joined the Prison Service it was seen as a genuine job for life with an index-linked pension and reasonable promotion prospects. The constant changes in conditions of service and pension over the years since I joined were not made with the intention of retaining staff. Many of the southern prisons such as Highdown, Swaleside and the Mount were particularly hard places to recruit large numbers in a short space of time. The Prison Service was not seen as a good job in this part of the country as you could find jobs easily and often with better pay and conditions. I came across this first at Brixton where the turnover of officers was a lot more than I had been used to in the North. The Prison Service was still a good job in the North, but even here there were better options in many cases. We had to consider the possibility of having to open much of the new accommodation with detached duty staff from around the country. This was a challenge going into the New Year. Detached duty was where you used staff from other prisons on a temporary basis to staff one of the new builds until they could recruit enough people.

Jenny and I had decided to move this year, as we had always said once our children were grown up we would move to the country. When we moved to our house in York it was a new house that was on a nice estate with one way on and one way off. After about seven years we found out that Rowntree's had a planning application in for opening up a piece of land that would mean opening up our estate to a pretty rough estate not far away. Up until this time, this estate might have been five miles away due to the fact there was a beck in between us. Rowntree's Trust is a very powerful organisation in York going back to the Rowntree's chocolate family. They had this land to build houses for a mix of people and many of them single parents. As much as I have no issue with this Trust providing houses for less fortunate people, when you choose to purchase your house in an area that you are told will be secluded and in a nice neighbourhood with no planning, you do get a bit miffed when powerful people get what they want without consideration for others. Once these houses were built we started to notice more yobs walking past our house and rowdy drunks late at night, as well as more burglaries and attempts. Some of the Rowntree's houses were occupied by single mothers and many of them seemed to attract partners who left a lot to be desired as to their social skills. The junior school my children went to was a nice school with nice children, and thankfully they had moved on before the children of these households started going to the school. Say what you like and call me what you like, but left wing social engineering does not work. The idea that you put yobs with decent people to make the yobs better people just does not work, and in my opinion works in the opposite in that it makes a nice area in to a crap one. I chose to pay a lot of money for my house to live in a nice area with nice people. We put up with the yobs while our children were going to school, but we had had enough and put our house on the market.

2008

We sold our house and moved in to a lovely house in a small village in East Yorkshire on the edge of the Wolds, where we still live to this day. The morning after the day we moved Jenny and I were in bed and I said, "Can you hear that?" She said, "I cannot hear anything," and I said exactly, it was so quiet apart from a few birds tweeting, no yobbos, no cars, nothing. We made an effort to join the village life and have made some great friends as well as my business partner of today which I will explain later. Living in a village like this was so far removed from my upbringing in a big city and even further removed from the life inside a prison. As I was still in the Prison Service when I moved here, it was great to come home to such a quiet and pleasant place. As I said above, we have made some great friends and we have a smashing social life. We have country walks on our doorstep and clean fresh air to breathe in every day. The only downside is the pub closed down about three years after we moved here which was a great shame as if it had been run properly it would have been a great asset to the village. I would guess the owners of the pub would disagree as they blamed the residents for not using the pub. The pub had not been decorated or upgraded since Guy Fawkes was a regular, and you were welcomed with a huge TV stuck in the corner with Coronation Street blaring out. Most people would go to a pub to get away from this. The lady who owned the pub is a lovely lady and an excellent cook but could not see that the surroundings, decoration and marketing of the pub was so outdated. I am not a beer connoisseur but the people who like their beer said it was awful. The first New Year we were there, I went in for a pint on Christmas Day dinner with my son and the place was empty. I asked the owner what it was like in here at New Year, as we thought it was a great way to get to know people and both of us could have a drink as we could walk home. The owner said it was great, so Jenny and I decided to go and find out.

We went to the pub about 9pm and it was empty apart from one family and a huge television. We thought we were maybe a bit early so I ordered a couple of drinks including a glass of red wine for me. I took one sip of this wine and shuddered. I said to Jenny, have a taste of this, it's bloody awful. She took a sip and said that is sherry, and not a good one at that. I hate sherry. It got to about 10pm and nobody else came through the door. Jenny and I sat there thinking this had to get better, but it didn't so we returned home, got a decent bottle of red out and spent the rest of the evening on our own enjoying a nice quiet time, saw the New Year in and went to bed. The people who own the pub are lovely people but they should have retired to a bungalow somewhere years ago and let someone take over the pub who could make it in to a really nice country pub with a great atmosphere and great food. It would have made the village an even better place to live than it is already.

About three weeks after moving here I had to drive to the Isle of Sheppey for a few meetings, so I was going to set off early and stay overnight. It was a freezing morning and I set off about 6am. I got to the end of the village where there is a junction and put my foot gently on the brake, whereas the car just carried on the ice as if I had no brake. I tried all the things people tell you about steering into the skid but this had no effect at all and the car decided to go where it wanted to go, and that was sideways into a ditch with a tree about two inches from my nose. I had to get out of the car on the passenger side and thankfully I was unhurt, but the car was rather poorly. I phoned Jenny and she came in her car with my son driving to pick me up. Thankfully I could use my wife's car instead, so I drove about 300 miles in a Mini. I have a bit of a dodgy back as it is and by the time I arrived on the Isle of Sheppey I needed a can opener to get me out of the car. Minis are great fun cars, but definitely not designed for long distance.

I spent this year travelling all over the country doing start up meetings at prisons with new builds taking place, assisting the prison teams to put together their bids for additional resources, how to project manage their own sites, deal with contractors and generally hold their hands through the process. We travelled to Burton-on-Trent on a regular basis as this is where our finance advisor was based, and we held regular team meetings all over the country as we lived in different parts of the country. We also had regular meetings with the wider Business Change team and these were held all over the country and often in very nice places. One of the best places we held a meeting was the Celtic Manor in South Wales. This was to be a venue for the

Ryder Cup in a couple of years. Celtic Manor was not just a golf course but it was a hotel, meeting venue etc. The accommodation, food and amenities were top class and we had a great couple of days. What this must have cost I wouldn't like to guess and quite frankly it was not the best way to spend the taxpayer's money. Throughout the year we had one of these meetings once a month, albeit not in as much luxury as the Celtic Manor.

I spent the rest of the year travelling up and down the country, meeting lots of people, problem solving and generally being out of my comfort zone as what we were doing had never been done before on such a scale. In effect we were like pioneers making the rules up as we went along. I was project managing about 15 separate sites around the country, from the building of one additional wing to nearly doubling the size of some prisons. The challenge was not just about the physical building but dealing with the different perspectives. The prison governors wanted to ensure they got as many resources as possible and the headquarters team who were responsible for the budget tried to do everything on as tight a budget as possible and we were in the middle negotiating on both sides, ensuring the prison governor had the correct resources and trying to convince headquarters to part with more money. Our role was in effect trying to please everybody so I became very adept at convincing people to accept a compromise to suit all parties.

2009

One of the biggest challenges of 2009 was recruiting all the staff needed for the additional building. This was not just prison officers but education, psychologists, offending behaviour programme staff and many more. As I explained earlier, matching the recruitment of prison officers with getting them trained ready for the new build opening was a logistical nightmare. To this end we ended up having to use a lot of detached duty officers. This is officers coming in from other establishments on a temporary basis for a couple of weeks at a time. This is not ideal, as it leaves the parent prison short and lots of different officers coming in each fortnight means they have to be inducted as they don't know their way around or the culture of the prison. This created another headache for us as many governors did not want to send their staff on detached duty, leaving them short and potentially affecting their regime.

The unions were equally unhappy as they said we should be recruiting staff. They did make a bit of capital out of this as they made a point to the senior managers of the service that the reason we could not recruit the numbers we wanted was the cuts to pay and conditions over the years had made the job unattractive. I must admit I think they had a point, and I don't think they made as much of it in the media as they could. Its that old saying, "If you pay peanuts, you get monkeys."

My job was to organise the detached duty in as fair and organised a way as possible to cause the minimum disruption. I had to get all the countries' staffing figures and try my best to spread the misery. As ever, the Northern prisons were the best off for staff as the job was still reasonably attractive to some people due to the lack of jobs in the North, and the pay was still reasonable compared to the South where there was more choice and often better paid jobs, making the Prison Service not high on the list of jobs to apply for. To be fair to most governors they did understand the situation and tried to be as helpful as possible. The recruitment of prison officers is a long winded and complicated system with all the security and other checks that have to be made, and then there is a long winded JSAC process similar to the one I explained earlier in the book for promotions. The service would not relax this ridiculous process to get people in quicker. Flexible thinking at its best!

Much of the new accommodation was starting to come to the end of the build and prisons started taking prisoners in. It was quite satisfying to see everybody's hard work and organisation coming to a successful conclusion. Part way through the year some of the bigger projects were put on hold or cancelled altogether due to the clever people predicting the rise in prison population changing their minds, saying it was not going to go up by as much as at first thought. I would say it had more to do with the fact they had run out of money, as they had not done their homework on how much all this was going to cost. As ever with large projects, government agencies overspend and nobody at the top takes responsibility for it or is pulled to task over it, but invariably they get promoted to another level of incompetence.

Towards the end of the year a lot of my sites were coming to completion or steps were in place to ensure the local teams knew what they were doing, so I was seconded to a team working on the new contract for escorting prisoners to court, between other prisons and deportations. This was another massive project and I was to work with them 2/3 days a week. I helped to put a number of the tender documents together for the companies such as Group

4, Serco etc. to bid for the various areas the team designated. These contracts were to be for ten years and were worth millions of pounds, so there was huge pressure from the very top to ensure we got the best service at the least cost on behalf of the taxpayer. This was a very interesting project and at times I was completely out of my depth, however I knew a little about procurement from my time on the Wolds bid team, but this was on another scale to that. I had to travel down to Peterborough twice a week to the offices of the team. Little did I know at the time that these offices were directly opposite Progressive Property, which would become a big part of my future life when I left the Prison Service.

Once again I had a good Christmas and New Year break.

Chapter 9

2010 to 2013

2010

I continued to work part time on the building programme and part time on the escort programme. Towards the end of 2009 I had been hearing all sorts of rumours that my role was now being classed as non-operational, even though when I joined the Business Change Team I was assured it was an operational position. The reason this was so important to me was the fact non-operational work did not count towards my pension retirement age of 55 years, so effectively meant I could potentially have to make those years up I spent on the Business Change Team. The service realised it had cocked up, so they gave everybody affected the option of going back into an operational role by a certain date or losing their pension rights. To this end, I was happy to go back in to a prison. Due to the fact it was the fault of the Prison Service we had been put in this position, it was their responsibility to find those of us who wanted to go back to a prison a position near to our home. We had to put our names in the hat with three prison options. I chose my three nearest to where I lived, except for Full Sutton. For personal reasons I did not want to return to Full Sutton.

All the Yorkshire governors met to discuss the people who were in the same position as me and have a bun fight about who should take who. The governor of Hull, according to him, asked for me to come to his prison. I have no idea if this was true or he was ordered to take me, but it suited me to go to Hull so I accepted. The governor was an old colleague from my Full Sutton days. He came to Full Sutton as a senior officer and to be honest I didn't really like him at this time, because he was so ambitious he thought of nothing else than his own career and would not allow anything or anybody to get in the way of that. I have nothing against people who are ambitious, in fact I respect that but in my opinion a personal ambition should not be at the expense of everybody and anything. He was a very capable person and, in my opinion, would have climbed the slippery pole on his own ability, so did not need to get on in the way he did.

I was due to start at Hull at the end May so in the few months before this I had a lot of work to do finishing some of my projects and handing over the others that were still to be complete. The one project I would have loved to see finished was Nottingham, because this was virtually increasing the size of the prison by half and the team there were a pleasure to work with. They were prepared to work with me, they understood the financial side of it, they negotiated in a sensible but tough way and made it so I enjoyed the journey down there and I am guessing they opened up their new prison with few problems and ran a great regime. Another prison I really enjoyed going to was Swaleside on the Isle of Sheppey. This again was a big build but the project manager there was really professional and worked with me to get the best for his governor. It was a hell of a place to get to from Yorkshire, but well worth it when you were working with good people. I also ensured that the detached duty system was working so my successor just had to follow this system. I also had to give up the other project, but feel I made a small but significant contribution to such an important contract. I am unsure if this contract was done to budget but the contracts were eventually awarded and seemed to be working OK.

I started at Hull prison on the 1st June. For those of you who do not know where Hull is, it is on the east coast of Yorkshire and gained its wealth from the fishing industry and many immigrants who landed there hundreds of years ago stayed to create their wealth. Hull has been a very wealthy city in the past with lovely buildings from this time, but now it is one of the poorest cities in Britain and has one of the worst educational records, with high levels of unemployment and poverty. Walking round Hull people watching is a sight to behold, especially in the summer months when the women don't wear a lot and there is flesh and tattoos everywhere. As for the men, if they are not drunk they are checking their veins to ensure there is enough heroin inside. I am of course exaggerating but I think you get the idea. Most Hull people will do anything for you and are exceptionally friendly, but like everywhere there are minorities of low life and the low life in Hull are pretty low.

Hull prison is a local Victorian prison similar to Strangeways and Brixton, so it was a bit like home from home for me. The original four wings are typical of their age, cramped with very few facilities for prisoners and staff but there are two relatively new wings and a new hospital which is airy, light with decent facilities for staff and prisoners. Hull has a big R43(a) wing, which is, as I explained earlier in the book, prisoners who request protection from other prisoners, generally for offence related reasons, i.e. sexual offences or being seen as informers or just poor copers, of which there were a lot in Hull. The hospital is a new building with excellent facilities for looking after the medical needs of prisoners and it had quite a large resident population with many of these absolute fruitcakes (not a medical term). Most of these, in my opinion, should not have been held in prison but could be better cared for in a special hospital and some of them possibly in the community, but it is easier for the courts to lock them up out of the way. The reception and visits areas were also fairly newly built so for an old local prison they were pretty good.

I met with the governor and we had a chat about old times like we were best mates. He knew I was there until I retired in about two to three years, and he was pretty good with me, offering to pay for any training or skills that may be useful when I finished. He also knew I would be loyal to the prison and would work to my full capacity as I have done throughout my time in the service. It is just a pity that loyalty and devotion to duty is never repaid by the leaders of the service. He was a shrewd character who knew I was going no further promotion wise and was winding down, so he gave me a lot of rope but at the same time knew I could be an asset to him. He asked me if I would manage the healthcare from an operational viewpoint and take some time to look at the prison performance and audits for an upcoming national audit visit. I was happy to do this on a short-term basis, so agreed.

The deputy governor was managing the healthcare so I had to have a handover from her. She was a lovely lady and very competent at her job. We knew each other from way back when I was a young officer and she was working in administration at Strangeways. She had taken the accelerated promotion route and the difference with her and many of the other people who took this route was she was not only an intelligent person but also very good with people, and it was not beneath her to seek advice from experienced managers around her. I have seen so many of these get-promotion-quick people come in and think because they have passed an accelerated promotion process this gives them instant experience in life and the Prison Service. The best ones were those who were prepared to watch, listen and learn before becoming experts. We spent a good bit of time together going over all the issues, the various characters, the politics, potential pitfalls and her generally advising me to aid my success. We always got on really well during the time we were at Hull together and I truly hoped she succeeded in her career.

I quickly came to realise managing the healthcare was a very different way of doing things than managing a prison department. The healthcare in Hull, as in all prisons by this time, was managed by health care professionals from a private company within the NHS. Many years ago prison hospitals were run by prison officers who went off to do a ten-week course and became hospital officers. It was ironic they were called hospital officers rather than health care, as there was not a lot of care took place in those days. The health care staff had a completely different mentality to prison staff in that firstly, they treated prisoners as patients, secondly, the decision making structure was more inclusive and questioning and finally they were even more PC, if that was possible, and they had even more targets and statistics than the Prison Service, if that was possible. On top of this there were so many meetings to attend. You have about three separate internal meetings a month with the healthcare staff, then about four external meetings with various agencies looking at quality, targets, efficiency, safety, performance and many more. As much as I appreciate there has to be checks and balances for such an important area as health, I do think they go overboard with it. I guess you cannot blame them with the compensation culture of today and greedy lawyers ready to pounce on the slightest mistake, not caring about the impact it can have on individuals just trying to do a good job in difficult circumstances.

The governor was very much into making Hull a true community prison, and he was very enthusiastic in working with external agencies making them very welcome to work in partnership with prison staff. He was very good at attracting funding both from the Prison Service and external agencies. He was also pretty good at hiding money as well, for the right reasons I would add. The Prison Service and government like the public to believe that governors have devolved budgets to spend as they see fit. This is far from the truth, as the governor is technically given a budget then central HQ dictate how the majority of it is to be spent. This leaves it very hard to be innovative. The prison cannot carry any funding over from one year to the next, so if you save money in one year you will be given less the next year, giving no incentive to save, and in fact it does the opposite where prisons will spend money for the sake of it to ensure they keep their budget for the following year. So around March of every year you see loads of new furniture, stationery and lots of other items appearing to ensure the budget is spent. What a stupid way to run a business. You feel any kind of free thinking or innovative thinking is pointless because everything is so centrally driven. I wanted to purchase some machines that allowed prisoners to book their own visits, order their goods from the prison shop, do their menus for the week, and submit applications and many more. The governor backed me on this and asked me to research it and price it up. I visited Doncaster prison, which is a privately run prison where they had some of these machines. They have one on each wing with a couple of prisoners who assist other prisoners how to use the machines, giving them a purpose and developing skills. These machines gave prisoners responsibility for their own lives and taught them skills they would need to survive outside, at the same time saving a lot of time consuming paperwork for prison staff, therefore making cost savings and providing excellent management information at the press of a button. My findings were that for the initial outlay to purchase the machines we would recoup this money within three years, then we would be in a constant cost saving after this, on top of the benefits to prisoners' skills. Not only would we save on the prison budget but there was a potential saving externally in lower levels of re-offending. I contacted an ex-colleague who was now working at area office about this project and he gave me instructions to forget it as HQ were looking at this as a project for the whole service. He then told me privately that it would never happen as there was no funding for it. We had worked out a way to pay for it, but were prevented from doing this because of the centralised buearacracy of the service. Even though they would have you believe governors had control over their own budgets. What a way to run a business, or should I say, how not to run a business or organisation effectively. Maybe instead of recruiting robots on the accelerated scheme they should have employed some good business brains?

The governor was getting a bit concerned about how the present Head of Residence was performing and asked me if I would take this position on. I said I would be delighted, as it was a role I could get my teeth in to and give me a bit of a challenge. I was also asked if I would keep the healthcare as well so I was going to be kept a busy boy. I felt at home in this role as I really enjoy the day-to-day involvement with staff on the front line.

Around September of this year I became the Head of Residence. My office was a lovely big office in the centre of the old prison where I had my own little kitchen, large desk and conference table for meetings and a big comfortable swivel chair that rocked backwards. I had responsibility for around 30 managers of differing levels and 150 officers and around 800 prisoners. I found Hull prisoners some of the most compliant I have ever worked with and the general relationship between staff and prisoners was good. As I said earlier, Hull is one of the most deprived cities educationally, and this very much reflects the prison population. Most of them know they will keep returning to prison as it is a way of life for them, so they understand keeping on the right side of prison staff makes their life easier when they return. I genuinely think many of them feel like it is one big family and they feel safe and comfortable in the prison. After all they get accommodation, warmth, food, companionship and a sense of belonging. This is something the chattering middle classes do not understand when they refer to prisons as horrible dirty places where people are treated badly and prison staff are all bullies (I generalise, I know). I recall when we received a number of prisoners as an overspill from Manchester. Some of them were a bit obnoxious and challenged/threatened officers. Many of the Hull prisoners set about them, saying, "These are our officers so don't give them a hard time." I never witnessed that attitude in any of my other prisons. Don't get me wrong, there were quite a number of wrong 'uns from Hull who were prepared to use violence against staff, but generally they were pretty compliant.

I was also responsible for the segregation unit and the management of C&R. Even though the use of C&R is very controlled and the training leaves the officer in no doubt about the rules governing its use, there are always some who will abuse their power if you let them. If the use of C&R is planned, for example a prisoner(s) is barricaded in a cell, we always film the removal of the prisoner(s). This is done to protect the prisoner and protect the staff from accusations by the prisoner, and it is very useful as a training tool as well as evidence if needed in a court or adjudication. When the officers have to enter a cell with a prisoner being aggressive, you find the biggest officer to go in first with the shield to pin the prisoner to the wall. This invariably means the prisoner puts up both hands to protect themselves, which means the next two officers coming in behind have two arms to get hold of and use the techniques of restraint they are taught. When C&R is used to its best effect it lets the prisoner know they have been naughty with a bit of legitimate pain but nothing lasting, and hopefully makes them think next time they want to be unreasonable and act like some wild animal or just a complete idiot. It does not always work and I genuinely think some prisoners actually enjoy the experience.

The segregation unit at Hull was quite a small one which I felt was a good thing as I have always felt large segregation units generally get filled because it is the easy way out to put a prisoner in one rather than try to work through what the issues are with them. The bigger the segregation unit, the more they get filled. Having worked at Brixton with a small segregation unit and other prisons with large units, experience showed me prison staff learn to deal with prisoners better and deal with difficult prisoners better when they don't have the easy get-out of putting a prisoner in segregation. This is equally true of Governor grades who find it easier to make a decision to remove a prisoner to segregation than try to work through the issue and keep a prisoner on the wing. Some prisoners do leave you with no option than to remove them, either for their own safety or other people's safety. I toyed with the idea of suggesting to the governor of closing the segregation unit and revolutionising the way we deal with difficult prisoners. I mentioned this to a few people and got the views of some officers and quickly came to the conclusion I was way ahead of the attitudes of most people, so decided to leave it as I was so close to retirement; why bother?

The segregation unit at Hull was the same as all others in that they were full of the desperate, the mentally ill, the misguided and the pure bad. I loved doing adjudications at Hull as many prisoners used to come in thinking they were the next Perry Mason. As I said earlier, the educational level of Hull generally is well below the country average so you can imagine there is not a lot of brain power going on within a prison environment. To be honest, many prisoners used to plead guilty as they were resigned to prison life and just went with the flow. Those that did plead not guilty usually changed their mind after a few questions as they could see their defence was going nowhere. The segregation staff took the attitude that if a prisoner had been placed on report he was guilty, and could not understand why I took the trouble to go through the process of asking searching questions of staff that placed prisoners on report and some felt I was the prisoners' friend. Even though I often explained my reasons to staff, and with the fact an adjudication is a legal process that can be challenged, they just did not get it. On some occasions I found a prisoner not guilty because the member of staff placing the prisoner on report had not followed the rules properly or had placed the prisoner on the wrong charge or the evidence was pretty ropy. Even though you explained this to the person, they still felt the prisoner should not have got away with it. Changing the attitude of segregation staff has always been a challenge in most prisons as we tend to employ a certain type of officer, generally big, tough and male. In saying that, I have come across some very dedicated staff working in these environments that have to put up with the most difficult prisoners in the system and often do it with humour and compassion.

A big part of my job was meetings. I chaired a number of meetings and attended many more. Meetings are obviously necessary for many reasons but I did feel the Prison Service had far too many and meetings that went on far too long. I attended the Senior Management Team (SMT), adjudication meeting, safer prisons, performance management, audit, three with healthcare, security, MQPL, race relations, POA/management, finance, efficiency, C&R, segregation, prisoner meetings. On top of this I met regularly with my managers, had bi-lats with my boss and staff below me as well as ad hoc meetings with anybody who knocked on my door. I have always been quite good at delegating, which was a skill I was thankful for being the Head of Residence, as I would never had gone home if I did not delegate effectively. So with attending meetings and dealing with up to 100 emails a day it was a busy old time, but to be honest I really enjoyed it.

Another year came to an end and retirement was getting nearer and becoming a bit of a reality now.

2011

2011 was very much the same as 2010: attending meetings, dealing with staff/ prisoner issues, doing duty governors, adjudications and generally keeping busy.

The governor left to take up a position at Full Sutton and our new governor was a person I knew very well and have mentioned in this book earlier as someone I worked with on the Wolds Bid Team. Not my favourite person, but quite frankly I didn't really give a monkey's who the governor was, as there was not a lot they could do to affect my life. I was looking to retire and there were no more promotions for me. I was good at my job and would continue to do my job professionally so whoever the governor was, it was irrelevant to me. It is always better if you have a good relationship with people as this makes life easier and the new governor and I had a decent professional relationship, but that was as far as it went and I think both of us were happy with this situation.

In June of this year my father passed away. He had a stroke some years before and had been in a wheelchair, he could not communicate and lived a pretty difficult last few years of his life, even though my stepmother did her best to make his life as normal as possible. She was absolutely brilliant with him as she basically had to put her life on hold to look after him. I just arrived at the hospital within about ten minutes of him passing away. It was a sad time but at the same time a relief that he was not suffering any more, so I said my goodbyes and shed a tear for a man who had always been there for me throughout my life. He was not a man who showed much emotion and did not demonstrate physical affection to his three children but he was a smashing father in many ways showing affection in other ways. RIP Dad, love you.

One of the things you had to do as a Governor grade was to conduct investigations into staff alleged misdemeanours and there seemed to be quite a lot at Hull. I used to enjoy doing these as they were quite challenging and interesting, putting together the facts based on interviewing people and doing a report at the end based on the evidence you found and making a recommendation for the governor to make a decision what action to take. I did one for Full Sutton prison. It was an Asian officer who accused the prison of being institutionally racist. The evidence that was presented to me by a lot of different individuals, with quite a number being black or Asian, was very compelling against this officer. They said he was lazy, spent weeks on sick leave, was often late for work, and generally he was useless at his job. There was also evidence to suggest he was working elsewhere while on sick leave. My evidence and recommendation led to him being sacked. I have no guilt that this man lost his job, as he was a disgrace and to use the race card in this way was equally disgraceful as people like him make it hard for people who have a genuine racial complaint. I can honestly say I very rarely came across people being openly racist, or even experienced it in the cloakroom culture, as some people would have you believe. I did come across these attitudes in my early days in the service, but thankfully we have come a long way for the better since then.

One good thing about Hull prison was the continued ethos of a community prison. We were very much into involving prisoners and their families in the prison community. I regularly held meetings with prisoner representatives from each area of the prison, listening to the issues prisoners had. I invited staff representatives from different areas of the prison to answer the issues prisoners had or explain why certain things happen. I made sure that any issues that we could not deal with at this meeting, they received an answer at the next meeting. Although prisoners were not always happy with the answers they received, by and large they respected the process and it created a better relationship between staff and prisoners leading to fewer incidents of indiscipline.

I had a very willing group of managers working for me on the residential team and I like to think I gave them good guidance and lead them in an inclusive way. I am a big believer in listening to people, asking them for their views and including them in the decision making process. I am also a person who believes in honesty and being able to express opinions in an open way, even if those opinions are not always what I agree with. I would rather have an issue in the open than let things fester. This has occasionally got me in bother. I had a manager at Hull who had been in the service for nearly 40 years, and to be honest was a bit of a drama queen. There was a particular issue that arose where he made quite a bad decision that could have had serious consequences. I asked him to come to my office to discuss this issue. I tried to get him to see the potential consequences of his decision and one an experienced manager should not have made. He would not listen to my advice and I suggested he was naïve in his decision making. He took exception to this and put in a complaint to the governor asking that I apologise to him. I refused to do this as I was not going to apologise for doing my job. The governor privately backed me but suggested this go to mediation. Once again an example of a senior manager going through the motions instead of dealing with this like grown men. I could not believe that I ended up sat in a room with this manager of 40 years' experience alongside an external mediator. He was adamant I apologise to him and at one point he was nearly in tears, saying he felt I had insulted him and had no respect for his position. I could not believe what I was doing here and refused point blank to apologise for doing my job. I wouldn't mind, but the two of us generally got on really well so why he wouldn't accept we had a difference of opinion here and move on I don't know. It was at this point I realised this job had finally gone bonkers and I really needed to get out. This situation was never resolved, as I would not apologise and he was adamant I should. I think the mediator had never come across anything so stupid and I could tell by her demeanour she felt this should never have got to this stage. I could not have agreed more. The manager was moved away from residential to some numpty job where he belonged. In private the mediation officer said she had never come across such a ridiculous complaint as this and didn't blame me for not apologising.

I promised the governor I would remain professional and carry out my job as if I were just starting and this is what I did throughout 2011. I put in the same amount of time as ever and worked diligently to try to improve things and suggest ideas, even though I knew I was not going to take them forward.

2012

2012, however, was going to be a bit different as this was going to be my last year in the Prison Service after over 33 years. I would be 55 years old in July, when I could retire, but I was going to do a little bit longer as there was a potential redundancy package coming that may give me a little extra cash. Early in the year my friend and neighbour, Graham, was looking to leave his business partner as they were becoming incompatible. Graham had been in the building industry for some years and is a quantity surveyor. I have always had a thing about property and have been a frustrated entrepreneur all my life, as I explained in Chapter 1 when I tried to purchase a newsagent and was told to go away by an arrogant and backward thinking bank manager. I approached Graham to ask him if he fancied joining forces to start investing in property. He said he did, so we became business partners and my journey to becoming an entrepreneur and businessman was beginning, even though I was still a prison governor.

At the beginning of the year I was still giving 100% but as the year went on I became more and more interested in my new future and less and less interested in anything the Prison Service had to offer. I was being paid by the Prison Service and had a responsibility to the governor and the staff I managed, so acted professionally at all times. I continued doing my job to the best of my ability, but to be fair to the governor I had to go and have a chat with him about halfway through the year to say I was losing my mojo and maybe he should look to replace me as Head of Residence, as this role needed someone who was going to give it 100% and take it forward from here. I was not the person to be taking anything forward other than my property business.

The governor could see my head was not really with the Prison Service, so he gave me a bit of a non-job. I had an office of my own out of the way where I did the odd small project and a number of investigations. I did an investigation at Leeds prison that took me out of the way and I was given as much time as I needed to do the investigation. Many investigations end up being longer than anticipated, as when you interview people you find you need to interview more. I did a thorough investigation and I explained to the deputy governor of Leeds that in my opinion, based on the facts I found, they had a problem with quite a number of staff and POA officials. I left my conclusion with them but got the impression the governor was going to cover it up and take no action. Did I care? Not a jot.

I spent a lot of my last few months at Hull locked away in my little office doing research on property and spending a lot of time on the internet. I still did my duty governors and adjudications as well as meetings like the SMT, but other than this I just wanted to go. I got to the point where I was coming and going as I pleased and spent many an hour viewing property when I should have been at work.

My new business partner, Graham, introduced me to the world of business networking in property and we started our education journey. He took me to Birmingham for a day's introduction to Homes of Multiple Occupancy (HMOs). These are large houses where you rent out individual rooms and they were very much flavour of the month with many property investors. The day's training we went to was at a hotel next to Birmingham airport. The room was full, with around 150 people. This was my first introduction to a guy called Simon Zutchi who had been investing in property for many years and had shrewdly seen there was a living to be made in educating others in the world of property investing, and by all accounts he was making a very good job of this, and a pretty good financial living. Simon came on stage with a lot of energy and I felt I was at some kind of American evangelist day with all the motivational talk and whooping that was going on. Simon then introduced a guy called Paul Preston, who came running on stage from the back of the room as we all stood up to applaud him on the stage. He stood on stage with his arms outstretched like an American Presidential candidate taking in the applause. Paul continued the high energy and American style presentation with the audience going along with it. Most of them were obviously more used to this than I was. I turned to Graham and said, "Where the hell have you brought me?" He told me not to be so cynical, open my mind and give it a chance. So I thought, OK, have it your way. To be fair the content of the day was pretty good and did give me a certain level of motivation to carry on. This was definitely different training to anything I ever did in the Prison Service.

Graham then took me to a property networking meeting in York which was another arm of the Simon Zutchi Empire. Networking was something

I was not particularly comfortable with but I was happy to give anything a try. I found it hard to network in the Prison Service, as many of the people I needed to do this with were often career climbers who were only interested in themselves and I didn't particularly like them. I know I should have just thought about my career, but I still wanted to keep a bit of pride. At these meetings you arrived a bit before the meeting began to chat, talk business and get to know each other. I found it a bit alien to just walk up to someone I had never met before and start talking to them as if I knew them, but that is what was expected so they did not find it rude that you just joined in the conversation. The meeting itself had two speakers, one for 25 minutes and the main speaker for 55 minutes with a bit of selling and other information in between. The main speaker at this meeting was a guy called Rob Moore from Progressive Property. I will say more about this gentleman later, but for now this was my first experience of him. He came in to the room wearing a bright striped shirt, expensive jeans and shoes. He was a tall slim man with a very confident air about him. He starts off telling the meeting he was a millionaire, driving around in flash cars, and came across as some big headed arrogant young man who only cared about himself and his greed. I really did not take to him at first, but after about 30 minutes he then calmed down and explained the reason he came across like this initially was to show the audience what you can achieve with hard work, education, listening and taking action on all aspects of the property industry. I will come back to Rob and Progressive as I move on to my new life after retirement.

As I was surplus to requirements at Hull, the governor asked if I would go to Wetherby for a few days as their SMT was having a few days of strategic planning in a local hotel. Wetherby was a young person's institution and I had never worked in this type of environment all through my service. I arrived at Wetherby and was briefed by one of the managers before he went off to the hotel they were meeting in. I had a tour of the prison and it reminded me more of a school than a prison. There was one of the units that had a large pond where some of the boys went fishing. I had never seen as many civilians working in one unit in a prison in my entire career. There was a mix of teachers, psychologists, social workers and others. What the cost of these places is I cannot guess, but maybe if we put the money in to schools we would stop many of them getting here in the first place. We always seem to spend more money after the person has become a criminal than preventing the person becoming a criminal in the first place. I am a big believer in trying to make these young people better citizens when they come out, not treating them with kid gloves instead of giving them some practical help and discipline that will make them better able to live in a tough world. If, in my opinion, you do everything for them and pussyfoot around them they come out expecting to be looked after and do not learn discipline, manners and how to assess the consequences of their actions. The welfare state has a lot to answer for making people incapable of looking after themselves and totally dependent on the state. How a fishing pond is going to give young people the skills to make a life in this world, I don't know. I am being a bit flippant here as I know there are lots of different things that make a person a better citizen, but I think we have forgotten the basics of life in favour of too much psychobabble. We humans are very simple creatures with very simple needs.

Doing adjudications in this place was a bit of a joke as the type of punishments you could administer had no deterrent effect whatsoever, therefore once again meaning there is little consequence for misbehaviour and these types of young people are just laughing at the prison system as they laugh at the judiciary, school and any other kind of authority. I am not advocating going back to Dickensian days, but young people need to understand there is a consequence to their actions. Instead of spending thousands on psychobabble we should be giving these young people practical skills to hold down a job, have the discipline to get out of bed in a morning, have respect for other people and property and tolerate different views and beliefs. Mindset is very important in all aspects of life and psychologists have a big input to this area of criminal behaviour. It is about balance, and I think we go too far down the social work side of the balance. Maybe we should even ask the young people what their views are on what makes a good citizen and work from there? I came away from my few days at Wetherby feeling we were making these people totally dependent on the welfare state and other institutions, giving them no values, no respect for themselves and others and no ability to stand on their own feet.

At one of the property networking meetings, I was advised if I do nothing else I should read a book titled *Rich Dad Poor Dad* by Robert Kiyosaki. I got this book on my Kindle and read it in a couple of days and spent the whole time shaking my head and thinking about my life, how I had done all the things the masses do and not the rich. This book is about assets and liabilities and how most people go through life collecting liabilities instead of assets. The basic difference is that an asset is something you make money from and a liability costs you money. He was a bit controversial in that he said your own house was a liability because it costs you money to run, where a buy to let property makes you a profit. Many disagreed with this, but I could see where he was coming from. Your house costs you money to run it; even if you have no mortgage you still have to pay bills, repair it etc. You have to do some of these things with a buy to let, but the difference is somebody else is paying for it and if you get it right you have some profit left over. I read another of his books called *Cash Flow Quadrant* which was equally as inspiring. I have read *Rich Dad Poor Dad* three times and I never come away from reading it without learning something and feeling inspired to improve in business and life. Even if you do not want to go into business, I recommend you read this book. As I said earlier about the boys in Wetherby the correct positive mindset is, in my opinion, 70% of what we do in life, work, business, and what the successful people have in abundance.

In both the above books Robert Kiyosaki puts a lot of emphasis on the way we are all brought up to think in terms of the conventional education, work, retire and in between collect liabilities instead of assets. He goes on to ask a number of questions such as, why do so many children hate school? Does school prepare you for the real world? Why do so many people hate school but love learning? Why do schools teach us little about money? Why are so many highly educated people not successful in the real world? Controversial questions but very interesting ones. He goes on to say how millions of people leave school and become trapped in jobs they don't like. I guess we are all part of the system, which is very hard to get out of, as human beings are very much conditioned to live their life as the state dictates. We get educated by teachers who are part of the system and have been brought up to think in that way, so they teach what they are conditioned to teach. Most teachers have little money. They specialise in teaching knowledge, but not in the use of that knowledge. Most people get no education at school or home about money, business, risk taking and being an entrepreneur/investor. The world needs both worker bees and entrepreneurs, so why don't our schools prepare people for both and educate them to make a choice? Many families who have no experience of being an entrepreneur or investor cannot understand why someone wants to take this path. Robert Kiyosaki suggests if someone wants to break free of this they should discount some of their families' values and views such as:

- But you have to have a job
- You're taking too many risks

- What if you fail?
- Just go back to school and get a degree
- Become a doctor, they make a lot of money
- The rich are greedy
- Why is money important to you?
- Money won't make you happy!
- Just live below your means, play it safe, don't go for your dreams.

Any of these sound familiar? Because they do to me.

Some other thoughts on knowledge/education:

The missing link in all systems of education known to civilisation today may be found in the failure of educational institutions to teach their students how to organise and use knowledge after they acquire it.

The saying 'knowledge is power' is only partially true. It becomes power only when, and if, it is organised into definite plans of action and directed to a definite end.

Henry Ford (of the car fame) was a man of little schooling so people assume he was not a man of education. The word educate is derived from the Latin, 'educo' meaning to educe, to draw out, to develop from within.

An educated person is not necessarily one who has an abundance of general or specialised knowledge, but one who has developed the faculties of their mind to acquire anything. Henry Ford comes within this definition of education. Knowledge has no value except that which can be gained from its application towards some worthy end. Sorry for getting a bit heavy there.

In the middle of the year we purchased a very run-down property in Beeston, Leeds. There was a lady and her son living there along with three dogs, four budgies, two rabbits and a lot of cockroaches. The cooker had layer upon layer of encrusted fat and other food items on it. The rooms were stuffed with rubbish and years of accumulated junk. The furniture was filthy, with a white leather sofa that was nearly black. This house was as bad as any prison cell and much worse than most of them. The smell of animals and stale food was stomach-churning. How anybody could live like this I am unsure. We bought the house at a price that reflected the state of it with the intention of gutting it and getting it looking great. We decided to do a lot of the work, or as much as we could, ourselves so I spent a lot of my weekends working on this house as well as working in the prison. This was a lesson we learnt about leveraging, i.e. while we are spending time on the house we are not looking for the next deal. Not only this, it took us nearly five months to get the house up to a standard to rent out. If we had set a team of builders to do it they would have done it in about six weeks and we would have earned about £2000 in rent. Lesson learnt, do what you are best at and hire out people who do what they are best at. We had the house up and running and a tenant moved in by November of that year. The tenants were a young couple who were very nice but turned out to be a bit of a pain in the rear. They would phone up at all times of the day, at weekends with stupid problems. They phoned me up once on a Sunday evening to tell me they had seen a mouse running across the kitchen floor. He wanted me to drive a round trip of 80 miles, to do what I am not sure. I think he thought the mouse was going to wait for me. Another time he phoned me up on a Saturday night to say the garage door would not open (it was an electric operated door). I asked him if he needed anything from the garage to which he replied no. I said I would come the following morning to look at it and he said why can't you come now? I explained it was 8pm on a Saturday and I had drunk a couple of glasses of wine and there was nothing that could not wait until the morning. There were many more incidences with this pair until they left 12 months later. At least they paid their rent and left the property in a decent state. The next tenants were fantastic and eventually bought the house, and we made a nice little profit.

I was 55 years old on the 4th July 2012, so from this date I could retire and what a feeling that was. I had kept hearing about a possible redundancy package coming out so decided to hang on a little bit to see if I would qualify as this would potentially give me an extra £25K. I had to give three months' notice to retire so I lasted until the end of August waiting for notice of a package. I was told it might be in January but nothing certain. I had completely lost all interest in the Prison Service so the only right thing to do was put my notice in, which meant I officially retired at the end November. Boy this time dragged. I was already doing a bit of a non-job so I came and went as I pleased and spent a lot of my time viewing property and preparing myself for my new life. I always said I would just walk out at retirement without a fuss and I told the governor this. To a certain extent he respected this, but on my last day at the morning meeting the governor did a little speech and I was presented with some gifts they had bought me, which was really nice. I gave a short speech to thank everybody and wished them good luck, as they were going to need it with all the changes coming, then walked out of the gate with little emotion for the last 33 years but lots of positive emotions for the start of a new life for me as a businessman/entrepreneur and freedom from bosses, bueffaracracy, political correctness, prisoners, whinging negative staff, feeling trapped and lots of other things. I sat in my car and thumped the air, put the radio on full blast and sang my heart out all the way home. I got home, gave Jenny a big hug and had a lovely glass of the best red wine. Nirvana had arrived. The feeling was as good as, if not better than, I had anticipated. So much pent up frustration over the last few years waiting for this moment; it was like I had been released from serving a life sentence myself.

We had booked a holiday to Cuba in December. This was just what I needed at this time. It gave me chance to reflect on my last 33 years and what I wanted to do with my future. Cuba is such a wonderful laid back, friendly place where the sun shone for the whole two weeks while it was freezing in the UK. The Cubans are some of the nicest, most genuine people I have ever met. They have nothing other than a lovely climate but genuinely seem to be happy. Most of the buildings in Havana look like a bomb has been dropped on them and the people have absolutely nothing. They are the best educated people in world and have a great free health service but nothing else. If this is true socialism, you can keep it. It was such a fantastic feeling coming back to the UK knowing I did not have to go back in to a prison or be told what to do by anyone (except Jenny of course). I truly cannot describe that feeling. It was Christmas when we got back, so it was about the middle of January when it really started to sink in that I was not on holiday but never going back inside a prison ever again (unless they lock me up for something!). We had a lovely Christmas Day at my daughter's house, who at this time was eight months pregnant and about to make Jenny and me grandparents, so life couldn't have been better.

2013

We had our first investment property up and running with tenants in, which made me feel good. This gave me such a sense of achievement that we had turned round this run down shit hole of a property into a lovely home for someone to enjoy. I never got this kind of feeling of satisfaction in all the 33 years working in the Prison Service. Graham and I had been going to property networking meetings for some time now and I was getting my head around the concept of these, and stopped being suspicious of people thinking their motive was like it is in the Prison Service, a selfish career one or look after number one; instead most people genuinely wanted to help you and encourage you to do well both financially and lifestyle-wise, whatever that was for you. Nobody was judging you, watching for mistakes or had the slightest concern over political correctness or other -isms. I met people who were very well off, successful businessmen and women who wanted to pass on their experience and knowledge to make me successful. I was not a threat to them getting promotion, or getting a certain job, but a colleague and friend. To add to this there was so much positivity around that my whole outlook both in business and in life was changing for the better.

On the 22nd January it most definitely changed for the better as my daughter made me a granddad to a beautiful little girl called Ava Rose. So another chapter of our lives started and the enjoyment this little bundle gives me and continues to is infectious.

Graham and I decided we needed to step up our education if we were to move our business to the next level. You remember I mentioned a guy called Rob Moore who was a co-owner of a company called Progressive Property. We decided to give these guys a go. Mark Homer was the other partner. Mark is a very private man who is happier in an office studying stats, doing deals and generally getting on with making money and growing his business which contrasted with the young, arrogant showman that was Rob Moore. I quickly came to realise what a fantastic team they made and why they were so successful at such a young age. Their drive and determination was infectious. We did a starter day with them at their office in Peterborough, which was a real eye opener about different ways to make money and do business in property. It was also very much hard sell of other courses at the end, but again their marketing technique worked for them. I learnt a little bit about joint ventures and how this was the way to go in the new world of broken and corrupt banks so I signed up for a Joint Venture (JV) day which Rob was facilitating.

A couple of months later I went back down to Peterborough for this JV day. It was a small group of people, so quite an intimate training environment. Rob came in the room with a bright striped shirt which I later found out was a Progressive way of standing out. He was not quite the same person I first came across at the York networking meeting. He was full of energy, confidence and had a certain way with him that made you listen to him. The day consisted of Rob explaining how joint ventures work in their many forms and I was particularly interested in how joint ventures worked with financial investors. One thing I remember Rob emphasising was the fact there is a lot of money out there. My initial thoughts at this time were: yes, and why would they share it with the likes of me? Rob must have been reading my mind as he said, "I know what you are thinking, why would these people give me money?" He went on to say why wouldn't they, if you have a good deal and are willing to pay a decent percentage interest or a share of the profit. After all, the banks were a waste of time for investing in. Fair point, I thought. He went on to explain all the different types of joint ventures and how to ensure the legal side was covered. He explained how to develop relationships with potential JVs, and the type of language to use. He equally said it was not just about the money but whether you can work with the person and always be ethical. It is not a good JV if you cannot get on with the person or they are interfering too much. It was all great advice and I decided to purchase some CDs which went in to more detail and provided all the relevant legal forms. I was due to go to Crete for three weeks to my brother-in-law's place a few weeks after this. I asked Jenny if she minded me taking these to listen to. She had no issue with that as she was happy sitting in the lovely warm climate reading her book. The property is on a hill overlooking a fantastic view across Souda Bay with hills on either side. So sitting there with my headphones on, in my shorts, looking at this lovely view, taking copious notes with a glass of wine was my idea of learning. I listened to these with a mind clear of any clutter or cynicism as Rob and Mark were not successful multi-millionaires by not knowing what they were doing.

I came home fully refreshed and ready to practise what I had listened to and taken notes on. Within about three weeks of getting home I used some of the techniques Rob suggested and we had the prospect of around £300K of JV finance if we could get the right deal. I was absolutely gobsmacked how using these techniques worked. I guess you do not ignore someone who has become a multi-millionaire from nothing within less than ten years. Another thing I quickly learnt was to copy what successful people do. That sounds pretty obvious but how many people actually do this? Most people just carry on doing what they have always done and listen to people who are not successful or just going through the norm of school, job, retire, moan about their job but do nothing about changing their life. To be honest this was me for many years and I knew nothing else. I was quickly changing my whole outlook to life and was meeting with very positive people who were determined they were going to be successful or were already successful. I see no point in having regrets but I wish I had found this life 30 years ago and I am sure I would be a millionaire businessman now. One of the things I would like people to take away from this book and my experiences of working in a very negative, politically correct, risk averse and bureaucratic environment that suppresses any innovation, to one working for myself and being free to think outside the box, is to take a few calculated risks. Be innovative and surrounded by positive and inspirational people who encourage and help you to be successful, it is never too late to change. This is very much about mindset. You can either go through life being negative, thinking the world is against you, blaming everybody else and accepting the norms you were taught at home, school, work etc. or you can be positive-thinking, accept that your successes or failures are in your hands, stop blaming the rest of the world, accept responsibility for your own life and keep going at all times. A piece of advice Rob suggested was stop watching the news, do not read newspapers and only read informative and positive things. I certainly agree with him about the news and newspapers, as journalists are some of the most negative people in the world who seem to think the public want to hear, see and read bad news all the time. Think about it the next time you read a newspaper or watch the news, and time how much good news there is. I would make a further observation. Mix with negative people and you will be negative yourself, mix with positive people and you will more than likely be positive yourself. Keep your mind clear of all the negative noise going on in life, think happy thoughts. I challenge you to spend the next seven days complaining about nothing and see how much better you feel at the end of it. Go on, do it! I realised very quickly how working in a negative atmosphere also affects your life outside work, and you tend to spend more time moaning and groaning about most things instead of looking at life in a more positive way. I guess the best person to judge my change in outlook is Jenny. I like to think I am no longer a Victor Meldrew (maybe sometimes) but I certainly feel better in myself.

Much of the talk on the property circuits was the strategy of Homes of Multiple Occupancy (HMO). These are houses where you maximise the rent by renting out rooms, rather than the whole house to a single family. There are a number of ways of doing this. You can purchase a ready made HMO, buy a large single house and convert to rooms, often using a room downstairs as a bedroom, or create more space by converting a garage to another room. You really need to have a minimum of five rooms to make it profitable as the landlord pays all the bills. We decided to look at Hull as the property prices are relatively cheap and we thought there was a good HMO market there. For our first one we decided to buy an existing HMO. It was a six-bed one with Polish tenants in place. It was a nice property and when full would clear around £600 per month. It started really well as the tenants were good ones who paid their rent and respected our property. Due to circumstances, we changed letting agents and decided to use some guys we met on the networking circuit. They came across as very innovative people who invested in property themselves and had big ideas of doing large scale projects and asked us if we wanted to be a part of it. The guy who owned the letting agent had a partner who was Polish, and she told him the tenants in our HMO were Polish chavs and we should remove them. We accepted this advice. It was the worst thing we did. It cost us quite a lot of money to empty the house before we started getting new tenants. These guys did not have access to the Polish community so tended to put local Hull tenants in. This was the start of this property being nearly ruined, regularly not getting the rent paid, showing no respect for the property and generally giving us a headache. We gave these guys the benefit of doubt for some time as they kept promising they knew what they were doing. It took us a while as we thought these guys could work it out, but in the end we had to part company and put right the mess these people had got us in. These people as far as I am aware are still trading as letting agents, which is a disgrace, but I am aware many other landlords are unhappy with the service they are receiving. They do say that one of the best ways to learn is by things not going quite right and making sure you don't do the same again, but learn from it and get better. This is OK, but I would much rather learn from someone else making the mistake first.

Well, the lesson we learnt from this was to do your due diligence on people as well as on the property or whatever business you are in. It has taken us a while but this property is now running well and making money. I talked earlier about JVs and the fact that even though someone has money and they may want to invest with you, you should do your due diligence on that person as you may find using their money was the worst thing you did. 2013 was an eventful year and very much a steep learning curve for me, but one I thoroughly enjoyed. One big thing I found out was about myself and how I can be a much better person in the right environment and with the right people. This year has taught me so much about how the Prison Service is such a negative place, and how it brings everybody down to their level of negativity compared to the people I associate with now. You do not realise when you are in such a negative environment just how much you are being dragged down, not just in your working environment but also your social one. I hope my long-suffering wife can see the difference in me as she deserves a medal for putting up with me all these years.

One thing has been brought home to me this year is how the British are so averse to talking about money and wealth compared to many other nations around the world. Why is this? I am not sure of the answer to that question. I always say the Labour party and its followers have politics of envy against the rich, the successful, and the talented. They say they are for the working person to make their lot a better one, but in my opinion they want everybody to be equal, but that is equally poor, they reject success, wealth creators and talented people. They and many British people who follow this doctrine cannot seem to accept that the talented people of this country are the ones making it possible for others to have jobs and all other things we take for granted. Many of those rich people give so much back to society that goes unnoticed. I would be interested to see how many of those people who shout about equality, unfairness etc. would share their £10m lottery win with the lazy and feckless who squander their money on useless things. I would like to show you a few points on how the rich think. If you don't agree that is fine, but at least give it some thought and look at your own life.

1. In a free market economy anyone can make as much money as they want.
2. Your background, education or IQ is irrelevant when it comes to earning money.
3. The faster way to make money is to solve a problem. The bigger the problem you solve, the more money you make.
4. Don't listen to the naysayers who tell you that life is supposed to be a struggle and that you should settle and be grateful for what you have.
5. Expect to make more money. For this one you have to think big £100K, £500K, £1m.
6. Lose the fear and scarcity mindset and start seeing money for all the good things. Freedom, opportunity, possibility and abundance.
7. Being rich isn't a privilege. Being rich is a right. If you create massive values for others, you have the right to be as rich as you want.
8. Don't wait for your ship to come in. You're not going to be discovered, saved or made rich by an outside force. If you want a lot of money, build your own ship. No one is coming to the rescue.
9. Stop worrying about running out of money and focus on how to make more. Constantly worrying about money is no way to live. Dream about money instead.

10. Stop telling yourself that getting rich is outside of your control. The truth is that making money is an inside job.

Steve Siebold

I would just like to qualify a lot of what I have said about money, wealth etc. Money is not everything in life. Being a good person, having a great family, being healthy and enjoying what you do is equally important. Finally to those who say money does not bring happiness, I would agree for those people who are unhappy anyway but I bet every one of you reading this book would be happier with money and wealth than without it. The other great thing about 2013 was the freedom I had to do what I want and have my destiny in my hands. That is priceless and felt even better in practice than all those years I spent dreaming when these days would come.

We bought a second property this year that we turned into a HMO. It was a three-bedroom house with a living room and dining room, so we turned the living room into a bedroom and the dining room into a living area, so we had four rooms to rent out. This property was a little too far from the university so we let it to blue collar workers. This is not the best property in the world, but by and large it works for us.

Towards the end of the year I attended a weekend training at Progressive Property. It was called, Multiple Streams of Property Income (MSOPI). It was a really good weekend, very intensive and interesting to listen to all the different strategies and options for building a business with property. We also talked about mindset, money management and other business issues. I came away from this weekend very positive and motivated to succeed and realised I was treating our business more like a hobby than a business. I gave this some thought, then had a meeting with Graham to discuss my thoughts on how we should take our business forward. I wrote a business plan with goals, objectives and a three year strategy. I also suggested we have two business meetings a month which would be minuted and actions to be carried out to push the business forward. We found this a really good way to push ourselves and we still do this to this day.

Chapter 10

2014 to 2017

2014

In 2014 Graham and I were looking to increase our knowledge, networking and portfolio so we decided to attend a weekend masterclass at Progressive Property. This was a really good weekend where we not only learnt many strategies for creating a business in property but also about the right mindset, and we networked with some great people. Both Rob and Mark, the owners of Progressive, take part in this weekend and they make you feel very inspired to succeed with Rob's enthusiasm and energy and Mark's knowledge of property and business. We also carried on with our networking, attending property meetings, learning lots of different ways to do things and meeting good people. I was really getting the hang of networking and found it interesting listening to people from all walks of life with different life experiences, but the one common factor was the positive attitude they all had and the desire to succeed. Many people I met were successful and wealthy people who I found were more than willing to offer advice and help in any way they could. This was unlike the Prison Service where many, not all, people were looking after number one. The difference with the property business and the Prison Service is you are not in competition with people in the property business as opposed to going for promotion in the Prison Service. Many people are going for the same position so that competition creates back stabbing, secrecy and sometimes hostility. Whatever happened to teamwork and looking out for each other?

We purchased another HMO this year. This is one we bought with investors as a JV. They put up the money and we do all the work and split the profit from the rent 50/50 and any uplift in equity the same. This was quite a rundown property, which required some work to bring it up to a decent standard. It was two small flats at the bottom with their own kitchen, shower area and living space, with three rooms upstairs and a bathroom, kitchen and separate toilet. It took a bit longer than we anticipated getting it up and running, but eventually we did. I was at one of our networking meetings when a guy stood up to ask if anybody was interested in the Green Deal. This was a government-sponsored scheme where you could apply for funding to insulate homes. I looked into this and it appeared we would be able to insulate the whole house for absolutely no cost to us. The insulation was on the outside of the house so it was like a big blanket round the house, then they rendered it, making it look really good. It cost around £18,000 and it genuinely cost us nothing. Effectively we got three lots of money as the house was, for council tax purposes, three flats. It took me a while to get my head round this and I kept questioning the guy I was dealing with that he was sure this was not going to cost us anything. Happy days. As with many things around property this has had its challenges but you have to be resilient, patient and most of all positive it will work. Property is not a get-rich-quick business but a slow one with solid assets. We have since split this property in to three self-contained flats.

We also JV'd with my stepmother on a small single buy-to-let in Selby, North Yorkshire. Basically she was getting nothing for her savings so I suggested she put it into property. She provided the deposit and we did all the rest. We give her 50% of the rental profit and a share in the equity growth if we ever sell it. We set this up with a Deed of Trust which protects her deposit and ensures everything is above board. We bought a tidy little two-bed house that was fairly modern and needed little doing to it other than a few cosmetics. Within two days of completing we had a young Polish couple renting it. They were a lovely couple who looked after the house like it was their own home. They have unfortunately left but we quickly got new tenants, this time a Polish family who are still there as I write this.

I carried on educating myself, attending networking meetings and generally throwing myself in to this business. It has its challenges and frustrations like most things worth striving for, but the difference with this is my success is down to me and not up to three people on a promotion board or some stupid JSAC. The choices I have are mine and I don't have to do what somebody else tells me to, I don't have to tread on eggshells about being politically correct or listen to people moaning about pathetic things. I don't have to be in any place unless I want to be and all I have is colleagues, business partners, professional people who work for/with me and people who help me along the way, not a boss in sight talking bollocks acting like an automaton having no independent thoughts but being a 'company man/woman' looking for their next promotion at any expense. Don't get me wrong, there are some very capable people managing at all levels in the Prison Service, but any flair and innovation is taken out of their hands to a centralist run industry that tells them how to do their job, how to think, instead of listening to their ideas and thoughts. What a waste of talent. My new world is full of talented, innovative people who use those skills to great effect to make a robust, profitable business and help others to do the same.

I continued to read motivational and mindset material and listened to podcasts in my car and at home. I regularly listened, and still do, to webinars which are good for information and encouragement. I will just give you a taste of things I now read and listen to. These are some extracts from a book by Richard Bandler who majors in Neuro Linguistic Programming (NLP).

Your fears, doubts, confusions, habits and compulsions are all by-products of how you are thinking, how you're thinking dictates how you're feeling and behaving in your life.

Learning/knowledge is the way to personal freedom. If the brain isn't given anything specific to work with, it processes nonsense.

Planning to succeed: All successful people have two important qualities.

- They know where they are going, and they are prepared to put in whatever work is necessary to get them from where they are now to where they want to be.
- Instead of thinking the thoughts that are not doing you any good, you get yourself to think the thoughts that will get you where you want to be.

You need to recognise and focus on what is important and rewarding, not on what's terrible about life.

The choice is simple: either you plan and take action to move you in the direction you want to go or you try to cope with the thoughts, feelings and experiences that threaten to overwhelm you.

Getting things done: Where people have problems getting things done, it's almost always because they have too much rubbish in their strategies.

Beliefs you need to abandon:

- I am not successful
- Being cynical about lots of things
- I will be happier if I am rich. Accept being happy is not just about money.
- Other people are naturally better at things than me
- I will never be able to do this

One person who I have mentioned before is Robert Kiyosaki who I find extremely interesting and motivational to read. The next book was *The Cash Flow Quadrant*. The quadrant is:

E   B
S   I

E is for employee

S is for small business

B is for big business (500 employees)

I is for investor

Each of us resides in at least one of the four sections (quadrants) of the cash flow quadrant, some in multiples. Where we are is determined by where our cash comes from. This is an easy way to categorise people based on where their cash comes from. The quadrant will show you where you are today and will help you chart a course for where you want to be in the future as you choose your own path to financial freedom. Robert Kiyosaki is not saying one quadrant is any better than the other, as it is about life choices and all of them have their strengths and weaknesses. Some people go between quadrants through their life, or even sit in more than one at any time. The vast majority of people around the world are happy to be in the E quadrant and that is perfectly fine if you are happy there. The problem is the vast majority of people tend not to like their job, moan about it all the time, watching the clock go round for home time and waiting for the weekend to arrive. Many of these people then moan about the owners of businesses and the bosses, getting envious of other people's wealth, but never doing anything about getting wealthy themselves. One thing they never consider is the wealth creators are the people who are making it possible for them to have a job. They are the people with vision, the ones who have taken risks, taken action, so please don't deny them the fruits of their hard work and endeavour as you may not have a job without them, or try to join them and become a B or an I in Robert Kiyosaki's cash flow quadrant.

I was beginning to realise there are a lot of people jumping on the training bandwagon in property. Some people were doing training with the likes of Progressive, Simon Zutchi and other reasonably reputable companies then setting themselves up as experts using the same material, having very little expertise or experience. So the learning lesson here is do your due diligence on the people you choose to train with. I also found there was a number of people standing up at networking meetings saying they were doing this, that and the other and how successful they were, looking for financial investors, but none of these people would show you the proof of their success. One thing about Rob Moore, he may be a big headed so-and-so at times, but he has got the track record and proof he knows his stuff and is very good at showing others how to be equally successful as long as you follow the system.

Graham and I were not moving on as quickly as we would have liked and tended to be a bit scattergun looking at the different strategies, finding we either did not like them or we were not too good at them, but tending to waste time getting not too far. I was beating myself up a bit about this situation but I guess a lot of businesses go down this type of road until you find where you want to be. I was beginning to think HMOs were not really where I wanted to be, or at least not the lower end of HMO as it reminded me too much of prisoners, moaning, whinging, no consideration for others and thinking the world owed them a living without any effort on their part. To be honest that was the homegrown Hull tenants, the Polish and other East Europeans were fine.

Around June of this year I was going to the gym, which I try to do about four times a week, and noticed a small school for sale. This was a lovely looking building that was built in 1858. I made some enquiries and it was the council who were selling it by tender. The tender had to be in by 14th Aug 2014. I got a bit excited over this and spoke to Graham about it. My initial thought was to put a tender together as a practice to see how we can improve when we are ready to take on this type of project. Graham did a great job with the detail stuff and he got an architect, Sean, to put some drawings together of our proposal at his risk. I dug around for the history of the building and did a bit of a write up about this and who we are etc. We put our tender bid in with not too much anticipation that we would be successful but to learn for the future. After a couple of weeks we were informed we had been shortlisted and they liked our scheme. After another couple of weeks I got an email from Graham saying, "Oh f—k, we have only won the tender." So it was decision time for us. We had no money and no builder and not much of an idea where to go from here, but the amount we bid for the property and Graham's figures for the build compared to the potential sale of the properties when built, Gross Development Value (GDV): we could not give this up. They often say a good place to be is out of your comfort zone as it makes you try harder. We were definitely out of our comfort zone but determined to make this work so got our thinking caps on. I had been having conversations with Rich who lived in between Graham and I about a possible JV with his dad's building company if we could find a suitable project. We met with Rich's dad, Paul, to discuss this project. He could see the potential in this straight away and said he was in. The next part was to find the money. Paul was prepared to put some money in and Graham and I could put some in so we could afford to purchase the building, now we needed to find the development finance. Paul came up trumps with a guy he knew who was prepared to loan £300K. This would get us to the point where we could sell some of the houses to pay for the rest.

This was the start of a fairly long process, starting with working with the architect to draft some plans for the planning process. We put together a really good scheme of the school being split in to four units with five new houses in the playground. This was in a conservation area, so we had to ensure the conservation officer was happy as well as the planning officer. For those of you who have never worked with planning officers, try to avoid them at all costs. As individuals they are nice people who are very helpful but they are of the mindset of local government, which means they do not have an independent mind but follow the convention and are incapable of making common sense decisions or no decisions at all without referring up the chain. Unfortunately in my new world I have to deal with planners so my advice to anybody who has to deal with them is to use a bit of psychology. The first thing I would do is go and meet them face to face, then you have a more personal relationship when you are talking to them on the phone and by email. Secondly play to their egos and ask for their advice, their opinions and help. Even if you know the answer ask them, this makes them feel in charge. Once you have this relationship then you are in a better position to challenge them. Better still, employ a planning consultant to do the work for you!

About six weeks in to the process we heard that a request had been made to English Heritage (EH) to have the building listed. Not knowing much about this, I set about trying to find out what the process meant and the potential for our site. We were not allowed to know who had put the request in and I found out anybody can do this at any time of the process. So if you had a vindictive person they could just do this for devilment and EH have to go through a very lengthy bureaucratic process. Even if they feel it will not get listed it still has to run the full course of the process. The gentleman at EH who was looking at this was very helpful, but would not tell me who had made this application or give me a clue if it would be successful. He did explain to me what constituted a building being listed and I felt our building did not fit this criteria but was reluctant at first to continue with the planning application. This process was dragging on and after a couple of months I asked the team if we should take a calculated risk and carry on with the planning application. We decided to do this and this turned out to be a good decision, as the EH application was rejected. I later found out it was the local council who applied for this and I believe there was a bit of malice in this as I found out they wanted the building. They could not afford the building and had no idea what they were going to do with it, and as it was the larger East Riding of Yorkshire Council that were selling it, this caused a bit of a rift between the two of them. All I can say is politicians, at all levels, make pretty poor business people and should stick to having meetings about meetings and attending civic ceremonies and let the people who are creating wealth and employment get on with doing that. This is a reason we should not nationalise any industry; politicians should stick to making legislation that makes it easier to do business and less bureaucratic, not running businesses. So it was two fingers up to the fuddy duddies in the local council and on with our project.

So 2014 came to an end and it had been a fantastic year for progressing our business, if a little fraught at times, but we remained positive at all times and were determined to be that way regardless of what was put in our way. Whenever I was feeling a bit down or unsure we were doing the right thing, I just thought of all the advice I had been given by other people, listened to motivational talks and attended networking meetings where I could chat to others, be inspired by them and come away motivated to succeed. Another way to make me feel better was to imagine I could still be in the Prison Service. That always made me feel much better.

2015

It was on with the planning process and all the other preparation and planning we had to do. Our architect Sean was doing a great job with a lot of patience as we kept changing things, as did the planners.

I had used my skills in project management (thanks Prison Service for this) to put together a project plan with the help of Graham and Rich. I used my organisational skills to make sure the others were on board and we all knew what we had to do and what others were doing. I organised a monthly project meeting to manage this process. We had to set up a Special Purpose Vehicle (SPV). An SPV, or a special purpose entity (SPE), is a legal entity created by a firm (known as the sponsor or originator) by transferring assets to the SPV, to carry out some specific purpose or circumscribed activity, or a series of such transactions. SPVs have no purpose other than the transaction(s) for which they were created, and they can make no substantive decisions; the rules governing them are set down in advance and carefully circumscribe their activities. Indeed, no one works at an SPV and it has no physical location. The legal form for an SPV may be a limited partnership, a limited liability company, a trust, or a corporation. Typically, off-balance sheet SPVs have the following characteristics:

- They are thinly capitalised.
- They have no independent management or employees.
- Their administrative functions are performed by a trustee who follows pre-specified rules with regard to the receipt and distribution of cash; there are no other decisions.
- Assets held by the SPV are serviced via a servicing arrangement.
- They are structured so that, as a practical matter, they cannot become bankrupt. In short, SPVs are essentially robot firms that have no employees, make no substantive economic decisions, have no physical location, and cannot go bankrupt. We set this up as a limited company called TeLo Homes Ltd. This was a mix of Teward Property, Graham's and my partnership, and Lofthouse Builders, Paul's business. So I became a Director of a company, in fact I became a Director of two companies, as Jenny and I had to set up a company to put in a Director's loan and we acted as consultants to TeLo Homes. Jenny also became a Director, much to her amusement.

We had to organise various suppliers from kitchens, bathrooms, to plumbers, electricians and roofers. This was a fairly long process as you had to go out to at least three suppliers for everything. Organising returns and following up on non-returns was nearly a full time job but I enjoyed the challenge, meeting different people and learning an awful lot. I came to the conclusion there must be plenty of work out there because many people just did not respond or said they were not interested. Painters and decorators were some of the worst to respond, so either they are pretty poor business people or there is plenty of work for them.

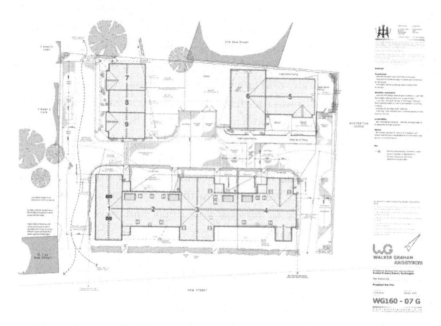

Site plan of our development

We eventually got to the point where we were happy with the plans and the planning officer agreed with it. We were about to go to the planning committee when the planning officer phoned to say his boss was not happy with a part of the plan. He wanted us to turn some of the houses round, which was a bit frustrating as he wanted us to put them where we originally had them, but our planning officer had told us to turn them around. Left hand, right hand came to mind. We asked to meet with the planning officer and his boss as a matter of urgency. We met with them and expressed our concern that they did not seem to be communicating with each other which was unnecessarily delaying our application. All he could say was they were short of staff. They were however sympathetic to our face but we knew the fact this was costing us time and money was irrelevant to them, as they appeared to have no concept of business, being public servants. We agreed to put the houses where they said, but because of this delay we missed the planning committee and had to wait another month. As we were about to go to the committee yet another caveat was put in there. Someone else decided one of the conditions would be that we could not occupy the new build properties until we had completed the school building. Well as you can see from the plans both from a health and safety and business sense you would work from back to front. Doing it the way the planners were saying meant we would not be able to occupy any of the houses until the whole development was finished, therefore we would not be able to generate any cash flow from sales to help fund the development costs. The reason for this was they felt if we did the new build properties first and sold them, we would not bother with the school building. The common sense of this was less than nil, as the school building was the focal point of the development, and how we would possibly sell the new builds looking at a grotty, graffiti-stained and run-down building, only the mind of a planner could come up with that. We went down the H&S route as we knew they would not be sympathetic to our cash flow issues, and asked if they would treat the big builders in this way. I suggest they would not as they would have clever and expensive planning consultants who would tie the planners in knots. They relented and let us occupy the two-bedroom ones, which was fine as we could work round this.

During the planning phase we knew that the local council had objected to the build due to the number of parking spaces. The Highways were content with our 12 spaces for nine houses and this fitted with the guidelines, but the local council still were not happy. I asked if I could attend their meeting where they discuss planning matters and address them and answer any concerns they had. I went along to this meeting and the room was full of these councillors with an average age of about 75 years, so very representative of the population. They were very friendly and let me introduce myself and the plans we had. One councillor came in the room about halfway through my talk. He did not introduce himself or apologise for being late, then proceeded to start texting on his phone. How this very rude and arrogant gentleman could possibly be informed enough to take part in the vote or subsequent discussion only he knows, but vote he did. They asked some reasonable questions and seemed happy with most of my answers, but I could tell there were a number of them who had made their minds up purely on the grounds they did not want us to do the development, and I am guessing it goes back to the fact they wanted the building for themselves. I knew that the larger council wanted this to go through and the Highways were on our side, so I played the game by being very business-like and answering all their concerns with great acting skills.

We finally went to the planning committee in June. We were allowed to give a three-minute presentation to the committee so I volunteered to do this. Graham, Sean and I went to the meeting in Beverley. We walked in to a huge room with about 15 members of the committee and a number of members of the public who were presenting their applications. It was finally our application which was presented to the committee by the planning officer and there were a couple of questions about parking which the guy from the Highways answered by saying they had no objections. I did my presentation. As much as the actual building, I explained we were local people who were very sympathetic towards a historic building that we would restore to a condition the town could be proud of, and it would last for generations as well as providing excellent quality housing on a brownfield site. It went through easily. What a great feeling this was; after such a long time and hard work we finally had some reality to work with. The three of us went to the nearest pub for a celebratory drink and to think about the next phase.

As I have mentioned in this book, Graham and I had done a lot of knowledge gathering and networking with the guys from Progressive. They do a 12 month programme called VIP. It is quite expensive and we had talked a lot about doing this programme to take us to the next level. Now we were moving in to the next level already, we felt it was probably time to do this. We signed up and went to our first meeting of the VIP in March. Basically the VIP is like a big club where you meet once a month, you get a mentor for 40 minutes on this day, lots of networking, updates, and interesting people talking about their experiences and sharing their knowledge. On top of this there is a closed Facebook page where you can go on and ask questions about property and other things. We met a real mix of people who were at different stages of their property/business journey but the one thing they all were was motivated, and very positive people who are great to be around. One thing I recall Rob saying some time ago was when you network, always be the poorest and least educated in the room as that way you learn a lot more. As you become wealthier and more knowledgeable, move to the next level where you are bottom of the pile again, so constantly learning from people ahead of you. That was great advice. If I am totally honest many of the people on the VIP were at a lower level to Graham and me, but there were those who were doing great things who we could chat with. I tended to equate the VIP to a university, where the contacts you made are there for life, so even though the 12 months comes to an end the access to your network continues. Our mentor was a great help as he was more a businessman than a property man, and he assisted us more towards the building a business side which is certainly what I needed.

One of the terms of the purchase of the school development was that we could walk away and have our deposit returned if we did not get planning permission, so now we had it we had to finish off the legal stuff and pay for the building. This done, the keys handed over, it was now over to Paul to start the build. There was lots of hard work and frustrations to come but I was really excited and inwardly proud of how far I had come in a relatively short space of time and doing something that I chose to do with people I chose to do it with. If you had told me I would be doing this in October 2012 when I was leaving the Prison Service, I would have laughed at you. So for any of you reading this who are fed up with your working life, sick of being told what to do by some clown of a boss, fed up of making somebody else rich: look at what you really want to do, educate yourself both in mindset and the practicalities of what you want to do and take action and do it. Don't get old and doddery and say 'if only I had done X'. Even if it doesn't work out, you have the satisfaction of trying. I bump into some of my ex-Prison Service colleagues from time to time and I listen to all the same types of moaning and groaning that I spent 33 years listening to, and often expressing them myself. I just smile to myself and realise I absolutely made the right decision to leave such a negative and destructive environment at an age when I could do something else with my life.

Once the build was underway I started to think about where we go next and looking at our next potential development. One thing we were becoming very good at was finding potential investors. I never had myself down as a networker when I was in the Prison Service, which was probably one reason I didn't progress quite as quickly as I should, and I didn't see the value in it, but in business it is vital and I quickly came to realise the potential and enjoyment of meeting interesting people whom you could potentially work with in the future.

One of the reasons for wanting to be successful financially is that Jenny and I love travelling, and want to see a lot more of this planet before we become old and senile. Because we are of a certain age, many of our friends go on cruises and tell us how wonderful they are and how we have to go on one and you will never do anything else. Well we decided to give it a go, even though I had massive reservations. We compromised by going to Miami, driving down to the Florida Keys for a time then back to Miami to cruise to the Caribbean for seven days to test it. Miami was a fantastic place and the Florida Keys were great, so we were in a great spirit by the time we went back to Miami to board the ship. Our ship was an American one so it was going to be full of Americans and Canadians. We arrived at the docks and saw our ship. It was absolutely huge and I was not getting a good feeling, but I was going to enter this adventure with an open mind and take it as it came. We eventually got through the boarding process and entered the ship. The facilities on the ship were like a top notch hotel and our cabin was really nice with an open balcony. The staff on board was very attentive and looked after your every need. The food was second to none and the entertainment in an evening was equally good. You can tell there is a 'but' coming, can't you? The one main fear I had about cruising was being trapped on this huge ship with thousands of people I didn't particularly choose to associate with. This fear soon became reality, as everywhere you went there were masses of people and some meal times were like the feeding of the five thousand. After a day and a half at sea we docked at our first port of call. You all pile off the ship like worker bees, wander around for a while, have a drink etc. and get back on the ship without really seeing anything of the place you have landed. The next day we docked again, got off and were harassed by the locals wanting to give us a taxi ride, sell us crap and generally take the contents of our pockets. After the last stop we had about two days at sea to get back to Miami. For two days we saw nothing but water. My one saving grace was the fact there was a nice gymnasium for me to get rid of some energy. Looking at the sea for two days, eating too much, being restricted to this ship was beginning to get to me a bit, so I was really glad we only did this for a week. I can see the appeal of cruises if you like to be pampered, fed excellent food, sit around, not have to think of anything and see a few places in a short space of time but for me it was just a glorious Butlins. We got off the ship and spent two days in Miami to chill out and get over the shock of the last seven days. Miami is a great place. I am a big believer in each to their own and for those who like that type of holiday it must be great, but I know someone who will not be rushing back to be a seadog.

As the year went on I continued to learn so much about business, planning, building, architecture, finance, networking and much more. Our monthly VIP meetings were always very interesting and I met many people from all ages, backgounds and abilities, but the one thing they all had in common was a very positive outlook and they were very motivated to succeed, which makes you feel the same and any negative thoughts are put to one side. I also learnt a lot about how finances work when you work for yourself and the one thing that is definitely worth paying for is an accountant. I was now in my element and my mind was working overtime on where Graham and I could go with our business. I sometimes get a bit carried away with my ambition but as long as you do your due diligence, listen to people who have been there and done it and surround yourself with good people, you will stand a good chance of succeeding.

By the end of the year our development was really taking shape and we were looking to market some of the houses. It is a great feeling to see what you have been working hard at, planning and being very patient with starting to take shape. Even though I had not physically done any of the build it still felt like I had produced something good and the satisfaction that you are providing lovely homes for people to live in makes you feel great. I never got this kind of feeling in the Prison Service as it was just a means to an end, i.e. making a living, whereas my new world was not just a job but a real reason to get out of bed in a morning. One other thing that was different in my new world was I associated socially with people in my network, whereas I very rarely met socially with colleagues in the Prison Service as all they tended to do was talk or moan about the job and had very few other interests. Not only that, I was not that interested in the Prison Service to make it my life. We had a great Christmas and the New Year could not come soon enough.

2016

Another year started and we were getting a lot of interest in our mews houses and sold all three of them, with two going to investors who wanted to complete before the new stamp duty rules came in. The Chancellor had brought a new tax law in that anybody purchasing a second home has to pay stamp duty on the whole cost of the house from the 1st April of this year. Prior to this date you only paid stamp duty on anything over £125,000 so it added a fair bit to the cost of the house. For some reason the Chancellor has a bit of an issue with landlords, as he is also introducing another punishment by not allowing mortgage interest to be offset as a business cost from 2017. It is, in my opinion, just a cynical way to create more money for the treasury and nothing to do with making it easier for first time buyers to purchase property. What a great way to hit some of your natural supporters at the time of the next election. Let's see if it backfires on this cynical Chancellor. These sales meant we had to get on and ensure we had these properties ready. We did get them ready and the owners were delighted with the quality. The satisfaction you get from making a quality house and watching people make homes with them makes all the hard work well worth it. To be honest when I say hard work, it is not really, as I enjoy my new world and do not see this as work but a pleasure.

We had no problem selling any of the other houses. The four properties in the school building were really nice and the people moving in to them gave us high praise for the way we treated them, the quality of build and attention to detail. It is fantastic to see a building that is getting on for 200 years old and going to ruin being restored for future generations to make homes in and enjoy their life.

Graham and I continued to do lots of networking and did a few talks on our projects and journey in property. This attracted quite a lot of people wanting to come and see what we do and ask us questions. Although this is quite time consuming, it is a pleasure to help other people as others have helped us. This is one of the things I find really inspiring in the business world, particularly in property, that people will help you and ask for nothing in return. Many senior people in the Prison Service would not get this mentality as they had one of protecting their precious careers and seeing you as competition for their next promotion. In business you can get things wrong and it is seen as learning, the Prison Service would be looking to discipline you at the first opportunity for any mistake.

We had our eyes on another property in the next town from us. This originally came to us as Graham was asked to look at it for someone else. We met a number of times with this gentleman but he was very indecisive and was due to go back home to Zimbabwe, where he lives. We felt this property was worth a look at so we asked this gentleman if he was not interested in it, did he mind if we took a look at it. He said he was not interested as the vendor would not reduce the price to his liking. The property is one half of a hotel that had planning permission for nine apartments and a commercial unit. We did our number crunching and decided we would put an offer in. Our offer was accepted and we agreed to exchange ASAP with a delayed completion until the end of August to give us some breathing space with our other development. Once again we are going to do this development without touching a bank for the finance, as we have our profits from the other development and private finance. I still have to keep pinching myself to believe how far we have come in such a short space of time. We exchanged on this property before the end of the tax year and paid our deposit so the owner could maximise his tax with an agreement we complete at the end of August.

We were off again with work to do and lots to learn. We came to a decision to operate slightly differently on this project as Paul, our other business partner and builder, felt the kind of work involved in this was not really the kind his guys did, so he would have to contract most tradesmen in anyway. Most of the work was a bit like a shopfit with stud walls, plastering, electrical, plumbing etc. and Paul's direct employees were more traditional builders. One thing we learnt from the previous project was to leverage as much work out as possible so we still had some planning issues, which we employed a planning consultant to deal with, and as we are three men we decided to go to an interior designer for the specification inside. Both these decisions were excellent ones and money well spent.

Graham did the tender paperwork for the initial strip out of the inside of the building as I was dealing with the legal stuff and for my sins, getting prepared for dealing with the utility companies who are an absolute nightmare, but I was beginning to love a challenge. We chose a young builder from Hull to strip the building and he did a fantastic job for what we thought was a very reasonable price. We then went out to tender for a contractor to do the refurbishment. I am lucky having Graham as a business partner as he knows a lot of people in the industry and so knew who to approach. We went to about five or six potential contractors and finally decided on a young chap from Hull who impressed us with his enthusiasm and knowledge. We took a bit of a gamble as this was the first time he had done anything like this as a principle contractor. At the end of 2016 we had a gutted building and a contractor in place to start in the New Year.

My daughter had purchased a new house with Adam, her partner, and although it needed a lot of work doing to it we got an invite to Christmas Dinner. Jenny and I had a lovely dinner with our family, our daughter, Adam & his daughter Grace, our son Alastair and the rather crazy three-year-old granddaughter Ava. Katy, my daughter, did a lovely dinner and as usual I ate far too much and just wanted to go to sleep. Ava of course had a different idea, so it was playtime instead. I am not complaining as I love her to bits and it is great to spend whatever time we can with her and all the family. You can replace money but you cannot replace time so these are precious moments to be cherished.

2017

Another year begins and another adventure in my entrepreneurial life to look forward to. As I said above, we learnt a lot from our last project and one of those was to leverage other people's time and skills. This does come at a cost but equally it frees up your time to do the things you are best at, which is far better financial use of my time. We had contracted the work out to Mike Lingard-Smith (MLS Group). Mike is a smashing fella and was very keen to do well and show he was good at what he did. He started to get his team together and by the end of January they were hard at it.

We still had a few planning issues to sort out but again we leveraged this to a planning consultant who took away all the concern and stress of dealing with council planners. Now that is most definitely money well spent.

Mike and his team got cracking with the build as Graham and I got on with looking for new projects, networking and managing the contractors. I am a bit of a head-in-the-clouds person at times, by which I mean always thinking of how to move forward with our business in a strategic way, often coming up with some wild ideas of getting way out of our comfort zone. Graham is the more detailed person who often brings me back down to earth with a more practical view on the world. I don't think it is a bad thing to think big and have goals in life, as long as you keep at least one foot on the ground. We continued to look at all sorts of potential projects and as I finish writing this book we are working hard to get some really good ones over the line, so hopefully my next book will be talking about even greater progress and multiple deals being done at the same time.

By the end of February we had finished the project at Pocklington, sold them all and had nine very happy new homeowners. This was a fantastic feeling and I had to pinch myself when I looked at the finished product to say I had been a part of making this happen. I never got this feeling in all the

33 years I worked in the Prison Service. But thank you, Prison Service, for making it possible for me to start a new life doing something I absolutely love.

Our development.

We are now at the beginning of June as I come to completing this book and the apartments are coming along at a pace. Mike is doing a fantastic job with the project on time and to budget. He is very much working with us and it is a pleasure to do business with him. We are planning to keep all the flats and the commercial unit, which will go in to our portfolio for a monthly cashflow. We are going to have a go at managing two of the apartments as serviced accommodation, which is similar to a hotel/holiday let where you can hopefully maximise the earning potential. I am very confident we will make this a success, but if not there is always a plan B of making it a single let.

As I am writing this bit of the book I bumped in to an ex-colleague from HMP Full Sutton in the supermarket. I asked him what he was doing with his life, to which he replied, I am still at Full Sutton but it is great because I am now part time and with my pension I am being paid the same as when I was full time. He said he was going to do this until he was 65 years of age, then go live in Spain. He said he was 60 years old so had another five years of working in prisons, albeit part time. I say each to their own but the thought of still doing that job at all fills me with depression, let alone doing it into my 60s. As long as he is happy that is all that matters, but it was obvious all he was looking forward to was reaching 65 and leaving whereas I just look forward to each day and the interesting things I will be doing. Whenever I talk to ex-colleagues like this I get a buzz, because I know how much my decision to retire at the first opportunity and chase my dreams and becoming a better, more positive person in the bargain was the right one. To be fair to this guy, he listened to my story since leaving the Prison Service, and he seemed genuinely pleased that I was making a success of my life and enjoying life; as he said, so many prison staff retire and go to pieces as they have nothing else in their lives, or nothing to get out of bed for in the morning. That makes me feel sad and if only I could reach out to them and let them know there is more to life than the Prison Service. One of the successful entrepreneurs I listen to a lot has a saying, "Don't do tomorrow what you did today, as all you will do is stand still." I find that very profound and more important, very true. Who knows where I will be in another three years, but one thing I do know is I will be moving forward.

In finishing off I would like to say why I have written this book. Firstly it is something I have always wanted to do, as I love books of all kinds and admire people who can write a story from their imagination. Secondly, I wanted to let people know what it is like to work in a prison from someone who has experienced it first hand without all the politics and bullshit. I have tried to keep it very realistic with no hype. Thirdly it has made me feel good getting some things off my chest, even if some may not agree with what I have written, but quite frankly I don't care what other people think as this is my experience and my opinion and observation of life working in a prison. Finally I wanted to let people who are stuck in a rut with their lives, at work, at home and generally, know that there is always time to change your life and outlook to life for the better by being more positive, stop listening to negative beliefs, have faith in yourself, don't have regrets when you get into later life, don't bother yourself with what other people are doing, stop blaming everyone else, just live your own life and most of all take action on what it is you really want to do in life. If you get knocked down, get up and start again, because if you do the right things, listen to the right people, you will be successful in life.

I have no idea who will want to read this book, but it has made me feel good writing it and I hope you enjoyed it.

As the Leeds United song goes, "Marching on Together."

One final thought: "Don't put off until tomorrow what you can do today."

THIS IS NOT THE END BUT THE BEGINNING OF A NEW CHAPTER IN LIFE.